I0759727

lonely planet

EPIC TRAIN TRIPS *of the* WORLD

Explore the world's most thrilling train rides and adventures

CONTENTS

 Everyday  Luxury  Epic

INTRODUCTION

Take a short stroll from the great London railway terminuses of Euston, St Pancras and Kings Cross and – on the side of a nondescript building on Gower St – you may notice a plaque. A rather sombre memorial commemorates the place where the first passengers paid to be hauled by a steam locomotive (cheekily named 'Catch Me If You Can') in the summer of 1808. Indeed, it was here that the first epic railway journey began. It was, it must be said, not a conventional journey. The track was just a circle, barely 30m in diameter – the train moved at roughly 12 miles per hour, and surrounding it were high walls, to keep this world-changing technology from the eyes of curious spectators (unless, of course, they paid a shilling to enter). Those who did pay were treated to some of the same sensations rail passengers experience today: the hypnotic music of clanking rails. The sensation of fresh air whooshing past their skin. The hiss of smoke and steam which – to those first awestruck eyes – must have seemed like it was summoned by a conjuror.

Now, well over 200 years after Catch Me If You Can was disassembled, other forms of transport have caught up – there is newer technology to entertain us. Our skies are filled with passenger jets: our roads will soon be busy with self-driving cars. In the 21st century passengers with enough money can – theoretically at least – pay to travel out of the earth's atmosphere and into space. And yet it is curious that the first herald of the industrial age – the railway – has not been superseded but in fact remains part of our lives. Trains carry billions of people across the planet – at work and at play, to family reunions and on great departures. Far more than cars and planes, they are freighted with romance and fantasy. The lines they travel are veins and arteries, moving people about the body of the land.

Flick through this book, and what catches your eye is the diversity of rail journeys on offer. For some they can represent the apex of luxury – with multi-course meals ushered to the linen-clad tables of the Hiram Bingham or the Rocky Mountaineer; or passengers retiring to their handsome quarters on the Ghan, the Blue Train or the Eastern and Oriental. For others they are the opposite of rarified travel, providing a window onto everyday life – be it sharing kebabs with locals amid snowy mountains on Turkey's Dogu Express, or playing cards as rice paddies flash past on Vietnam's storied Reunification Express.

Now, in the age of high-speed rail, there is no shortage of lines that reach dizzying velocities. You can whoosh from Paris to the Mediterranean on a TGV; from the neon lights of Tokyo to the temples of Kyoto on a Shinkansen service. At the same time, there are still dawdling railways that plod on only a tad faster than that first one on Gower St. You might feel your ears pop as you inch into the clouds on an Indian hill railway like the Darjeeling Himalayan; you will doubtless feel grateful for the slow-motion travel as countryside vistas unfurl on the Welsh Highland Railway.

Railways still have not reached the end of the line. Maglev lines – where trains levitate above the track – offer a glimpse of possible futures. And, in an age when air travel is inflicting damage on our planet, railways are being sought out by many as a more sustainable answer. But even putting technology aside, trains endure two centuries on as the most human form of transport. You cannot so easily take a wander, eat a meal with cutlery, strike up a conversation with a neighbour opposite, or doze on a bed in an aeroplane or a car. And though such things are possible on a ship you will be gazing at featureless seas, not at a world unravelling in real time before your eyes.

It just so happens that my favourite railway journey – the Caledonian Sleeper – departs from Euston, only a 10-minute walk from that sombre plaque. I'm often daydreaming about boarding a train: passing under departure boards, squeezing through corridors to find my bunk. And sipping single-malt whisky in the dining car, as London suburbs flash past with the promise of opening the curtains on the Highlands the following morning. Catch me – if you can. **OS**

HOW TO USE THIS BOOK

This book offers a selection of epic railway rides across six continents – from basic to luxury, slow to fast and from the proudly historical to the positively futuristic. It's important to note that train travel is constantly evolving – while some services are suspended, other lines are being extended – so always do your research before travelling. For each route, as well as practical details, our authors have penned three extra routes along similar themes – so you can find the right epic train trip for you.

Clockwise from left: Meet at St Pancras station in London for Eurostar departures; Vietnam's Reunification Express hugs the coast; a view of the Simonsberg peaks from South Africa's Blue Train to Cape Town.

Opening spreads from left: The Shivalik Deluxe Express from Kalka to Shimla, India; sightseeing from Canada's Rocky Mountaineer; a Japanese Shinkansen train speeds past Mt Fuji; Portugal's pretty Linha do Douro.

AFRICA

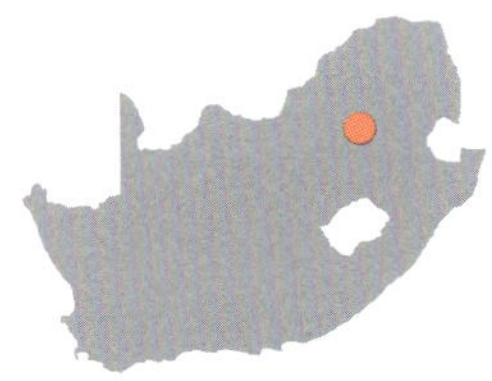

SOUTH AFRICA'S LEGENDARY BLUE TRAIN

Pamper yourself with a once-in-a-lifetime adventure on the Ritz of the African railways – complete with cocktails, silver service and an optional safari.

'Good evening, sir,' says the bartender of the Club Car, as he mixes another cocktail with a flourish. 'Might I get you something to drink? A cognac, perhaps? A Scotch? We have a fine selection. Or would you care for a cigar? Cuban, of course.'

I order an old fashioned and sink into a burnished leather armchair, watching people play cards and backgammon while I wait for my drink. Lamplight gleams off hardwood panelling. The murmur of conversation fills the carriage. Ice chinks in heavy crystal tumblers. If I didn't know better, I could convince myself I was in a London gentleman's club – but I'm not. I'm in the middle of the African bush, dressed not in safari gear, but a suit jacket, puffing on a hand-rolled cigar as I watch the sunset over the veld.

The Blue Train is full of incongruities like this. It travels through some of South Africa's wildest landscapes, but it's also one of the world's most indulgent trains: Africa's answer to the Orient Express, with more than a whiff of Agatha Christie about it. I half expect to see Hercule Poirot toddle past, twirling his moustache as he cogitates his latest case. In the dining car, gourmet menus of Karoo lamb, ostrich steak and barbecued kudu are served on bone-china plates and glinting silverware. In the cabins, there are Egyptian cotton sheets, fluffy pillows and squishy, surprisingly capacious beds. In the marble-tiled ensuites, scented salts and monogrammed towels are laid out with military precision; some bathrooms have full-size tubs. And passengers also have their own personal butler on hand to polish shoes, plump cushions and turn down the sheets at bedtime (with the obligatory chocolate placed on the pillow, of course).

My steward for the journey is Henry. Originally from Cape Town, he feels like he's found his calling on the Blue Train. 'I love all the

history and tradition,' he says, as he shows me back to my cabin on the first night, now transformed from a thoroughly comfortable sitting room into an even more comfortable bedroom. 'We say it is a five star hotel – on wheels!' One day, he hopes to become train manager, he says, but for now, he's happy butlering – although, he adds in a whisper, he still hasn't quite mastered ironing the creases in his trousers. He brings me a nightcap of hot chocolate and says goodnight, and I soon fall asleep to the steady rock and clatter of the train.

This legendarily luxurious train dates back to the early 1920s. It was conceived for a wealthy clientele who had made their fortunes plundering South Africa's mineral deposits: businessmen, speculators, prospectors who'd struck lucky. The Union Express, as it was then known, made its inaugural journey in 1923 from Johannesburg to Cape Town (in the opposite direction, it was the Union Limited). Carriages featured the latest mod cons, including hot and cold running water, ceiling fans and air-conditioning. The train had its own dining room, saloon and gaming parlour; it's rumoured that a Friesian cow was stabled permanently on board to ensure a supply of fresh milk for breakfast.

Nicknamed the Blue Train on account of its regal navy-and-gold livery, the service offered the last word in luxury, but it's had a somewhat checkered history, having remained in service throughout the apartheid years. Refurbished in 1997, it now runs several times a week between Cape Town and Pretoria, crossing four provinces (Gauteng, North West, Northern Cape and Western Cape) en route.

"It plonks you in a grandstand seat for a spectacular procession of African landscapes, packing in a continent's worth of scenery – from mountains, plains and lakes to parched desert..."

The journey is spread over three days, with two nights spent on the train in your own plush, private cabin. Departing in the early morning from the coast of Cape Town, the train arrives 54 hours later among the pink jacaranda trees of Pretoria. Along the way, it plonks you in a grandstand seat for a spectacular procession of African landscapes, packing in an entire continent's worth of scenery – from mountains, plains and lakes to parched desert and open savannah. You might even spot some African wildlife as you speed by, from wildebeest to springboks, impala to flamingos.

KIMBERLEY AND KRUGER

En route from Cape Town to Pretoria, the Blue Train makes a stop in the old prospecting town of Kimberley, home to some of South Africa's richest diamond deposits and the famous Big Hole, said to be the deepest pit ever dug by man. North of Pretoria, a few trains every month continue into Limpopo Province, where you can arrange private safaris into Kruger National Park to spot the Big Five.

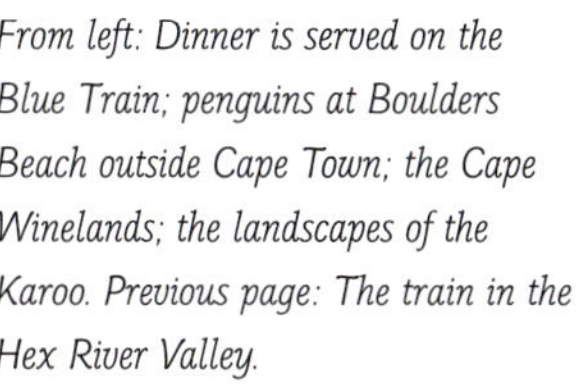

From left: Dinner is served on the Blue Train; penguins at Boulders Beach outside Cape Town; the Cape Winelands; the landscapes of the Karoo. Previous page: The train in the Hex River Valley.

The pampering is, of course, part of what makes the Blue Train experience so special, and – along with the amazing scenery – it's undoubtedly the main draw for many of the passengers. Over evening cocktails in the Club Car, I get chatting to a few of my fellow travellers: Henry delights in informing me that the train never exceeds 55mph (88km/h) to avoid disturbing its clients' conversations. Among my companions is Maggie Ryder, a silver-haired New Yorker who's taking the trip as part of a year-long, round-the-world retirement adventure with her husband Bill. 'We've always dreamed of taking the Blue Train,' she says, sipping her second negroni as we trundle over the parched, sunbaked Karoo plains. 'It's like stepping back in time. All the luxury makes you feel like a movie star. And I just love travelling by train, anyway. It gives you time to think.'

It's hard to quibble with Maggie's rather poetic point of view. We chat for a while longer, then sit back and sip our drinks in contented silence, gazing dreamily out of the observation windows as darkness falls over the savannah. The land shifts through a rainbow of colours – cadmium yellow, tangerine, rose pink, blood crimson, then pitch black. Stars spot the sky, slowly massing into constellations. The Milky Way appears. In the distance, pink lightning flickers over the plain.

The Blue Train doesn't come cheap, but if you ask me, this is one railway trip that's worth the spoil. **OB**

Start/Finish // Pretoria/Cape Town
Distance // 994 miles (1600km)
Duration // 54hr
Ticket types // There are two cabin classes on the Blue Train: Deluxe and Luxury. The main difference is space: Luxury suites are 3ft (1m) wider and find space to cram in a full-size bath and double bed.
How to book // Book direct (bluetrain.co.za), ideally several months in advance.
When to go // The Blue Train runs year-round. May to September is best for wildlife spotting in Kruger National Park, but it can also be a busy time to travel.
Things to know // Formal attire is obligatory in the dining car: either jacket and tie, or an evening dress.
More info // South Africa Tourist Board (southafrica.net); Kruger National Park (sanparks.org/parks/kruger).

Opposite top: The Rovos Rail Observation Car is a fine place to spend an evening. Opposite below: The distinctive livery of the Shosholoza Meyl trains, seen in Johannesburg.

MORE LIKE THIS
SOUTH AFRICAN RAILWAY RIDES

ROVOS RAIL

The Blue Train is far from the only luxurious rail experience Africa has to offer. Rovos Rail offers a whole catalogue of incredible pan-African train trips, lasting two days to two weeks: you could travel across the dunes of Namibia, steam to Victoria Falls, travel over the Cape Mountains or cross the Great Rift Valley. The 15-night African Trilogy route is arguably the pick of the trips. It starts in Pretoria and takes in sights including Kruger National Park, the kingdom of eSwatini, the Drakensberg Mountains, the Kalahari Desert, Namib-Naukluft National Park and the seemingly endless Namib Desert. Sleeper cabins are just as plush as the Blue Train: Royal Suites even find space for a full-size, freestanding clawfoot bath.

Start // Pretoria
Finish // Walvis Bay
Distance // 3100 miles (5000km)
Duration // 15 nights

GAUTRAIN

This high-speed commuter line, completed in 2010, has a very different ethos to the Blue Train: it's geared for efficiency rather than luxury, and was built as part of a wider project to inject investment into Gauteng Province by linking Johannesburg and Pretoria with OR Tambo International Airport. The project aimed to reduce local residents' reliance on their cars; the highways around Johannesburg are notoriously nightmarish, and it was hoped that the Gautrain would alleviate some of the worst problems. But it came at a cost: originally budgeted at R3.5 billion, the line eventually came in at an eye-watering R25.4 billion (US$3.66 billion). The jury is out on whether the Gautrain has been worth the investment: the railway has been criticised for being too expensive for many locals, and for excluding the townships where most people live.

Starting // Johannesburg
Finishing // Pretoria
Distance // 50 miles (80km)
Duration // 35min

SHOSHOLOZA MEYL

Offering a decidedly more functional experience than the Blue Train, these intercity services link Johannesburg with Cape Town, Durban and Queenstown. The name derives from South African dialect: 'Shosholoza' comes from a song about train workers, while 'Meyl' means long-distance train. There are two service levels: Sleepers (with two-, four- and six-person compartments) and Sitters (where you just get a seat). Unfortunately, following serious crashes in 2018 and 2020 and the fallout of the pandemic (when whole sections of the track were looted), the services are currently in a mess: seat numbers have been reduced, and sleeper services stripped back. The service has even been suspended on several occasions, so check for updates (shosholozameyl.co.za) before you travel. If it's running when you're there, it's a fun – and incredibly affordable – way to explore the country.

Starting // Johannesburg
Finish // Cape Town
Distance // 994 miles (1600km)
Duration // 3 days

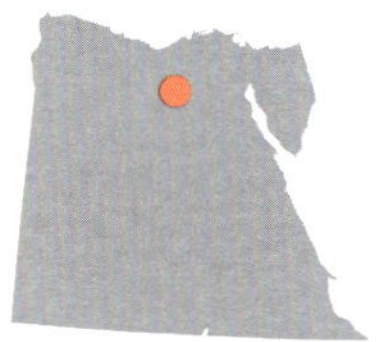

A RAILWAY RIDE INTO ANCIENT EGYPT

Egypt promises a trip back in time like few other places, and even on the train, travellers soon rewind all the way to the pharaohs.

They say opposites attract, and my love affair with Egypt constitutes perfect evidence. I'm an introvert and a planner, but as soon as my flight lands in chaotic Cairo, I realise that all notions of who I think I am have parachuted out the window somewhere over the Mediterranean. The way I operate elsewhere won't work here.

Egypt – and its capital in particular – can be a tough place to love. It pushes your buttons and gets under your skin. You can resist and get dragged under or take some notes from the Nile and simply go with the flow. Maybe the first thing you'll do when you arrive is watch your life flash before your eyes because your taxi driver is playing real-life Grand Theft Auto. Perhaps you'll get sucked into a perfume scam after the shop owner's cousin's friend's brother's cousin's friend buys you some falafel to lure you into the store – two actual events from the last time I was in the city.

On this trip, I wanted to take the sleeper train from Cairo to Aswan, as far south as you can go on the Egyptian railway and the last major tourist town before you reach Sudan. Trying to book a ticket online in advance had proved fruitless (see what happens when you try to plan?), so my first adventure was heading to the train station to find out what was still available.

At Ramses Station, I get lost trying to find the ticket window – but I do discover the Egyptian Railway Museum. Egypt was the first place in Africa and the Middle East to have a railway network, started by the Ottoman overlords in 1851, who contracted British engineer Robert Stephenson to make it happen. The first routes were not south along the Nile to the historic sites that are magnets for today's visitors, but towards

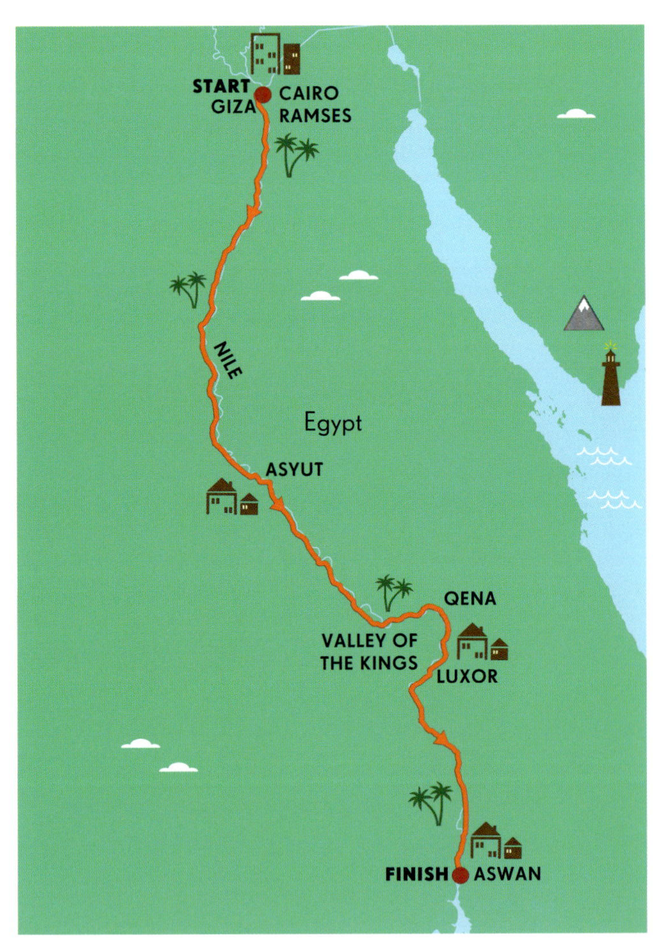

the more important waterways of that era for the shipping needs of the British: north towards the Mediterranean and east to the soon-to-be-completed Suez Canal.

When I finally find the ticket counter, plenty of sleeper berths are available for the next evening's departure, and so, 24 hours later, I return to Ramses with my backpack.

Built in 1892, Ramses Station has a restrained Islamic-style exterior with blue tiling and pointed arches – but inside, it goes full Las Vegas casino. On the ceiling, illuminated metal palms fan out from a glass icicle-looking spike, like a pyramid that's been held upside down too long. The striking features look like they could be art deco but were actually done in 2014, much to the chagrin of Cairo's architectural preservationists.

I use my rudimentary knowledge of Arabic numbers to track down the platform and check the departure time. I've gotten here early, but soon enough the scheduled departure arrives and passes – as do another 37 minutes. Finally, the white and green carriages with 'sleeping car' painted on the side in English and Arabic appear. With a single step on board, I've time-travelled four decades into the past as I walk down the narrow corridor laid with the white-dotted maroon carpet that every hotel had in the 1980s. In fact, these carriages were built in East Germany, when that was still a thing. I find my pint-sized room, which has two beige seats and a beige-blanketed upper bunk that's been pulled down, ready for an overnight guest. Though it's bland, it's clean.

The train lurches forward, but we soon stop at the next station, Giza, about 6 miles (10km) from the Great Pyramid. More international travellers pile on – many Egyptians can't afford this trip, which is priced for the foreign market, exponentially higher than the standard daytime trains that make the same journey. Once we're in motion again, Mohammed, the sleeping car attendant, brings my dinner, a tray with containers of meat and rice. I eat and gaze out the window.

TRAIN STATION HISTORY LESSONS

The exterior of the train stations in Giza and Luxor have been designed to look like pharaonic-era temples with monumental columned entrances. Above the entry door is Nekhbet, the vulture goddess with wings spread as a symbol of protection. In Luxor's version (the one in Giza is the same shade as the stone), she clasps two shen rings, symbols of eternity whose shapes are also found in the ubiquitous cartouche, and plumed sceptres in her talons.

From left: The Nile at Luxor; inside Cairo's dramatic 1892-built Ramses Station; sunrise over the Pyramids at Giza. Previous page: Exploring the Karnak temple complex.

As we edge towards the end of Cairo's sprawl, the buildings get shorter and the lights become fewer. After an hour, the darkness is all-consuming, and with nothing left to look at but my own face reflected in the window, I climb up to my bunk.

The wild Nile snakes its way through a cross-section of Egypt, leaving a ribbon of lush, fertile land in its wake. The train tracks aren't far from the river, and for much of the journey, they parallel a manmade agricultural canal that channels water from it.

The sun has been peeking through the window for hours by the time I wake up at 7am, and I stand in the corridor outside my room where the windows are bigger and showcase the more interesting side of the scenery.

The train trundles past farmers' fields, where people are hard at work while water buffalo lazily swat away flies and scarecrows wearing djellabas (long traditional robes worn by men) silently stand sentinel. I feel as if I'm watching a scene that has taken place countless times for thousands of years.

Most of my fellow foreigners disembark in Luxor, humming with excitement for dusty days of sightseeing in the Valley of the Kings and getting lost in the millennia-old Karnak temple complex, which we've just passed on the train. But I remain on board for several more hours, reaching Aswan around midday. After our late start in Cairo, we haven't made up any time; in fact, we've fallen even further behind as our iron horse passes through station after station and the hours and desert landscapes roll by. But what use is a timetable when you're travelling through centuries? **LK**

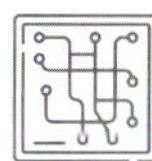

Start/Finish // Ramses Station, Cairo/Aswan Station
Distance // 549 miles (879km)
Duration // Around 14hr – pack your patience as the train is often delayed.
How to book // Abela Trains (abelatrains.com). The website is annoyingly buggy and often doesn't work. If that's the case, go to your departure train station a day or two in advance. At Ramses Station, the dedicated sleeper train ticket counter is a small room on the west side of the building – you don't need to enter the main train station hall.
Things to know // Foreigners are required to pay in US dollars, not Egyptian pounds, for train tickets. You might also be able to pay in euros or using a credit card at the station in Cairo.

Clockwise from top: Pompeii with Vesuvius rising beyond; the Temple of Diana in Mérida, Spain; the Swanage Railway passes under Corfe Castle.

MORE LIKE THIS
RAILWAY LINES NEAR HISTORIC RUINS

CIRCUMVESUVIANA TO POMPEII, ITALY

Make an easy day trip from Naples on the Circumvesuviana, a slow local train so named because it runs close to Vesuvius, the volcano that of course erupted in 79 BCE and buried several ancient Roman cities, including the most famous, Pompeii. Within minutes on foot from the station, you're at the entrance to the ruins and ready to walk in the fateful footsteps of the unknowing victims of that historic disaster. A separate line from Napoli Garibaldi runs to Herculaneum, another ancient ash-covered city that's closer to Naples but less visited than Pompeii.

Start // Napoli Garibaldi Station, Naples
Finish // Pompei Scavi Villa dei Misteri Station
Distance // 17 miles (28km)
Duration // 40min

MÉRIDA TO ALMADÉN, SPAIN

Founded in 25 BCE as a retirement retreat for Roman soldiers who had successfully served the empire, Mérida is today the capital of the Spanish province of Extremadura, whose name is said to derive from the Latin meaning 'extremely difficult' because of the long, exhausting march from Rome to the empire's western frontier. These days, travellers will find that getting here by train is quite simple, and a full display of Roman remains is visible right from the station and your window seat. The 82ft-high (25m) arched Aqueduct of the Miracles harkens back to this era, as does Mérida's exquisitely preserved 1st-century BCE theatre, still filled by 21st-century audiences on summer evenings. After a gorgeous ride through sunbaked Spanish landscapes, discover the main attraction in Almadén which, in contrast, is far below ground: a former cinnabar (mercury sulphide) mine in the city whose name comes from conquerors who came to the Iberian Peninsula centuries after the Romans – it means 'metal' in Arabic.

Start // Mérida
Finish // Almadén
Distance // 135 miles (217km)
Duration // 2hr 30min

SWANAGE RAILWAY, ENGLAND

Bookending one end of England's Jurassic Coast – the country's first natural World Heritage Site, dotted with sea-sculpted bays, beaches and cliff faces full of fossils – Swanage is the beginning of a steam- or diesel-powered train trip that runs past the stony, sombre ruins of Corfe Castle. Constructed by King William the Conqueror in the 11th century, the structure is one of the most iconic landmarks in Dorset. Centuries later, it was home to Sir John Bankes, King Charles I's right-hand man during the 17th-century Wars of the Three Kingdoms, when Corfe Castle was besieged by parliament's forces. This journey is short but scenic, and the heritage railway also puts on themed events, such as afternoon tea in a Pullman observation car, rallies showing off steam machines of all sorts and family-friendly dinosaur experiences.

Start // Swanage
Finish // Norden
Distance // 9.5 miles (15km)
Duration // 25min

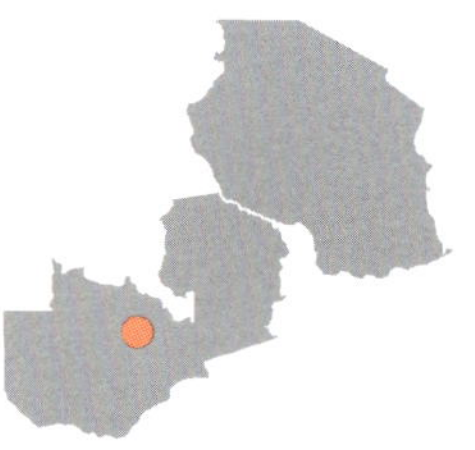

A TRUE AFRICAN ODYSSEY ABOARD THE TAZARA

A colourful route through Southern and East Africa's greenest backcountry, the Tazara's unpredictability makes it one of the continent's greatest railway adventures.

Time and the Tazara (TAnzania ZAmbia RAilway) are interesting companions, and fans of a particular brand of slow – sometimes very slow – travel will have a ball. If you're looking for a journey with plenty of time to gaze out the window at the gently passing East African countryside, then the Tazara is for you. It's also for adventurers who don't mind a few bumps in the night, savour grabbing fresh-cooked snacks from vendors on platforms and enjoy sharing a drink and a joke with strangers in a resolutely retro dining car. If you're ready to leave reliable schedules and smooth journeys behind, an unforgettable experience awaits.

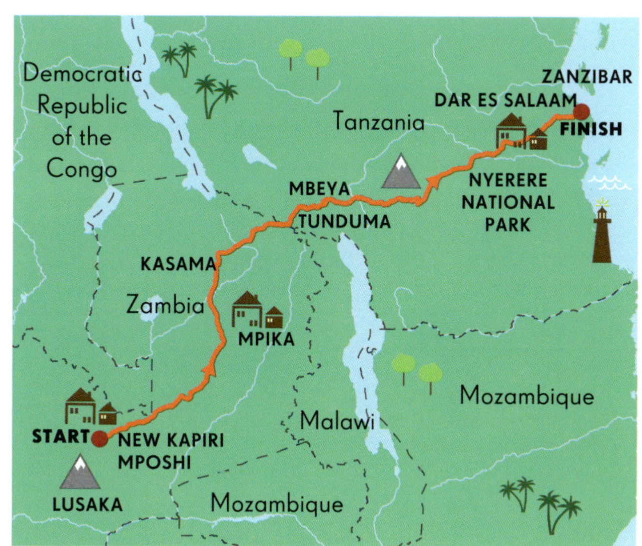

Most overseas travellers ride the Tazara as part of a wider African adventure. Appearing on some maps as the romantic-sounding Great Uhuru Railway, it's a convenient bridge from Zambia's accessible national parks to Tanzania's principal city, Dar es Salaam, from where Zanzibar's fabled Stone Town and Indian Ocean beaches are a fast-ferry away. I was looking forward to spending at least two days heading north across the plains of Zambia and then snaking through Tanzania's southern highlands, with the potential for wildlife spotting while passing through Nyerere National Park.

The Tazara is, in fact, served by two trains: one express (known as the Mukuba) that covers the 1156-mile (1860km) journey in just 46 hours, and the Kilimanjaro 'Ordinary' train that takes a few hours more. Both run weekly in each direction. Timetables should, however, be treated cautiously. Though the track was completed as recently as 1976, the service is unreliable and prone to holdups. There can be engine breakdowns, freight-train derailments (or wild animals) blocking the line and border delays. Extra patience, provisions to last at least a day and a sense of adventure also need to come along for the ride.

It pays to be comfortable, so spring for a First Class berth if possible. While this in theory means sharing with three others, in practice, there was no more than one other fellow rider with me at any one time. The extra space was perfect for lazy, meditative hours spent looking out of the window while lying horizontally.

On boarding, I couldn't help but get excited. I was in departure mode: sitting upright and ready for the off. But nothing happened. So we waited for a few minutes, then a few minutes more, and then it didn't feel much like anything would happen for a while. An hour after our scheduled departure, however, we lurched into life and rumbled out of New Kapiri Mposhi, travelling through a soft, warm twilight for the first few hours, followed by a swift plunge into near-total night. I strolled down to the dining car, where a gathering of characters were settled in for the night, swapping stories and laughs over cold beers. The occasional lurch to a halt in the pitch darkness of the bush felt part of the fun.

Journeying through the night made it difficult to tell how fast we were going, though the odd trackside light and sign of habitation suggested a steady, if not smooth, passage. Whenever we sped up, things got pretty bouncy. While I drifted off to sleep, occasional bumps in the night became par for the course. Periods of not moving at all made snoozing a little easier.

The following day we were due to arrive at the border after breakfast, but the delays meant this was now a lunchtime appointment. There were around 20 minutes allocated on each side, which felt optimistic – and so it proved. We disembarked at Nakonde to exit Zambia and again on the other side at Tunduma, where the station hall served as an immigration office. By the time all the paperwork was fixed and we rolled on into southern Tanzania, it was mid-afternoon.

From here on, progress was steady. We entered rolling highlands scenery, passing through the country town of Mbeya, the line's highest station at around 5578ft (1700m). Like other halts, this was a chance for a leg stretch and to check out some platform food. Quite the variety: bananas and mangos, snacks

CHANGING TRACKS

The days of unpredictable services on the Tazara may be numbered. In early 2024 the railway looked to be edging towards a cooperation agreement with the Chinese government, similar to the one that led to a rejuvenation of the Ethio-Djibouti Railway that connects the Ethiopian capital, Addis Ababa, to Djibouti's eponymous port city. In time, expect track and rolling stock renewal and faster journeys.

Clockwise from top: Food vendors greet a train; idling at the old gold mining town of Mbeya; a giraffe in Nyerere National Park; wildebeest are sometimes glimpsed from the train. Previous page: Rolling through the bush.

and hot meals cooked over stoves, beer and water. Like most of the stops en route, the platform scene was full of life and noise: passengers coming and going, cargo being loaded on and off the train, and people just turning up to observe the commotion.

Leaving Mbeya, we embarked on the upland section of the line, threading through several tunnels as we passed the southern flank of the Udzungwa Mountains. In daylight, I was told, there were lovely views to a backdrop of hills, but our train passed through at night, leaving us with chill and mist as proof of the higher, colder terrain.

At some point during this second night, I had the happy realization that thanks to the slow running, we'd be passing through Nyerere National Park during daylight. This meant the chance to spot wildlife while skirting the edge of the park's swamps, rivers and grasslands. For a few hours, the journey became an impromptu train safari, with zebra, a variety of antelope, giraffe and rumours of more spectacular animals holding up the train's passage as they crossed the tracks. These delays, and a few more extended pauses at stations along the way, added up to an extra night on board before an early morning arrival into Dar es Salaam. The animal-spotting more than made up for this.

Tanzania's largest city made for a noisy finish point, enveloping our arrival into its daily business. Despite the elongated journey, I dawdled at the station, sad to leave the Tazara behind, unsure if I'd become institutionalised or had simply fallen in love with this leisurely journey across two beautiful countries. **TH**

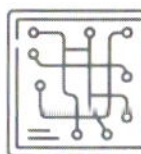

Start/Finish // New Kapiri Mposhi, Zambia/Dar es Salaam, Tanzania

Distance // 1156 miles (1860km)

Duration // 46hr (expect delays)

Ticket types // First Class berths accommodate four people; Second Class, six. It's possible to book a whole compartment by buying extra seats.

How to book // Make reservations by email, or book at stations in Zambia or Tanzania.

When to go // The dry season, from June to October, is the best time to travel.

Things to know // Use waiting time at the border to change money; only Zambian kwacha are accepted on board while the train is on the Zambian side of the line, and vice versa with Tanzanian shillings.

More info // Tanzania Zambia Railway Authority (tazarasite.com).

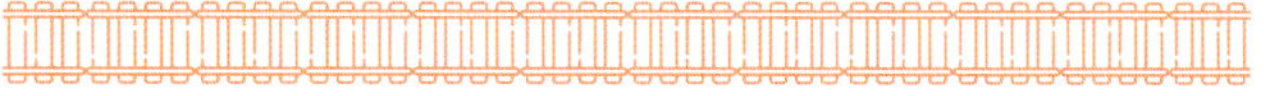

Opposite top: Hamburg's iconic Elbphilharmonie concert hall. Opposite below: Crowds flowing across Prague's Charles Bridge.

MORE LIKE THIS
CROSS-BORDER ODYSSEYS

UZBEKISTAN & KAZAKHSTAN

This efficient and modern service makes its way over one long day from Tashkent, Uzbekistan's capital, to Almaty, the largest city in Kazakhstan. It's almost (but not quite) a sleeper – on current timings it departs Tashkent in the early hours and arrives late at night into Almaty, having paused for around two hours for Uzbek border formalities and for another hour upon entering Kazakhstan. Along the way, there's plenty of time to sample the vast menu in the dining car, but the main attraction is losing yourself in the scenery as your eyes wander the endless grassland of the steppe, so symbolic of travel across Central Asia. This train is an excellent add-on to a few days exploring the historic cities of Uzbekistan: Bukhara and Samarkand are within easy reach of Tashkent by regular and convenient fast trains.
Start // Tashkent, Uzbekistan
Finish // Almaty, Kazakhstan
Distance // 458miles (738km)
Duration // 17hr

GERMANY & SWEDEN

This Swedish Railways (SJ) service, one of the darlings of the new European night-train scene, has grown in popularity and scope since its launch in 2022. From Hamburg – an excellent place to board if arriving from points south or west – the train heads into Denmark and makes an early hours crossing of the Öresund Bridge to Malmö. Beyond this southern tip of Sweden, morning views of Nordic forests and lakes root travellers in their surroundings until the train pulls into Stockholm Central, located in the middle of the tangle of waterways and islands at the heart of the capital. Private operator Snälltåget also operates seasonal night services on this route; check out this alternative train if your timings or availability don't work out on the SJ train, or if you want to try out Snälltåget's own highly regarded restaurant coach.
Start // Hamburg Hauptbahnhof, Germany
Finish // Stockholm Central, Sweden
Distance // 504 miles (811km)
Duration // 15hr 20min

BELGIUM & CZECHIA

A gallant start-up in a scene dominated by state-owned railways, the European Sleeper from Brussels to Prague has proved an invaluable addition to the continent's roster of night trains. With stops in Antwerp, Rotterdam, Amsterdam, Berlin and Dresden, this thrice-weekly option has reinstated a route phased out in 2008 but resurrected for climate-conscious passengers. Connecting Europe's two premier beer destinations – Belgium and Czechia – you'll get a guaranteed unforgettable sundowner whichever way you travel. Note that on alternate days to the European Sleeper service, there is also an Austrian railways (ÖBB) Nightjet service running from Brussels or Paris as far as Berlin, though taking a different route via Liège and heading down the Rhine to Mannheim.
Start // Brussels Midi, Belgium
Finish // Prague Hlavni, Czechia
Distance // 807 miles (1300km)
Duration // 15hr 20min

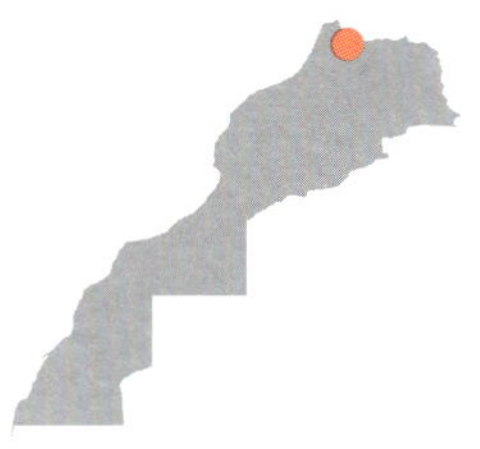

ACROSS MOROCCO ON THE HIGH-SPEED EL BORAQ

You can still take the Marrakesh Express of the 1969 song, but sleek El Boraq, Africa's first high-speed train, now cuts that journey time in half.

I've spent many long hours on Moroccan trains over the last 20 years or so, but now I'm taking a maiden voyage on El Boraq from Tangier to Casablanca, followed by the Al Atlas train from Casa to Marrakesh. Named for the lightning-fast, mythical creature that whisked the Prophet from Mecca to Jerusalem to heaven and back in the space of one night, El Boraq was inaugurated in 2018 and currently runs between Tangier on the Strait of Gibraltar and the country's largest city, Casablanca, on the Atlantic.

It took some years to build up to that launch, completely overhauling existing stations and laying the fast track. Stations in the cities of Tangier, Kenitra, Rabat and Casablanca had to be rebuilt to accommodate El Boraq. In future, the high-speed service will be extended to the tourism magnets of Marrakesh and Agadir. There's talk, too, of joining Africa to Europe with a line between Madrid and Tangier via a tunnel under the Strait of Gibraltar in time for the 2030 FIFA World Cup, hosted by Morocco, Spain and Portugal.

Most visitors to Morocco come to explore the ancient cities full of Islamic architecture with exquisite, sculpted plaster, colourful mosaics and painted wood, to trek the rugged High Atlas Mountains or to ride camels in the Sahara. But there's another side of this fast-developing country to discover that might come as a surprise: it's modern, forward-thinking and investing heavily in infrastructure like city tramways, impressive ports – and the high-speed train. Today I'm in the new Tanger Ville Station; it's enormous, modern with lots of glass, tall palm trees and other leafy plantings, the wide concourse surrounded by shops and fast-food outlets. As

Mate

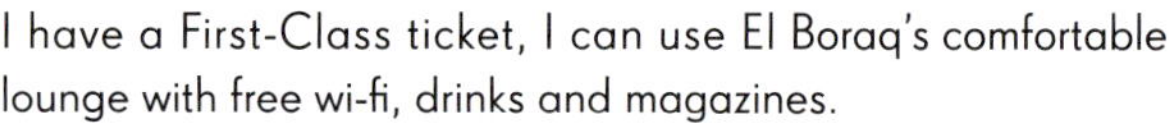

I have a First-Class ticket, I can use El Boraq's comfortable lounge with free wi-fi, drinks and magazines.

Twenty minutes before departure, we're called onto the platform, First-Class passengers using a door from the lounge. As I've bought my ticket online, I just have to show it on my phone at the ticket check. And there's the train. It's smooth and shiny, a silvery grey with green and orange streaks down the sides. If it looks familiar, that's because it's a repurposed TGV Euroduplex, or double-decker, just as you'd see in France, tweaked to accommodate local conditions.

I leave my suitcase on the luggage rack near the doors and find my seat. It's certainly very comfortable, with two chairs on one side of the aisle, and one on the other. I flick the footrest down, open the table and plug in my phone. The seats recline, there's an overhead luggage rack for small bags, a reading light and a window blind. So far, so impressive. I start chatting with the woman next to me, Fatima-Zahra, who tells me she's been visiting her parents in Tangier and is now going back to Casablanca where she works as an English teacher. This train has made visiting her family easier now that the journey is so much shorter – two hours instead of five or six – but it comes at a price that many Moroccans can't afford.

"The route takes us southwards along the Atlantic coast, past the seaside resort of Asilah with its pretty white medina..."

The route takes us southwards along the Atlantic coast, past the seaside resort of Asilah with its pretty white medina and pirate history. Beyond it, we gain speed as we approach the fast section of track, and suddenly we're travelling at 199mph (320km/h) – the train is smooth and silent, while the view outside is blurred. After a while, I walk through to the buffet car for some coffee and breakfast.

We reach the busy market town of Kenitra in 50 minutes, and after that our speed is reduced to 100mph (160km/h), though there are plans to upgrade the next section of track between Rabat and Casablanca. As we near the former, capital of Morocco, we pass the new 55-story, 820ft (250m) Mohammed VI Tower and the nearby Grand Théâtre designed by Zaha Hadid, one tall, black and powerful, the other sensual, low-lying and white. The sea views after Rabat are striking, and easier to see now we're travelling at a gentler pace. We pass the industrial town of Mohammedia and the beaches where Casablancais spend summer weekends before El Boraq pulls into Casa

TRAIN ETIQUETTE

As the seating arrangements on Al Atlas trains are compartments of six to eight people, it's a more convivial atmosphere than on the modern El Boraq, and you're more likely to get chatting with your fellow travellers. If you take your own food on board, take a bit extra so you can share with others in your compartment. During Ramadan, the buffet car is closed and there's no snack trolley.

Clockwise from top left: The Djemaa el Fna in Marrakesh; Marrakesh Station; Tangier medina; Casablanca's King Hassan II mosque; platforms at Casablanca's station. Previous page: Marrakesh medina.

Voyageurs Station on time after a journey of just two hours and 10 minutes – less than half the five hours the ordinary train takes.

But I'm not planning to be in Casablanca for long. After a change of platforms I board the Al Atlas train to Marrakesh, Morocco's most alluring destination. We leave the coast and travel inland, heading south where the landscape varies between desert-like scrub and farmland, punctuated by small towns and villages, each with their mosque minaret. There are just three stops at the towns of Berrechid, Settat and Ben Guerir. Eventually, the impressive, snow-capped High Atlas Mountains come into view once we get close to Marrakesh where I'm welcomed by another airy, well-planned station with lots of taxis outside to take me to my hotel.

But if you do have that Crosby, Stills & Nash song in your head, or would rather save the cost of a night in a hotel, the nostalgic Marrakesh Express sleeper between Tangier and the Red City is for you. It departs Tanger Ville at 11.45pm each night, and pulls into Marrakesh Station at 9.10am the next morning. You can take a Second- or First-Class seat, or a bunk with a freshly laundered sheet, pillow and blanket. It's a slow train and makes six stops during the night, but you won't notice as you'll be gently rocked to sleep as the train clicks over the rails. **HR**

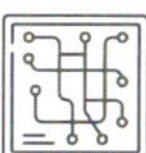

Start/Finish // Tanger Ville Station/Marrakesh Station
Distance // 312 miles (502km)
Duration // El Boraq Tangier to Casablanca, followed by Al Atlas Casablanca to Marrakesh: 5hr 30min/Marrakesh Express: 9hr 16min overnight
Ticket types // First or Second Class. On El Boraq, First Class has three seats per row; in Second Class, it's four. On Al Atlas trains, First Class has six-seater compartments, while Second Class compartments seat eight.
How to book // Buy tickets at a station or online at oncf.ma. Book sleeper compartments in person at a station or at marrakechtickets.co.uk up to two months in advance, and be sure to take your passport when booking.
When to go // Spring and autumn are the best months, but mountain-top snow sparkling in the sunshine makes winter popular too.

Opposite top: The gates of the Royal Palace in Fez. Opposite below: Voyageurs Station in Casablanca, Morocco.

MORE LIKE THIS
MOROCCAN TRAIN TRIPS

ORIENTAL DESERT EXPRESS

A DH410 diesel locomotive with a maximum speed of no more than 31mph (50km/h), plus stops to clear sand from the track, mean that this journey can take 10-12 hours. It passes through spectacular desert landscapes in Morocco's far eastern region, and includes a photo stop at the 1214ft (370m) Tiouli Tunnel, built in 1930 and the only one on the route, and at Tendrara, where a sequence from the James Bond movie *Spectre* was shot. Carriages formerly reserved for the Moroccan royal family, including a dining car, make for a comfortable ride. You'll need to find a travel agent or railway enthusiasts club offering this journey as it's by charter only, and often part of a longer trip.
Start // Oujda
Finish // Bouarfa
Distance // 179 miles (288km)
Duration // 10-12hr

CASABLANCA TO FEZ

The Casablanca to Fez route is served by the Marrakesh-Fez Al Atlas train as well as by trains starting in Casa, setting off from Casa Voyageurs Station. An electric locomotive capable of 100mph (160km/h) hauls around nine carriages, of which two are First Class, hugging the coast north to the capital, Rabat, and then, at Kenitra, turning inland. It then runs east through farmland to Sidi Kacem, a wide loop around Meknes to accommodate the topography, and on to Fez. The inland section becomes greener, the hillsides dotted with olive and citrus trees, and plenty of vines around Meknes. There's no dining car, but a man with a trolley sells soft drinks, coffee and tea and snacks. First Class compartments have comfortable, reclining seats, six to a carriage, while Second Class has eight, though some carriages are open plan.
Start // Casa Voyageurs Station, Casablanca
Finish // Fez
Distance // 199 miles (320km)
Duration // 3hr 30min to 4hr

FEZ TO OUJDA

A diesel DH420 locomotive labours its way up from Fez into the foothills of the Rif Mountains to the northern city of Oujda over 205 miles (330km) of unelectrified track. The line winds slowly around hills and rivers, taking six hours to complete the journey, the best part of which is the landscape and the backward views of the train itself winding around rocky outcrops. Between the oasis of Sidi Harazem and Oued Amlil, a spectacular viaduct carries the train across part of the Idriss I Dam. The fortified city of Taza is perched up high, commanding the surrounding country. Here you'll skirt the edges of the lush Tazekka National Park. There are flat-topped mesas in the distance, near the Algerian border, while the riverbanks are rimed with pink-tinged salt. Oujda boasts a refurbished station, its futuristic white curves spanning the tracks.
Start // Fez
Finish // Oujda
Distance // 205 miles (330km)
Duration // 5hr 30min to 6hr

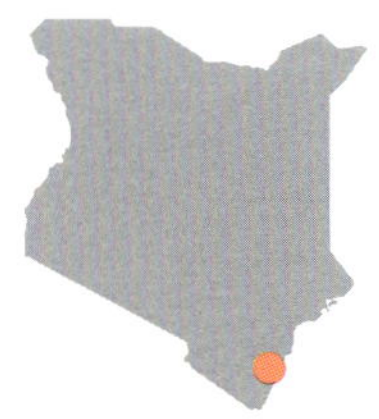

INTO KENYA ON THE MOMBASA-NAIROBI SGR

The 'Lunatic Express' was Africa's most legendary railway – in recent times it's been reinvented as a slick modern service, shuttling between Kenya's two biggest cities.

The train in Mombasa was unrecognisable from the one I had boarded years before.

I remembered the old Nairobi-Mombasa line as a great shambling dinosaur of a railway. A line where tumbledown coaches clung tenuously to rickety rails. On which the dining car swung like a ship in a storm and passengers did their best to doze in compartments, with sleep interrupted by a chaotic symphony of creaks and crashes. Delays were sometimes hours, but often days.

What was on offer now, though, was a new incarnation; not the narrow-gauge line I had once ridden, but a sleek new standard-gauge railway (SGR), Chinese-built and opened in 2017. A journey on this Mombasa-Nairobi SGR (also known in its new guise as the Madaraka Express) presented a bold vision of 21st-century Kenya – purring trains, futuristic stations, businesspeople coming and going from the Indian Ocean to the Central Highlands. At the same time, the ghost of the old line could still be glimpsed, its rails rusting in the grasses parallel to our path. Ride on the new SGR and you can still hear stories of its former incarnation – known as the 'Lunatic Express'.

My journey started in the port of Mombasa where a tangle of estuaries empties out into the Indian Ocean. For centuries, Kenya's second city was a springboard for those seeking to plunder the riches of the interior. You can get to grips with this history amid the sun-bleached battlements of Fort Jesus, a 16th-century bastion occupied by the Portuguese and the Omanis before it fell into British hands in the last years of the 19th century. I explored its turrets and crenellations, then ambled east, down Haile Selasissie Road to the old Mombasa Station. It was the British who resolved to build a railway into the Kenyan hinterland, aiming partly to disrupt the slave trade in this part of the continent, but mostly to project British power to the great lakes of East Africa and keep a step ahead of their German colonial rivals. Tracks were first laid in Mombasa in 1896 and reached the shores of Lake Victoria five years later.

The line the British built became most famous as a train for tourists. Throughout the first half of the 20th century, the so-called 'Lunatic Express' earned its reputation thanks to a madcap assortment of aristocrats and adventurers who came from Europe and North America to ride the pioneering route. Safari back then meant shooting game, even from a train –

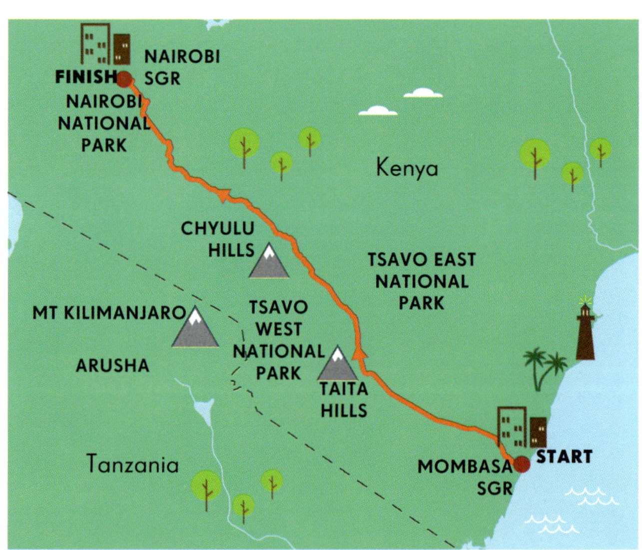

"Once upon a time, however, wildlife encounters in these parts were of a much more dangerous kind."

pith helmeted hunters rode on a garden bench mounted on the locomotive, taking aim at elephants along the way – but the wildlife sometimes fought back: rhinos often charged the trains and giraffes chewed lineside telegraph lines. The Lunatic Express (known officially as the Uganda Railway and locally as the Iron Snake) has a legacy stained by the British colonial exploitation of Kenya. It was also partly responsible for creating the modern concept of safari. For some, the railway was a passport to a land of adventure: it introduced outsiders to the primeval kick of encounters with big beasts.

Trains today only depart the old Mombasa Station to link to the new 21st-century one, an out-of-town, space-age structure. Soon my train rolled out of Mombasa SGR terminus and green creeks turned to the scrub of the interior. Classic East African vistas unfurled – savannah, baobab and watering holes – highlighting another advantage of the modern SGR: it's a daytime train unlike its sleeper predecessor meaning passengers can savour the scenery along the way. Two hours after leaving Mombasa the Taita Hills rose up, their cool heights home to rare plant species. Then we travelled the boundary between Tsavo East and Tsavo West National Parks: the former Kenya's largest; the latter one of its most beautiful, a tapestry of rolling hills and extinct volcanoes. Both are rich in wildlife including elephant, rhino, lion and leopard. Sometimes passengers spot zebra or impala out of the window. Once upon a time, however, wildlife encounters in these parts were of a more dangerous kind.

GAUGING THE FUTURE

It's hoped the Mombasa-Nairobi SGR will be just one part of a new East African standard-gauge network that will stretch from Kenya into neighbouring Uganda, and onward into Rwanda, Burundi and South Sudan. At the time of writing, work was underway on the section from Nairobi to the Ugandan border at Malaba – the other segments remain very much at the planning stage, having hit financial stumbling blocks.

Clockwise from top: looking out over the savannah; a rhino in Nairobi National Park, on the edge of the capital; the new SGR station at Mombasa; much of the route is elevated. Previous page: a male lion in Tsavo West National Park, Kenya.

A dark chapter in the construction of the 'Lunatic Line' concerns the 'Tsavo Man Eaters' – a pair of lions who reputedly killed scores of Indian labourers in 1898. The two were hunted down and their taxidermied remains are now stored in the Field Museum in Chicago. Other man-eating lions continued to stalk railway workers. In 1900, a British officer named Charles Henry Ryall camped out inside a railway carriage armed with a rifle, intending to lure in a troublesome lion known as the 'Kima Killer' by offering himself as bait. Unfortunately he had fatally dozed off by the time the lion crept aboard.

Such grisly histories were far from passengers' minds as we passed by the Chyulu Hills – a volcanic ridge Swiss-cheesed by lava tubes. On clear days travellers can spy Kilimanjaro, its snows marking the Kenyan border with Tanzania. The final approach to the capital saw the trains skirting the edge of the Nairobi National Park before ending at another futuristic station on the edge of the town.

Nairobi owes its existence to the railways – it grew from a little halt on the line to the great metropolis of the present day – and right in the centre is the original Nairobi Central Station, with the excellent Kenya National Railway Museum next door. Here you can trace the lineage of the modern SGR and walk among ancient steam locomotives and rolling stock, parked among jacaranda trees in bloom.

Among them one particular carriage caught my eye – the little grey truck in which one Charles Henry Ryall had fallen asleep, and a hungry lion stepped aboard. **OS**

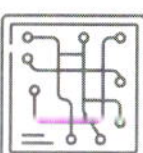

Start/Finish // Mombasa SGR Station/Nairobi SGR Station

Distance // 360 miles (579 km)

Duration // 5hr 10min

Ticket types // Trains on the Mombasa-Nairobi line divide between First Class – spacious with reclining seats – and a slightly more cramped Second Class, which squeezes five seats into a row, rather than four. In First you can access the buffet car: in Second you make do with a trolley. Unlike the old railway, there are no sleeper services.

How to book // You'll need to use an agency to pre-book tickets from outside Kenya – try East Africa Shuttles (eastafricashuttles.com).

Things to know // Allow plenty of time before departure due to airport-style security checks. According to reports, alcohol is not allowed on board.

Opposite: Passengers boarding a train at Dar es Salaam's Central Station.

MORE LIKE THIS
EAST AFRICAN TRAIN TRIPS

NAIROBI TO KISUMU

You can still get a taste of old school Kenyan narrow-gauge trains in the country's west, boarding the overnight sleeper from Nairobi Central Station to Kisumu. Schedules were a little unclear at the time of writing, but the 'Kisumu Safari Train' is thought to depart the capital on Friday evenings – so sadly darkness will have descended by the time you reach the hippo-dotted expanse of Lake Naivasha, the highest lake in the Rift Valley. The train continues in the small hours past the shores of Lake Nakuru, traditionally home to vast flocks of flamingos, with a fine national park encircling its shores. All being well it will be breakfast by the time the sleeper reaches the greatest lake of all, Victoria, and terminates at the easy-going city of Kisumu. Spend an idle weekend here before catching the return train back to Nairobi on Sunday evening.
Start // Nairobi Central Station
Finish // Kisumu
Distance // 134 miles (216km)
Duration // 12hr

DAR ES SALAAM TO KIGOMA

For most railway fans, Tanzania is synonymous with the far-roaming Tazara services that head south from Dar es Salaam across the border into Zambia. Fewer make the journey due west from Dar to Kigoma on the Central Line, a project inaugurated during German colonial rule. It takes the best part of two days to travel the width of the country from the Indian Ocean to the great inland sea of Lake Tanganyika – on the way you pass the capital Dodoma and skirt the edge of the Muhesi Game Reserve. The end destination is a pleasant town whose station sits right on its freshwater port. Scan the quays for the *MV Liemba* – the ancient ship that was the inspiration for *The African Queen* – which takes passengers south to Zambia. As in Kenya, this old metre-gauge railway is being shadowed by a more modern standard-gauge 'SGR' route under Chinese construction.
Start // Dar es Salaam
Finish // Kigoma
Distance // 780 miles (1255km)
Duration // Around 2 days

NAIROBI TO NANYUKI

It takes about an hour to fly from Nairobi to Nanyuki, a little market town pitched under the northern slopes of Mt Kenya. If you're not in a hurry, though, you could board the eight-hour train which – like its little counterpart heading to Kisumu – conveniently makes a weekly departure from the capital on Friday and returns on Sunday. It's a long, meandering journey from the outskirts of Nairobi into the Highlands proper – soon Mt Kenya appears out of the right-hand window and the green heights of the Aberdare Range lurk in the distance to the left. Nanyuki can be used as a base for scaling the mountain which gives the country its name.
Start //Nairobi Central Station
Finish // Nanyuki
Distance // 110 miles (177 km)
Duration // 7hr 49min

DAR-ES-SALAAM
NEW YORK
2
2103

AMERICAS

A CANADIAN CLASSIC: THE ROCKY MOUNTAINEER

Few train trips can offer such a wealth of wild scenery as this one – let alone the chance to spot a grizzly from your seat.

'Moose to starboard!' hollers passenger Don Smith, as he holds aloft his lens and snaps off frames like a machine gun. 'He's a beauty!' he adds, sending everyone thronging to the right-hand side of the carriage, cameras whirring. Oblivious to its sudden celebrity, the moose in question ambles across a meadow munching grass, antlers held aloft, framed against a backdrop of green pines and snowy mountains. It looks like it's posing for a magazine shoot. Encounters like this are par for the course on the Rocky Mountaineer. One minute you're sipping a cocktail: the next you're squished against the window, watching elk grazing on the riverbanks, mountain goats on the slopes, ospreys nesting in the treetops. The apogee of the Rocky Mountaineer Wildlife Spotters' Club is a sighting of a black or grizzly bear, but you'll need good luck – and a decent lens – to see one.

With experiences like these, it's little wonder that the Rocky Mountaineer is considered Canada's premier train trip. Though it's

ROCKY MOUNTAINEER

officially been running since 1990, the railway's history actually stretches back more than a century earlier – all the way to Confederation, in fact. Its route tracks the old Canadian Pacific Railway (CPR), the pioneering line over the Rockies which, in 1886, completed the long-mooted dream for a trans-continental railway connecting Canada's Pacific and Atlantic coasts.

Sadly, CPR trains only haul freight these days. If you want to ride the route as a passenger, the only way to do so is aboard the Rocky Mountaineer – and thousands of people pay very handsomely for the privilege every year. Unlike the cramped carriages and steam locomotives of old, however, today's version of the train is an unabashedly luxurious experience. Waistcoated hosts provide a running commentary on the scenery as you hurtle along. Concierges mix cocktails and deliver snacks to your seat. Three-course meals of sockeye salmon and caribou steak are served on starched white tablecloths in the dining car. Every creature comfort is catered for: air-con, reclinable seats, padded antimacassars, USB ports. Best of all, the carriages sport domed bubble windows that offer wraparound views of the scenery. One thing's for sure: you won't be roughing it on the modern Rocky Mountaineer.

There are several possible routes through the mountains. The classic is the 'First Passage to the West', which traces the CPR from Vancouver over the Rockies to Banff, with an overnight stop in Kamloops. Three times a week from April to October, the train departs like clockwork, with a kilted bagpiper on the platform to give it a traditional Highland send-off.

From here, the train begins the long haul into the Rockies. The first day, we cover the land west of the Continental Divide, roughly following the course of the Fraser River. Quintessentially Canadian landscapes flash past: rivers, forests, plains, prairies. After a while, it's hard not to become a bit blasé about the scenery – and then, as we round another bend in the track, a jaw-dropping vista arrives to jolt my retinas from their complacency. A waterfall, bursting like a thunderstorm down the mountainside. A gorge, dropping away into mist like a Tolkien illustration. A lake, shining like glass in the sunlight. At Hell's Gate, the Fraser River is forced through a gap just 112ft (34m) wide, resulting in a foaming tumult of whitewater. At Cisco Crossing, two bridges cross the river at the same point, the result of rival railroad engineers who refused to collaborate. And as we pull into Kamloops for the night, the mighty Rockies loom like battlements along the skyline.

On day two, the alpine scenery hits overdrive. As we roll through Revelstoke, Glacier and Yoho, it becomes hard to hold onto a useful sense of scale. Surely a mountain can't be quite that large, I ask myself? Isn't that river just a bit too loud? Are trees normally so tall? Is there usually that much sky? Riding the Rocky Mountaineer is like being a passenger on a model railway whose creator has got their proportions muddled: between Revelstoke and Golden, we cross Stoney Creek Bridge, which was the highest timber bridge ever constructed

COMPLETING THE CPR

At Craigellachie, a plaque and monument commemorates the driving-in of the 'last spike' on the Canadian Pacific Railway. On 7 November 1885, Scots-Canadian businessman Donald Alexander Smith, co-founder of the project, hammered a ceremonial spike that completed the trans-Canadian railway – five years ahead of the deadline. Unfortunately the spike bent while he was banging it in, and it later had to be discreetly replaced.

Clockwise from top: Lunch is served; bighorn sheep glimpsed from the train; crossing Stoney Creek bridge; canoes at Lake Louise; the interiors in Gold Leaf class. Previous page: The Rocky Mountaineer at Morant's Curve.

when it was completed in 1885. Later rebuilt in steel, it still feels improbably, dizzyingly high. At 270ft (82m), it's only a smidgen shorter than the Statue of Liberty.

The most memorable engineering feature on the route is at Kicking Horse Canyon. Gouged from the mountainside by its namesake river, this precipitous ravine presented a formidable challenge to the CPR's builders, and was nicknamed the 'Big Hill' for evident reasons.

Here, the railway negotiates a 1 in 25 gradient; the first train to attempt it derailed, killing three people. Brakes frequently overheated; breakdowns were common. Eventually, a plucky engineer called JE Schwitzer devised a clever series of corkscrew shafts, modelled on a Swiss railway design and now known as the Spiral Tunnels, which tame the gradient by circling through the mountainside.

Beyond Kicking Horse Pass, the Rocky Mountaineer hits the home stretch. Lake Louise blurs past, framed by 9843ft-high (3000m) peaks. Glaciers flash and glitter on the mountainsides. The blue waters of the Bow River surge into view. The train rounds the flanks of Castle Mountain, following a famously photogenic bend in the river known as Morant's Curve (after Nicholas Morant, a CPR staff photographer). At last, the train pulls into Banff Town, two days, 36½ hours, and 594 miles (956km) after it departed from Vancouver.

Yesterday I was standing with my toes in the Pacific Ocean; today I'm breathing pine-scented air in the middle of the Rocky Mountains. It's been quite a commute. **OB**

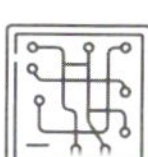

Start/Finish // Vancouver/Banff Town
Distance // 594 miles (956km)
Duration // 2 days
Ticket types // There are two classes. Silver Leaf passengers travel in a single-decker coach, with meals and snacks served at your seat by train attendants. Gold Leaf buys access to the premium double-decker carriage, with a viewing deck on the first level and a dining room below.
How to book // Book direct (rockymountaineer.com); last-minute deals are sometimes available.
When to go // May to September are the most expensive months; discounts are available in April and October. The train doesn't run November to March.
Things to know // Tickets include meals, drinks and overnight accommodation in Kamloops.
More info // Visit tourist board sites for local inspo: Banff & Lake Louise Tourist Board (banfflakelouise.com); Jasper (jasper.travel).

Opposite top: A Rocky Mountaineer train on a 'Journey Through the Clouds' departure. Opposite below: Silver Leaf class on the relatively new journey through the United States.

MORE LIKE THIS
OTHER ROCKY MOUNTAINEER ROUTES

JOURNEY THROUGH THE CLOUDS

This is an alternative to the classic Canadian Pacific route. Initially, it follows the same journey as the 'First Passage to the West' along the Fraser Valley, but at Kamloops, it veers northeast along the North Thompson River and loops over the mountains to Jasper. Arguably, it's even more scenic than the better-known route. You'll pass Pyramid Falls, where a waterfall thunders down a glacial valley to rejoin the Thompson, and get a grandstand view of Canada's highest peak, Mt Robson, at 12,973ft (3954m) – known to climbers as the 'Great White Fright'. There's wildlife-spotting potential around Moose Lake and Yellowhead Pass, while Jasper Town is an outdoor adventure hub.
Start // Vancouver
Finish // Jasper
Distance // 559 miles (900km)
Duration // 2 days

RAINFOREST TO GOLD RUSH

Coast, forests and mountains all feature on this three-day Rocky Mountaineer route, which factors in overnight stops at the ski town of Whistler and the logging centre of Quesnel before finishing in Jasper. The first day tracks the coast, with views of Horseshoe Bay and Howe Sound unfolding en route to Whistler. Day two is devoted to the gold country: 150 years ago, the area around the Cariboo Plateau was the epicentre of BC's great gold rush, and huge fortunes were made and lost by prospectors here, especially around Barkerville. Day three is for nature: as you cross the Rockies and continue to Jasper, you should have a great chance of spotting iconic BC wildlife including bears, wolves, moose and bald eagles.
Start // Vancouver
Finish // Jasper
Distance // 717 miles (1153km)
Duration // 3 days

ROCKIES TO THE RED ROCKS

Inaugurated in 2021, this is the first Rocky Mountaineer train to run south of the border, tracing the Colorado River, crossing canyons, badlands, deserts and mountains along the way. The journey begins in the desert city of Moab, Utah, and ends 354 miles (570km) east in the Mile High City, Denver, Colorado, crossing the Continental Divide en route, and overnighting in Glenwood Springs. From spooky sculpted hoodoos to red-rock canyons and natural arches, it's a landscape made for photographers and geology buffs. Standout sights include Mt Garfield, the high point of the Book Cliffs; and Ruby Canyon, famous for its strange rock towers, carved by aeons of wind and erosion. Railway nerds will appreciate the 'tunnel district' – a 13-mile (21km) stretch featuring 30 tunnels blasted through the rock.
Start // Moab
Finish // Denver
Distance // 354 miles (570km)
Duration // 2 days

RIDE THE HIRAM BINGHAM INTO THE INCAN HEARTLAND

Take a swashbuckling journey by rail through the Peruvian Andes on the Hiram Bingham, arriving at the foot of the South America's great lost city.

In 1911, the American Hiram Bingham set out on an expedition in the Andes, tracing the Urubamba River downstream. It would have been a journey of considerable hardship that involved crossing swollen currents, hacking through thick jungle, clambering up merciless mountains and swatting away insects. But he was spurred on by rumours of Inca ruins in these hills. Eventually he found his holy grail in the lost city of Machu Picchu, whose overgrown masonry he brought to the attention of the wider world.

Contrary to popular belief, Bingham didn't rediscover the Inca citadel (locals had always known of its existence). Nor was he even the first modern explorer to set eyes on it after the citadel was abandoned in the 16th century. Nonetheless, he is part of the legend of Machu Picchu, even lending his name to a luxury train that roughly retraces his route, from the city of Cusco (where he first heard whispers of its existence) to the little station at Aguas Calientes, at its base. The train I encountered on the edge of Cusco was emphatically not a train of any hardship, nor for that matter was it in need of rediscovery. Enduringly popular since its creation in 2003, the luxury Hiram Bingham train sees history and high-rolling combine. Short of the ceremonial processions of Inca emperors, it's the most stylish way to arrive.

I was escorted to my linen-clad table, adorned with fresh flowers. A cocktail menu appeared from nowhere; pisco sours materialised moments after. Bingham's story is a powerful one, and some fellow passengers are attired in the cosplay of explorers like him – fedora hats, utility jackets with multiple pockets. Others are smartly dressed for the occasion – the Hiram Bingham is a Belmond service and sister of the Venice Simplon Orient Express. Like its sibling, this Peruvian train also conjures up echoes of a golden age of travel (which, in truth, never actually existed upon these rails), the decor on board more suggestive of transcontinental odysseys rather than a three-hour jaunt. Not that this bothered passengers on my northbound departure to Aguas Calientes, all giddy with

anticipation of arriving in Machu Picchu. The most stylish part of the train is at the rear, in the polished wood of the bar car where cocktails are shaken, and in the observation carriage, which has a little balcony where you can look out to the retreating track as you might a ship's wake.

We began by trundling through a valley floor chequered with farmland. It wasn't long before we were acquainted with the raging current of the Urubamba River and entered the Sacred Valley of the Inca – the heartland of the great civilisation. Reaching its peak in the 16th century, the Inca Empire stretched from modern Chile to Colombia. Its people were master stonemasons – and with a railway ride through the Sacred Valley you can see their genius for construction. The Hiram Bingham passed through the village of Ollantaytambo, whose ancient terraces served as both fortress and temple complex. Higher still were the ruins of Pinkuylluna, clinging to a vertical cliff. It was an appetiser for the more famous stones of Machu Picchu – though many eyes on board were instead drawn to the menus before them, whose appetiser was Andean cured trout.

Effort is required not to spill food on the Hiram Bingham – it's sometimes a bumpy ride on this narrow-gauge line, the tracks just 3ft (1m) wide. The benefit of this gauge is that it allows the railway to twist and turn sharply in tandem with the meanders of the Urubamba – sometimes we disappeared into tunnels and cuttings, before being reunited with its furious current on the far side. The line was laid in the decade after Bingham first encountered Machu Picchu – by the time the tracks reached Aguas Calientes, the city above had been cleared of foliage and was gracing newspaper and magazine covers across the world.

"Grab yourself a window seat and press your face close enough to the glass, and you might still entertain fantasies of being an explorer..."

In the 21st century, trains are the only practical way to reach Machu Picchu (unless you hike the Inca Trail): here and there we passed PeruRail and IncaRail locomotives that service the thousands who forgo the expensive Hiram Bingham. It's a well-travelled route. But grab yourself a window seat on any kind of train, press your face close enough to the glass to blot out

EL ZIG ZAG

A highlight of the train ride to Aguas Calientes is ascending 'El Zig Zag' – a series of switchbacks climbing the escarpment on the edge of Cusco. Unfortunately, the Hiram Bingham skips this feature entirely, instead starting from Poroy Station, a short taxi ride out of town, but more basic PeruRail trains do travel this section soon after departure from Cusco San Pedro Station.

Clockwise from top left: The Hiram Bingham's Observation Car; looking into the narrow-gauge coaches; rolling stock at Aguas Calientes; fruit for sale in Cusco. Previous page: Clouds smother the lost city of Machu Picchu.

your fellow passengers and you might still entertain fantasies of being an explorer, following the great Urubamba on its downstream voyage.

After Piscacucho, the flanks of the mountains closed in, the snowy peak of Nevado Veronica reigning over the sky. More Inca ruins loomed high above – Patallacta, Chachabamba, others out of sight. The landscape became greener as the dusty slopes of the Andes gave way to the greens of another ecosystem. You could sense the Amazon basin drawing nearer. For Hiram Bingham passengers the journey ends short of the great jungle, at Aguas Calientes, where everyone boarded waiting buses to navigate the switchbacks up to Machu Picchu itself.

The Inca had many strongpoints, but timing was unfortunately not one of them. Their empire flourished at the precise moment the Spanish landed in the Americas. The new arrivals had advantages such as iron swords and the wheel, but it was diseases the conquistadors brought which also sealed the Inca decline. In the centuries that followed, the temples and terraces of Machu Picchu were left alone atop their mountain perch, with only the call of the condors. These days there are new sounds: the bustle of tourists and the rattle of wheels on iron rails. **OS**

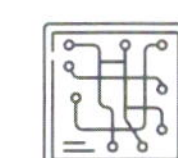

Start/Finish // Poroy Station (outside Cusco)/Aguas Calientes
Distance // 57 miles (92km)
Duration // 3hr 30min
Ticket types // Tickets on the Hiram Bingham are all inclusive. As well as meals and most alcoholic drinks, the price covers transfers, admission and guiding at Machu Picchu itself, plus afternoon tea at Belmond Sanctuary Lodge by the city gates. To keep costs lower, consider a one-way journey on the Hiram Bingham, returning on one of the cheaper trains. PeruRail and IncaRail also travel on the same line and cater for a variety of budgets: PeruRail's Vistadome coaches are perfect for mountain views. Note that only Peruvians can board local trains in the Sacred Valley.
How to book // Direct with Belmond belmond.com

Opposite top: Gazing out at the altiplano from the Andean Explorer. Opposite below: The intermittent service into the Andes from Lima.

MORE LIKE THIS
RAILWAY HIGHS IN PERU

ANDEAN EXPLORER

Belmond's other Peruvian offering is the Andean Explorer, launched in 2017 and proudly claiming the distinction of being South America's first luxury sleeper. In a part of the world sorely lacking in trains, it's a more than welcome addition – while the narrow-gauge Hiram Bingham goes northward from Cusco, the standard-gauge Explorer swings south. A classic two-night itinerary sees the train speed through snow-capped mountains to Puno and the shores of Lake Titicaca, before dog-legging to the country's second city of Arequipa. On the way expect stops to enjoy more Inca ruins and Titicaca boat rides, though it's hard work prizing yourself away from this beautiful train with its handsome bar, comfy compartments and even a spa carriage, where you can enjoy a massage as the sierras slip by.

Start // Cusco
Finish // Arequipa
Distance // 450 miles (724km)
Duration // 3 days

LIMA TO HUANCAYO AND ON TO HUANCAVELICA

The railway linking the Peruvian capital Lima to the highland city of Huancayo was once the highest in the world, though it's since been eclipsed by another in Tibet. It is nonetheless a truly epic ride – beginning in Lima's magnificent art nouveau Desamparados Station, the train soon leaves the desert country of the coast to traverse the high passes of the Central Andes, dotted with lonely mining settlements. From the likable city of Huancayo a second line links to Huancavelica across the altiplano, extending the adventure. It's a journey of dizzying statistics – reaching ear-popping elevations of 15,692ft (4783m) – but there's a sad postscript: the traditionally unreliable departures from Lima had totally ground to a halt at the time of writing, reportedly due to landslides on the line. Only a small part of the Huancayo to Huancavelica line was operational. Here's hoping these trains climb to lofty elevations once again.

Start // Lima
Finish // Huancavelica
Distance // 286 miles (460km)
Duration // Around 24hr

TRAM 97, LIMA

The Peruvian capital once boasted one of the continent's best tram networks, with four lines shuttling to distant corners of the city. After booming in the early 20th century, the trams were suffering by the 1960s, and eventually shuttered for good after a succession of strikes, paving the way for the reign of the motorcar (a story familiar across South America). There was, however, a notable survivor. Head to the bohemian Barranco district and you can see tram number 97 – a restored Italian-built machine that rumbles along 1968ft (600m) of track in an evocation of days past. You can find it parked outside the Museum of Electricity, where you can also inquire about departure times.

Start/Finish // Barranco
Distance // 1968ft (600m)
Duration // 10min

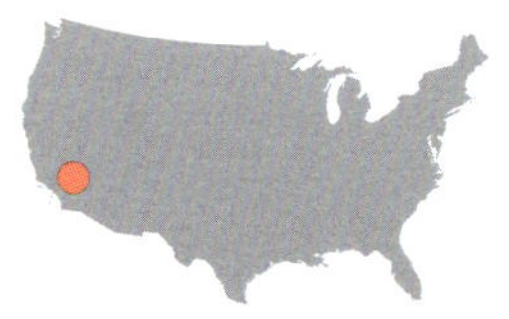

FLY AWAY ON THE CALIFORNIA ZEPHYR

An Amish couple, a Japanese student and I walk into a dining car. This isn't the start of a bad joke but a classic moment on the USA's longest-running daily train service.

Riding the California Zephyr made me fall in love with the United States again. Like the country, it's not perfect – in 2023, only 33% of trains arrived on time – but it's ripe for adventure, gifting that sense of possibility and showing off a diverse cross-section of the nation, both in the landscapes and the passengers, that you won't find anywhere else.

Though it clocks in at 2438 miles (3924km) and takes upwards of two days from start to finish, the California Zephyr is not a train to hop off and on, but instead a journey to see through to its conclusion. This is arguably Amtrak's most scenic route, passing through major cities, two snow-capped mountain ranges (the Sierra Nevada and the Rockies), high-desert ghost towns and empty, lonely prairie. The train feels like a wonderful combination of a bar on wheels, a rowdy classroom and a wildlife-spotting safari, a motley crew lounging in the observation car that offers a handful of booth tables, nearly floor-to-ceiling windows and swivel seats facing outward.

In the waiting hall at the train station in Sacramento, I gaze at a beautiful wall-spanning mural commemorating the city's 1863 ground-breaking ceremony for the first Transcontinental Railroad – the California Zephyr partly follows in its tracks. When the double-decker train arrives, I board, along with docents from the nearby

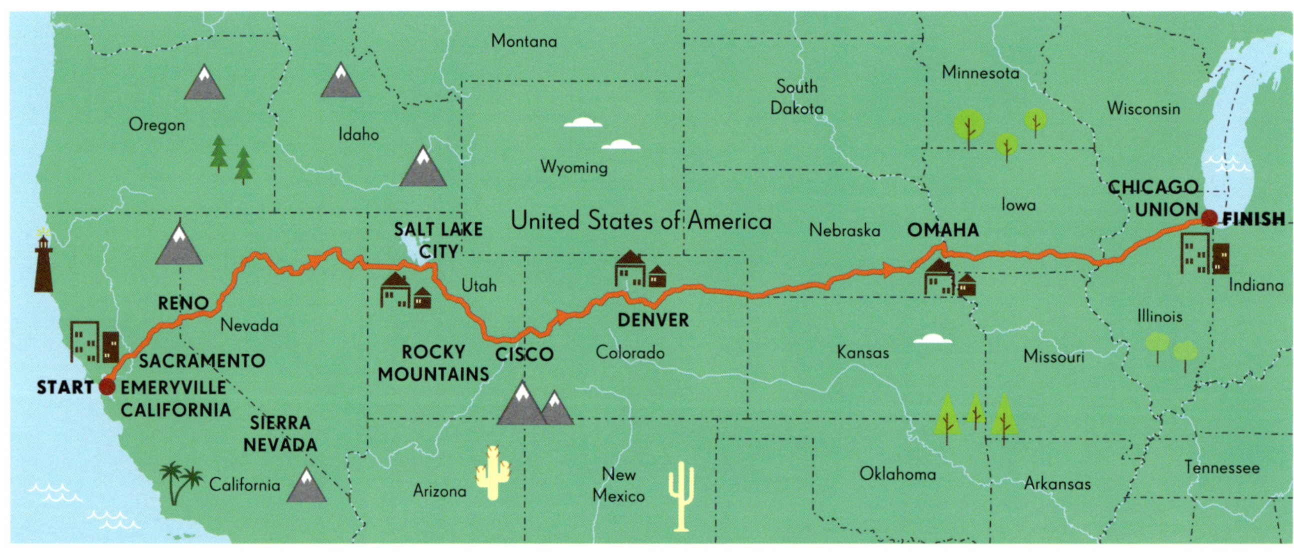

California State Railroad Museum. Once the engine springs into action, so do they, narrating the scenery and history for the happily captive audience for several hours until we cross the state line from California into Nevada. Along the way, the train twists and turns through the canyons of the Sierra Nevada, at one point even passing under the lift cables of the Soda Springs Ski Resort. On the other side, the tracks closely follow Donner Pass Rd, named for the infamous group of pioneers whose wagons got snowed in and who had to turn to cannibalism in the 1840s.

After the docents depart in Reno, the stories continue – this time our own personal histories, swapped among passengers. Americans don't shy away from spilling their lives to strangers, and I get to know the California Zephyr's cast of characters: a 60-something man going to meet his daughter-in-law and grandson for the first time after resolving a long estrangement from his son; a well-travelled woman tired of making the drive from the coast to Chicago; a retired couple giddy about the beautiful blooms they saw at an orchid festival in San Francisco; a man who knows all about the healing power of magnetic bracelets and proclaims himself a prophet who is spreading the word. A large family of traditionally dressed Amish – women in bonnets and plain dresses and men with long, untrimmed beards and suspenders – are playing card games on the way home to Pennsylvania Dutch Country after the mother had a medical procedure in California.

"The stories continue – this time our own personal histories. Americans don't shy away from spilling their lives to strangers, and I get to know the California Zephyr's cast of characters..."

One woman is more interested in reading a book called *The Art and Science of Grazing* than talking. Two Japanese students who are not totally fluent in English must wonder what kind of sitcom they have stumbled into. Where else in the world could this group of people have ever come into contact?

By the end of the day, the train has crossed over another state line into Utah, and those gathered in the observation car watch the cotton-candy pink and orange sunset over the alien-like salt flats. After dark, I retreat to my roomette, one of Amtrak's sleeper cabins, and call it a night.

In the morning, I head to the dining car for breakfast. The tables seat four and, like a singles mixer, Amtrak puts random parties together, so I scoot across the vinyl seat to make room for one of the Japanese students as the middle-aged Amish couple squeeze in on the other side. We nod to each other in familiarity and then gasp in surprise as we spot a herd of antelope grazing just outside the train window. Our breakfasts arrive, and the Amish recount their sighting of wild horses the night before.

I can't resist spending another day in the observation car. A new conductor boarded overnight in Salt Lake City and, clearly perked up from his morning coffee, he calls out all the wildlife he's seeing over the intercom as if we're on a group safari. Oohs and aahs rise from the growing crowd, passengers shouting out to the group as they spot more animals.

As we roll towards the Rockies, the conductor carries on: 'There's Cisco, Utah – don't blink. You'll know when we pass it. It looks like it's out of *The Hills Have Eyes*. Population: 1.' The observation car starts playing a collective game of 'I Spy', trying to figure out where the one person lives.

The tracks meet the Colorado River and they sync in parallel unison for hundreds of miles, overlooked by bald eagles. Once we're in the mountains, the train slows to a crawl, and some of the jagged canyon walls edge in so close that it feels like they are going to scrape the windows at any moment. On the other side of the Rocky Mountains lies their geographical opposite: the flat expanse of Midwestern prairie that accompanies us the rest of the way to Chicago.

Riding the California Zephyr is a reminder that the journey is the reward, a maxim that's too often not the case when travelling. The comradery makes it feel like you're part of a bigger whole, an unforgettable moment in time perhaps never to be repeated – at least not until the next California Zephyr sets off on its 52-hour cross-country journey. **LK**

UNITING THE UNITED STATES

The California Zephyr follows part of the route of the Transcontinental Railroad, the USA's first cross-country span, which opened in 1869. The Central Pacific Railroad and the Union Pacific came together in Utah and the tracks were completed with a ceremonial Golden Spike. Today, Golden Spike National Historical Park, an hour's drive outside Salt Lake City, commemorates the great occasion.

Clockwise from top: Skyscrapers in San Francisco; Burnham Harbor in Chicago; Denver's Union Station; Glenwood Springs. Previous page: A train passes through Ruby Canyon.

Start/Finish // Emeryville (San Francisco Bay), California/Union Station, Chicago, Illinois
Distance // 2438 miles (3924km)
Duration // 52hr
Ticket types // Both Coach and private rooms are available.
How to book // On the Amtrak website (amtrak.com)
Things to know // Private room prices can be sky high (upwards of $1400 for two passengers), but this rate includes all meals in the dining car, available only to those with private rooms. Though Amtrak's Coach seats are comfy, spending consecutive days attempting to sleep in them can be rough. Budget travellers should consider the USA Rail Pass, which offers 10 journeys within 30 days for $499. If you travel the whole California Zephyr route, that's just one journey. The catch? You must ride in Coach.

Clockwise from top: Steaming ahead on the Durango & Silverton Railroad; a conductor on the Cumbres & Toltec Scenic Railroad; a historic reenactor on the Georgetown Loop Railroad.

MORE LIKE THIS
HERITAGE RAILWAYS IN THE ROCKIES

DURANGO & SILVERTON NARROW GAUGE RAILROAD

Opened in 1882 to haul silver and gold out of the San Juan Mountains, the Durango & Silverton Narrow Gauge Railroad is a must-do in southwestern Colorado. Vintage steam trains – ride in the open-sided car for the full coal-flecked experience – chug their way through dense forests and along a roaring river and granite mountain cliffs, tracing needle-thin dynamite-blasted passages. The standard round-trip journey is a full day excursion and takes three and a half hours each way, plus two hours of free time in Silverton to grab lunch and soak up the Rocky Mountain scenery before heading back to Durango, itself a train town founded in 1881 by the Denver and Rio Grande Railroad.
Start // Durango
Finish // Silverton, Colorado
Distance // 45 miles (72.5km)
Duration // 3hr 30min

CUMBRES & TOLTEC SCENIC RAILROAD

Originally an extension of the Durango & Silverton line, the Cumbres & Toltec Scenic Railroad is the longest and highest elevation narrow-gauge steam train ride in North America. Engines pull passengers up the epic 10,022ft (3055m) Cumbres Pass, assisted by helper locomotives up the 4% grade. Roll through the mountains and past wildflower-filled alpine meadows, rushing creeks and historic sheep ranches while keeping an eye out for elk and bears. Iconic moments along the way include crossing the 137ft-high (42m) Cascade Trestle Bridge and Tanglefoot Curve, a tight loop that nearly sees the train folded in half. At a plodding 12-15mph (19-24km/h), trips require a full day, which includes a one-hour break for lunch midway at Osier and stops to fill the steam engine's water tanks.
Start // Antonito, Colorado
Finish // Chama, New Mexico
Distance // 64 miles (103km)
Duration // 7hr

GEORGETOWN LOOP RAILROAD

Take a break from driving on Colorado's Interstate 70 with a ride on the Georgetown Loop Railroad just outside of Denver. Corkscrew train tracks navigate a few miles of the Rocky Mountains through Clear Creek Canyon between the old mining towns of Georgetown and Silver Plume. Although this railway was used for hauling out ore, it was also one of Colorado's original tourist attractions. Steam engines puff up 600ft (183m) of elevation, through steep grades and vertigo-inducing bridges above fast-flowing creeks. The whole experience takes about two and a half hours, with a mine tour sandwiched between two 30-minute journeys. There's also an overlook from the interstate to watch the steam trains on their journey through the canyon from above.
Start // Georgetown
Finish // Silver Plume, Colorado
Distance // 4.5 miles (7km)
Duration // 2hr 30min

3748

ACROSS PATAGONIA ON LA TROCHITA

A harsh Patagonian landscape of wind-battered pampas and snow-topped mountains, punctuated by isolated little train stations, awaits intrepid travellers who make this legendary train journey.

The wee hours of the morning find me alone on the platform at middle-of-nowhere Ingeniero Jacobacci Station. Legendary travel writer Paul Theroux disembarked a train on this very spot as part of his cascade of rail journeys across South America, later noting this place as particularly desolate in *The Old Patagonian Express*. I'm attempting to recreate his classic 1978 train journey.

I watch the Tren Patagónico disappear into the pre-dawn darkness, billowing a ghostly cloud of steam, heading for the mountains surrounding San Carlos de Bariloche. A few people got off with me, since the only long-distance train left in Patagonia is still the most convenient way for locals from isolated towns to get home after studying in Viedma or Bariloche. They've now disappeared as well, and I'm left to shiver beside my backpack, the temperature around freezing.

I've hours to kill before my connection arrives, the famous La Trochita, literally 'little gauge', named after the 29-inch (75cm) track (*trocha* in Spanish) on which it runs, and dubbed 'the Old Patagonian Express' by a local lad in conversation with Theroux back in the day. I walk up and down the platform to keep warm and look up at the night sky, which is the clearest I've ever seen on the outskirts of a town. As a kid in the Soviet Union, I first saw the Southern Cross constellation at Moscow's planetarium, and promised myself that one day I'd see it for real. I see it now, and feel that familiar exhilaration that comes from being in a new place, alone, under a blanket of stars.

'Are you waiting for La Trochita?'

My stargazing reverie is interrupted by a stooped man.

I nod.

He turns out to be José, the station master, and since his office is officially open to the public twice a week between 3am and 5am, he invites me to warm up, proffering a flask of hot water, accompanied by a cup densely packed with the ubiquitous yerba maté (a herbal drink immensely popular in Argentina).

'Sugar?'

'No, thank you.'

He looks at me approvingly.

'Porque la vida ya es bastante dulce!' (Because life is sweet

enough already!)'

As I sip the bitter brew, I feel myself waking up. José is within his right to shut his office at 5am and go back to sleep, but he takes pity on me and we continue talking until the sun rises.

Come mid-morning, a bus load of day-trippers from Bariloche and I watch expectantly as La Trochita finally makes an appearance. The black locomotive pulls up with a mighty belch of steam, hissing as we board the compact, wood-pannelled carriages. Having ridden steam trains in other parts of the world – Wales, Russia – I feel an instant affinity with this leviathan from the past, and think that it was deeply unfair of Theroux to have described this beauty as a 'demented samovar on wheels'.

Our destination, Ojos de Agua, is a mere 26 miles (43km) away, but we can't be going faster than 20mph (30km/h). Ignoring the merry hubbub around me, I stare out of the window, entranced by the raw beauty of the landscape. As we chug across the huge Pampas plains, battered by the Patagonian wind, with snow-sprinkled mountains in the background and the odd sighting of a fleet-footed *ñandú* (small ostrich), I revel in this vastness – something that I often yearn for at home in built-up, crowded England.

Ojos de Agua, a couple of streets parallel to a river tributary, isn't much to look at compared to the pretty little mountain town of Esquel – the original home of La Trochita – which I later reach by bus from Bariloche, after returning to Ingeniero Jacobacci.

From Esquel, I make the hour-long journey on another remaining section of the original La Trochita line to Nahuel Pan – a smattering of wind-battered, red-roofed wooden cabins, home to thirty or so Mapuche families. Among the tiny town's craft and food stalls, the longest wait is for *choripan* (grilled chorizo with chimichurri sauce in a bun). I overhear two of my fellow travellers

THE STORY OF LA TROCHITA

In 1978, Paul Theroux made the journey along the original 402km-long (250 mile) route plied by La Trochita between Esquel and Ingeniero Jacobacci. It was once the world's longest narrow-gauge steam-train line, with six stations. In 1993, the railway line was privatised and, as a result, fell into disuse, with three segments of the track (Esquel/Nahuel Pan; El Maitén/Ñorquincó; Ingeniero Jacobacci/Ojos del Agua) converted to tourist-only services in 1994.

Clockwise from top: A ñandú with its young; steaming into Esquel; a German-built Henschel engine provides motive power. Previous page: Light on the Andes as a train passes by.

discussing the merits of Mapuche-made *bara brith* (Welsh-style fruitcake) and how it compares to what they'd tasted in Gaiman, a Welsh settlement elsewhere in Patagonia. Turns out that they're Welsh themselves and travelling in the footsteps of extended family members who'd moved to Argentina generations ago.

I poke my head in the dusty two-room museum dedicated to the cultures of the Mapuche and Tehuelche – the original inhabitants of the Pampas – and end up chatting to the elderly curator. He tells me that La Trochita is Nahuel Pan's lifeblood, that the locals have been reliant on the train for decades.

'When the train was derailed several times by the wind, we really felt it,' he says.

This seems entirely believable as the creaky wooden carriages had shaken and juddered during La Trochita's wheezy ascent up the valley from Esquel.

'Does it break down these days?'

'Sometimes, yes. Then we have to wait for the replacement part to be handcrafted, since they are not industrially produced anymore.'

On the way back to Esquel, I watch La Trochita round the many bends in the track and drink in the landscape of bare hills, scrub and pastures full of sheep, trying to tune out the wandering minstrel who's busily serenading my fellow passengers. Silhouetted against the snowy mountains is the hovering dark form of a condor: like the train, another enduring symbol of this harsh and beautiful land. **AK**

Start/Finish // Esquel/Nahuel Pan; El Maitén/Ñorquincó; Ingeniero Jacobacci/Ojos de Agua

Distance // 11 miles (19km); 22 miles (35km); 27 miles (43km)

Duration // 3hr return; 5hr return; 6hr return

Ticket types // Theoretically, La Trochita trains come with First Class and Second Class carriages (the former with padded seats), but in practice, tickets are all the same price.

How to book // Book online via latrochita.org.ar for the Esquel/Nahuel Pan and El Maitén/Ñorquincó segments. Meanwhile, trenpatagonicosa.com.ar/la-trochita has the reservation phone number for the Ingeniero Jacobacci/Ojos de Agua segment.

When to go // Winter (June-September) is ideal for snowy views. In spring and summer (October-February) the Pampas comes alive with wildflowers and you're more likely to spot wildlife. In February, El Maitén hosts Argentina's National Steam Train Festival.

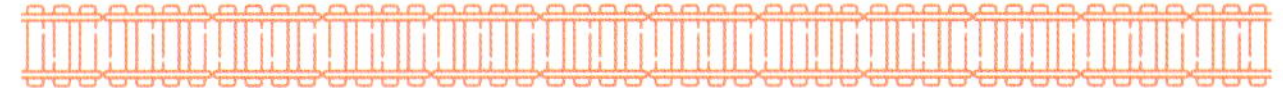

Opposite: The 1913-built steam engine that is a feature of journeys on the El Valdiviano route.

MORE LIKE THIS
SOUTH AMERICAN STEAM

SÃO JOÃO DEL REI TO TIRADENTES, BRAZIL

The oldest still-operating train in Brazil, the 19th-century Maria Fumaça ('Smoking Mary'), as the locals affectionately call it, connects the historic gold rush town of São João del Rei to Tiradentes where graceful 18th- and 19th-century buildings sit against a backdrop of blue-tinged mountains. Hissing and belching great clouds of vapour as it makes its slow, ponderous way through the lush, winding valley of the Serra de São José, the Maria Fumaça passes through tunnels and traverses bridges framed by subtropical vegetation. As you cross one of the oldest gold mining areas in Minas Gerais state, peer out of the train window at rusted mining equipment and other detritus of gold miners' dreams littering the landscape; you may even see some present-day *garimpeiros* (gold panners) trying their luck. São João's train station Museu Ferroviário sheds light on railway history in Brazil.
Start // São João del Rei
Finish // Tiradentes
Distance // 8 miles (13.5km)
Duration // 35min

EL VALDIVIANO, CHILE

Dating back to 1899, the golden age of Chile's railways, the El Valdiviano route was the last link in the chain that connected the country's main port, Valparaíso, and the capital, Santiago, with the port of Puerto Montt. Diesel locomotives covered the route of over 620 miles (1000km) in 14 hours, but the route fell into disuse in the 1980s before being revived in 1999. Today, it's operational on Saturdays and Sundays in January and February, pulled by a British-made steam locomotive from 1913, with passengers accommodated in vintage cars. During the five-hour round trip along the Calle-Calle River, travellers alight in Pishuinco and Huellelhue to shop for crafts and sample regional gastronomy.
Start/Finish // Valdivia
Distance // 36 miles (58km)
Duration // 7hr

TREN DE LA SABANA, COLOMBIA

Connecting Colombia's capital with the historic town of Zipaquirá, famous for its cathedral carved from salt, the Tren de la Sabana has been traversing the savannah between the two cities for many decades, reaching its maximum extension of 124 miles (199km) in 1953 and contributing massively to the economic development of Bogotá and its environs. The line's importance waned over the years, with faster four-wheeled transport taking precedence, and it went out of operation in 1991, along with Colombia's National Railway. In 1993, the first of five renovated steam locomotives was launched by Turistrén. These days, diesel locomotives ply the route on weekends, providing a fun day out for local families and other train lovers, with a brass band entertaining passengers. On the way back from Zipaquirá, the train stops at the appealing village of Cajicá for lunch.
Start // Bogotá
Finish // Zipaquirá
Distance // 33 miles (53km)
Duration // 2hr 30min (return)

620

CALIFORNIA DREAMING ON THE SUNSET LIMITED

Lap up the long-distance life riding one of the USA's most historic rail routes between the Big Easy and the City of Angels.

Thanks to the arrival of the aeroplane, it barely takes five hours to cross America these days. Most people don't even give it so much as a second thought. They hop on a flight in New York after breakfast and arrive in Los Angeles by lunchtime, covering an entire continent in less than a quarter of a day.

It wasn't always like this: 150 years ago, crossing America was still an epic undertaking that was measured in weeks, rather than hours. Most people never made it out of their home state, let alone across the country. But in 1894, the completion of a new railway line made it possible to cross the country in days – an achievement which, at the time, must have seemed as futuristic as space travel. That railroad was the Southern Pacific Railway, and while it wasn't the very first trans-American route (that distinction belongs to the Pacific Railroad, completed in 1869), it was the fastest by a country mile. Four years later it was renamed the Sunset Limited. It's been running non-stop ever since.

It is, in fact, the longest continuously operating named train route in all of the US. On its coast-to-coast journey, it travels

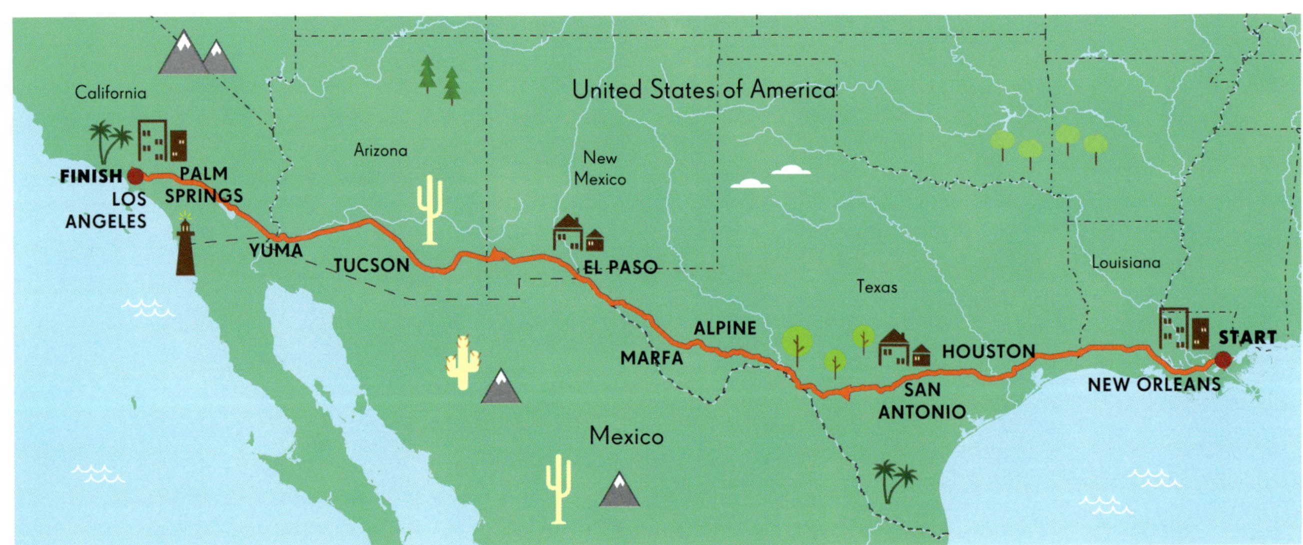

> *"If Jack Kerouac had written* On the Rails, *rather than* On the Road, *he would have set it on the Sunset Limited."*

through five states – Louisiana, Texas, New Mexico, Arizona and California – and crosses a trio of America's greatest rivers (the Mississippi, the Colorado and the Rio Grande). It also traverses the Continental Divide and spans four time zones. From mesas to mountains, deltas to deserts, plains to pine forests, there is no better way to appreciate the American landscape in all its variety and strangeness. And it's been a lifelong ambition of mine to ride it.

Most travellers take the train in an east–west direction, following a similar route to that of America's early pioneers. The journey lasts 46½ hours, with two sunsets spent on board (alternatively, since the train runs three times a week, you can hop off and back on to allow yourself more time to explore). Overexcited by the adventure ahead, I spend a little too long carousing in the French Quarter in New Orleans the night before departure, and very nearly miss my eastbound train, just about clambering aboard the sleek, silver double-decker carriage a minute or two before it departs. I climb the ladder-like steps and settle into my Superliner cabin which, while small, has everything I need: a WC, a banquette that transforms into a bed and, most importantly, a widescreen window that will provide me with my very own private-cinema-booth view onto America over the next three days.

It's the vistas that make the Sunset Limited special: if Jack Kerouac had written *On the Rails*, rather than *On the Road*, he would have set it on the Sunset Limited. One day you're rolling through the Louisiana bayous. The next you're careering into cowboy country, or lost in the middle of the desert. The hours roll by, and the great American landscape just keeps on rolling on: sunbaked plains, snaking creeks, dry gulches, gold rush towns, hazy mountains. City after city trundles by (Houston, El Paso, Tucson, Palm Springs), as do scarcely-heard-of towns (Marfa, Alpine, Lordsburg, Benson). We pass Fort Davis, where bands of Apache and Comanche raiders once roamed, and Texas Rangers patrolled. We trace the banks of the Rio Grande, skirting the Mexican border past Big Bend National Park. We cross the Chihuahuan Desert, populated by extra-terrestrial-looking succulents and saguaro cacti straight out of a Wile E Coyote cartoon. And like so many train-hobos before me, I discover there's something uniquely, seductively, addictively hypnotic about seeing America by rail – and it's not just down to the metronomic clack of the wheels. It's to do with the super-sized nature of the place: the endless horizons that stretch out in all directions to a never-ending vanishing point. When the landscape just seems to go on forever, you stop worrying about where you happen to be, or how long you've been travelling, or how far it is to the journey's end. You exist in the moment, in the 4ft-wide (1.2m) frame that's become your only window onto the world. Grandiose as it sounds, there's

DESERT STARGAZING

With fantastically clear skies and minimal light pollution, the Chihuahuan Desert is one of the top places in the southern US for stargazing. Three of America's most powerful telescopes are located at the McDonald Observatory (mcdonald observatory.org) in Fort Davis, just a short drive from Alpine Station on the Sunset Limited route.

From left: A station attendant at Alpine Texas; a GE Genesis locomotive hauling the Sunset Limited; a musician at New Orleans. Previous page: Echo Park Lake in Los Angeles.

something almost Zen about travelling on the Sunset Limited.

In the observation car, I get chatting to Bob Glaser, who's that rarest of American oddities – a committed train traveller. He's been obsessed with locomotives since he was a boy, and reckons he's ridden pretty much every named line in the Lower 48.

'America has totally forgotten about its railways,' he says. 'But without them, this country simply wouldn't be what it is today. They paved the way west. They carried the steel and timber that built our cities. America literally owes everything to its railways, but for most people, they're just a footnote in history. I think that's a damn shame.'

The hours blur past like a dream. Almost before I know it, we're rattling into the suburbs of Los Angeles. The city's sprawl unfolds around us, a tangle of freeways, low-slung buildings, canyons rising into the hills. The electric-blue Pacific Ocean glints in the distance. We hit Union Station at 5.35am, and as I step out into the hazy morning light, LA's peculiar aroma – smog blended with a soupçon of sea-salt – hits my nostrils. Being stationary again feels profoundly weird. It'll take some getting used to.

As I walk under the station's arched art deco windows, my hobo spirit inevitably kicks in. I feel a sudden urge to keep moving. In that moment, I'd keep on riding the rails forever, given half a chance. **OB**

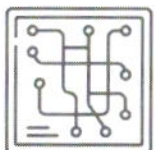

Start/Finish // New Orleans/Los Angeles
Distance // 1240 miles (1995km)
Duration // 46hr 35min
Ticket types // You can just book a seat on the Sunset Limited, but cabins are more comfortable. Superliner Roomettes have two fold-down berths and shared toilets; more spacious Superliner Bedrooms have private bathrooms; Family Bedrooms have four bunks and shared toilets.
How to book // Book direct (amtrak.com/sunset-limited-train).
When to go // Trains run year-round, but fares vary according to demand.
Things to know // The Sunset Limited runs three times weekly (Monday, Wednesday and Saturday from New Orleans; Tuesday, Friday and Sunday from Los Angeles).
More info // Amtrak Guide (amtrakguide.com).

Opposite top: The Empire Builder passing near West Glacier, Montana. Opposite below: The Southwest Chief beneath a mesa.

MORE LIKE THIS
USA SLEEPER SERVICES

EMPIRE BUILDER

Like the Sunset Limited, this country-crossing train follows a very historic route. For much of it, you'll be tracing roughly the same course as Meriwether Lewis and William Clark, the first men to cross though the wild American west all the way to the Pacific Coast. Introduced in 1929, it was designed as the signature passenger train of the Great Northern Railway, and it still carries around 340,000 people every year, making it by far Amtrak's busiest long-haul line. It starts in the Windy City, Chicago, and ends in either Portland or Seattle, depending on your preference. Unsurprisingly, there are some seriously big views along the way, with the Mississippi River, the plains of North Dakota, Glacier National Park and Mt Hood all putting in an appearance.

Start // Chicago
Finish // Seattle
Distance // 2206 miles (3550km)
Duration // 46hr

SOUTHWEST CHIEF

Another once-great American railway that has been running in some form or other since 1936 (although not always under the same name, or even exactly the same route as the one which it follows today). Originally named the Super Chief, the train was inaugurated in 1936 as the premium service on the long-defunct Atchison, Topeka and Santa Fe Railway, which was acquired by Amtrak in 1971. It tracks the American Midwest, with key stops including Kansas City, Albuquerque and Flagstaff – and an optional side excursion to see the Grand Canyon should you wish (which you absolutely should). Like the Sunset Limited, it's a Superliner Sleeper service: originally it would have had Pullman carriages, but nowadays it's double-decker all the way.

Start // Chicago
Finish // Los Angeles
Distance // 2265 miles (3645km)
Duration // 40 hours

TEXAS EAGLE

The Texas Eagle makes a great alternative route (or a potential add-on) to the Sunset Limited. Leaving from Chicago, the train travels through St Louis, Little Rock, Dallas, Fort Worth and Austin before hitting San Antonio. Here it links up with the second half of the Sunset route, allowing you to continue all the way to the Pacific. If you do, you'll be notching up a railway milestone – end-to-end, the Chicago to LA route is the longest continuous train trip it's possible to make in North America, at 2728 miles (4390km).

Start // Chicago
Finish // San Antonio
Distance // 1306 miles (2102km)
Duration // 32hr

MEXICAN RAILWAYS' LAST STAND: EL CHEPE

Chug from desert to Pacific coast via the rim of one of the world's deepest canyons, the Barrancas del Cobre, on Mexico's last true long-distance passenger train.

The desert can be cold. I felt this shivering in the 5am chill outside Chihuahua's railway station. I was a Latin American novice, having visited only border city Ciudad Juárez before, already in love with the place's feisty green salsas and flaming pink bougainvillea. Yet I was conscious, waiting while the train I was soon to board was prepared – as though the driver did not have complete confidence in his locomotive travelling 400+ miles over the Sierra Madre Occidental mountains to the Pacific Ocean – that I was about to experience much more of this region's colour in a short space of time. Perhaps my shivers were also anticipation.

We left on time. This was Mexico's last great train ride – certainly its last genuine historic passenger service beyond Mexico City's commuter lines – and a matter of much pride to the smartly attired and gracious staff, who were not about to let this vestige of rail heritage be found wanting.

The Ferrocarril Chihuahua al Pacífico is a mouthful even for Mexicans, who affectionately abbreviate the service to 'El Chepe', derived from its rolling stock reporting mark CHP. But its twice-weekly 14-hour trundle, against the odds of the mightily tricky topography of the Barrancas del Cobre (Copper Canyon) that it negotiates along the way, is more straightforward. A reliable fixture in the nation's transport network, El Chepe has been running faithfully since 1961.

I was taking El Chepe Regional – a sedate service aimed at locals, with more stops – on leg one to canyon-rim adventure hub Creel. I wanted to spend longer on this ravishing route than the single day afforded by the all-in-one run. I would then take the fancier El Chepe Express to Los Mochis after a couple of days' outdoor action. The regional train passengers were an interesting assortment: an El Fuerte family revelling in the overly icy air-con; businessmen heatedly discussing freight logistics to Baja California; an elderly couple who sighed, smiled and fondly nodded at almost every vista our carriage yielded. And well might they have marvelled. Even the uncelebrated parts of El Chepe's route are special. We passed the fertile farmland of Ciudad Cuauhtémoc, centre of Mexico's main Mennonite population, bathed gold-green in the morning sun. Snippets of Plautdietsch, the Low German dialect many Mennonites still speak, entered the mix of passenger conversation, before the climb up into increasingly craggy countryside around cattle-ranching town Creel.

'You have come,' exclaimed Ivan, owner of Creel adventure outfit 3 Amigos. 'When so many pass straight on through – congratulations! Most tourists stay away from northern Mexico because of what they hear on the news about drug wars, but this is only in a few places in over a million kilometres! And there is too much to miss out on here!'

Creel's myriad canyon adrenaline rushes include a day trip to Mexico's highest full-time waterfall, Cascada de Basaseachi, or multiday adventures along the bottom near Batopilas, where the climate dramatically shifts from sharp, alpine-like climes around the canyon top down to stickily tropical. But I opted for an afternoon mountain bike ride a few miles out of town to the wacky rockscape of Valle de las Ranas y los Hongos (Valley of the Toads and Mushrooms), named after the maddest-looking rhyolite formations here. I also saw the Rarámuri, the canyon's historic inhabitants. Smiling and clad in dazzling reds, blues and greens, they were here laying out handicrafts, including bark carvings fashioned from mountainside pine trees, on the rocks.

The Rarámuri were also vending their wares when I saw them two days later on leg two of the train ride at Divisadero. You can disembark for 20 minutes at this canyon-rim station to clock views that tumble away to a canyon bottom over 6000ft (1828m) below at this point. Here, thrill-seekers can tackle hair-raising Parque de Aventuras Barrancas del

RARÁMURI RUNNERS

It's said the Indigenous Rarámuri people retreated to the canyon-carved Sierra Madre Occidental highlands after the Spanish arrived in the 16th century. Despite this seclusion, their athleticism is well documented. Rarámuri means 'runners on foot' in their language and Rarámuri men traditionally ran ultramarathon distances of 200 miles (320km) to hunt or transfer messages between canyon communities.

Clockwise from top: a service departs; the train at Los Mochis; Cusárare waterfall near Creel. Previous page: The looming cliffs of Copper Canyon; Basaseachic waterfall.

Cobre, an adventure park where ziplines with some of the planet's deepest drops crisscross the canyon. But now I was a passenger on the touristy El Chepe Express. And the whole set-up felt more gimmicky. With rolling stock replete with leather seats, HD screens and a bar-cum-terrace, this was a train for privileged travellers: a luxury option, I felt, rather than a salt-of-the-earth passenger service.

Views were astonishing all the same. Seated on the left from Creel to Los Mochis, I was in prime position for the finest of them. And for me these happened not at the canyon top, but rather as the locomotive commenced its descent from the Sierra Madre Occidental. This is the part that fires up the railway buffs, where the majority of the route's 86 tunnels and 175 bridges can be found and the train is transported through precipitous rock walls and down switchbacks, canyon-bottom rivers gleaming like dainty threads below. Engineering highlights include the 3074ft (937m) La Pera tunnel, discombobulating passengers with its horseshoe shape that leaves those emerging with the scenery they imagined would be to their left, off right. And there's also the longest bridge on the line, Puente Agua Caliente, spanning 1637ft (498m).

Finally, as evening shadows lengthened with the setting sun, we shunted into our final destination, mountains behind and glimmering Pacific ahead. As I stepped out onto the palm-flanked streets, it struck me that there could scarcely be a greater set of contrasts between embarkation and disembarkation. El Chepe had linked together so much for me. And the fact that there was no other passenger train like it between here and Panama City, almost 3000 miles away, meant that this was an experience that was very unlikely to be matched. **LW**

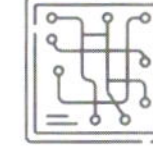

Start/Finish // Chihuahua/Los Mochis
Distance // 405 miles (652km)
Duration // 14hr 30min
Ticket types // Chepe Regional trains offer Tourist Class and Economy Class, and cover the whole route year-round; Chepe Express has First Class, Executive Class and Tourist Class, travelling the Chihuahua-Divisadero route in high season (August and September) and the Los Mochis-Creel route at other times.
How to book //Go to chepe.mx
When to go // Spring (March to May) and autumn (September to November) offer the most pleasant temperatures for hiking and other outdoor activities.
Things to know // The full route can be done on Tuesdays/Saturdays (from Chihuahua) and Wednesdays/Sundays (from Los Mochis). Chihuahua state time is one hour ahead of Sinaloa state.
More info // visitmexico.com; amigos3.com

Opposite top: A spirited ride on the Jose Cuervo Express. Opposite below: Views of shipping on the Ferrocarril de Panama.

MORE LIKE THIS
LATIN AMERICAN JOURNEYS

JOSÉ CUERVO EXPRESS, MEXICO

Tequila aficionados might immediately recognise the José Cuervo brand – and Mexico's 'Tequila train' gets its passengers intimately acquainted with the drink. Trundle through prime tequila-growing terrain in Jalisco state between Guadalajara and the town of (you guessed it) Tequila. This region gave Mexico its best-known booze and most famous folk extravaganza, mariachi, and you'll be dosed with both on this train, tequila and traditional music tour. Once in Tequila, indulge in a tasting at La Rojeña tequila distillery, get free time for a round-town look, catch a mariachi performance and be bussed out to the blue-green agave fields for a tequila-making demonstration. Of the four train classes, most luxurious is the Elite Wagon, its open bar stashed with special José Cuervo bottlings. Note, the two and a half hour train trip is done one-way (you return to Guadalajara by bus) and as part of the all-day itinerary described above.
Start/Finish // Guadalajara
Distance // 43.5 miles (70km)
Duration // 2hr 30min

FERROCARRIL DE PANAMÁ, PANAMA

Running alongside the Panama Canal is this set of rails going Pacific to Atlantic in under an hour – by far the fastest land-based way of accomplishing this feat. The trip isn't just about the geographical satisfaction and the fact you'll be clocking vessels negotiating the world's most-famous manmade waterway (which, incidentally, the railway predates by 50 years) for much of the ride. There are big wow moments too, such as when you bisect the Culebra Cut through a mountain range and when the train crosses vast Lake Gatún by causeway. In Colón you can visit the mid-18th-century, UNESCO-listed military fort of San Lorenzo. Plump for a morning service, a day in and around Colón and an early evening return, or take out-and-back family-oriented Saturday services during certain months.
Start // Panama City
Finish // Colón
Distance // 48 miles (77km)
Duration // 45min

TREN MAYA, MEXICO

Perhaps the most ambitious rail infrastructure project in recent decades anywhere in the Americas, Tren Maya has managed to get passenger trains linking up tourist locales across southeast Mexico's rugged and ravishingly beautiful Yucatán Peninsula. Hot spots Cancún and Playa del Carmen, with their big hotels and sandy beaches, are now connected through proud provincial capitals Mérida and Campeche and major Mayan archaeological complexes Chichén Itzá and Palenque. The route from key international arrival point Cancún Airport to Palenque in jungle-clad Chiapas became operational in 2024, along with the Cancún-Playa del Carmen leg along the Caribbean seaboard. An eastern loop via Tulúm, connecting with the Cancún-Palenque line at Escárcega, is planned. There are two to six daily services, depending which stations you are travelling between.
Start // Cancún Airport
Finish // Palenque
Distance // 523 miles (842km)
Duration // 10hr

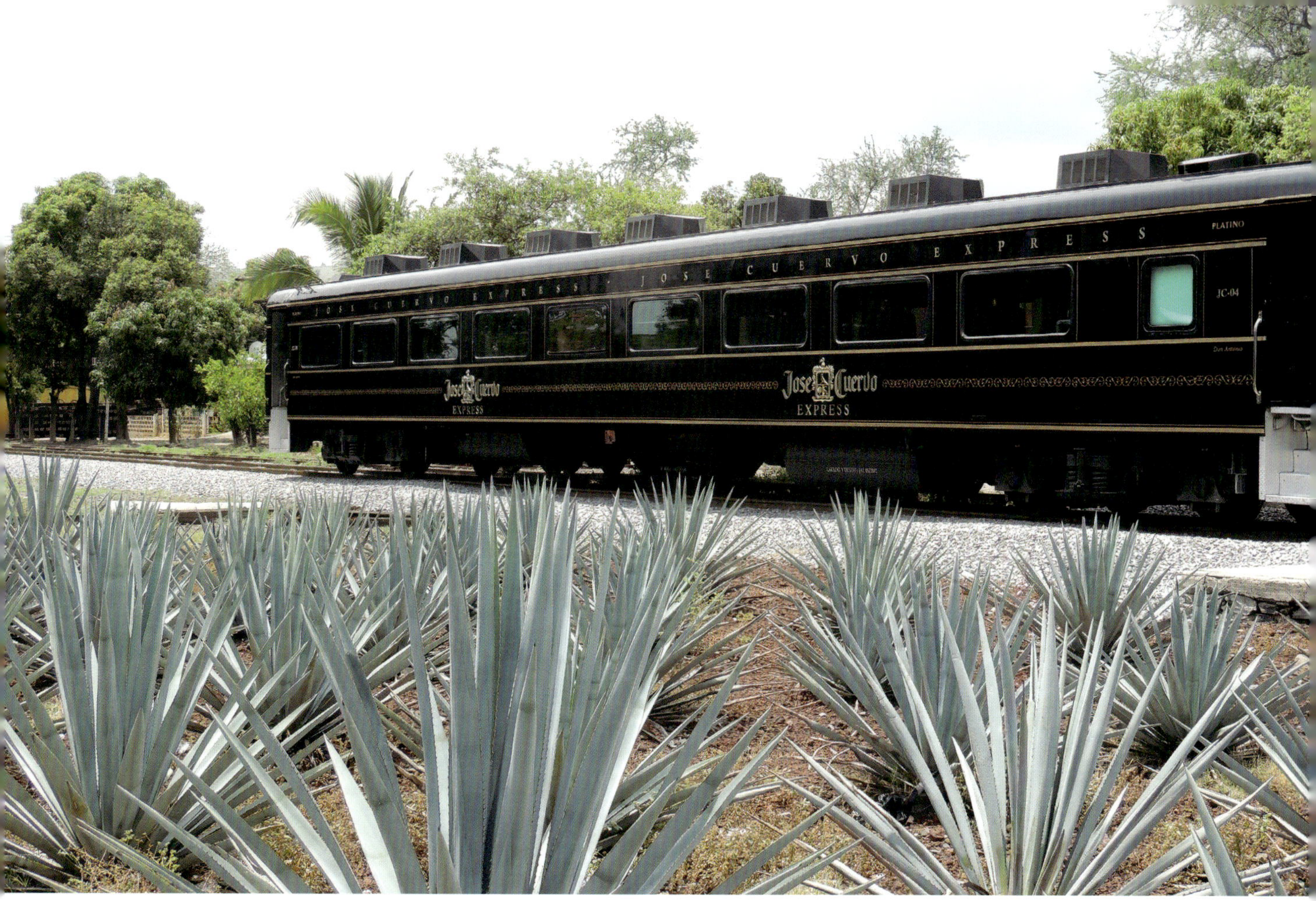
JOSE CUERVO EXPRESS
Jose Cuervo
EXPRESS
PLATINO
JC-04

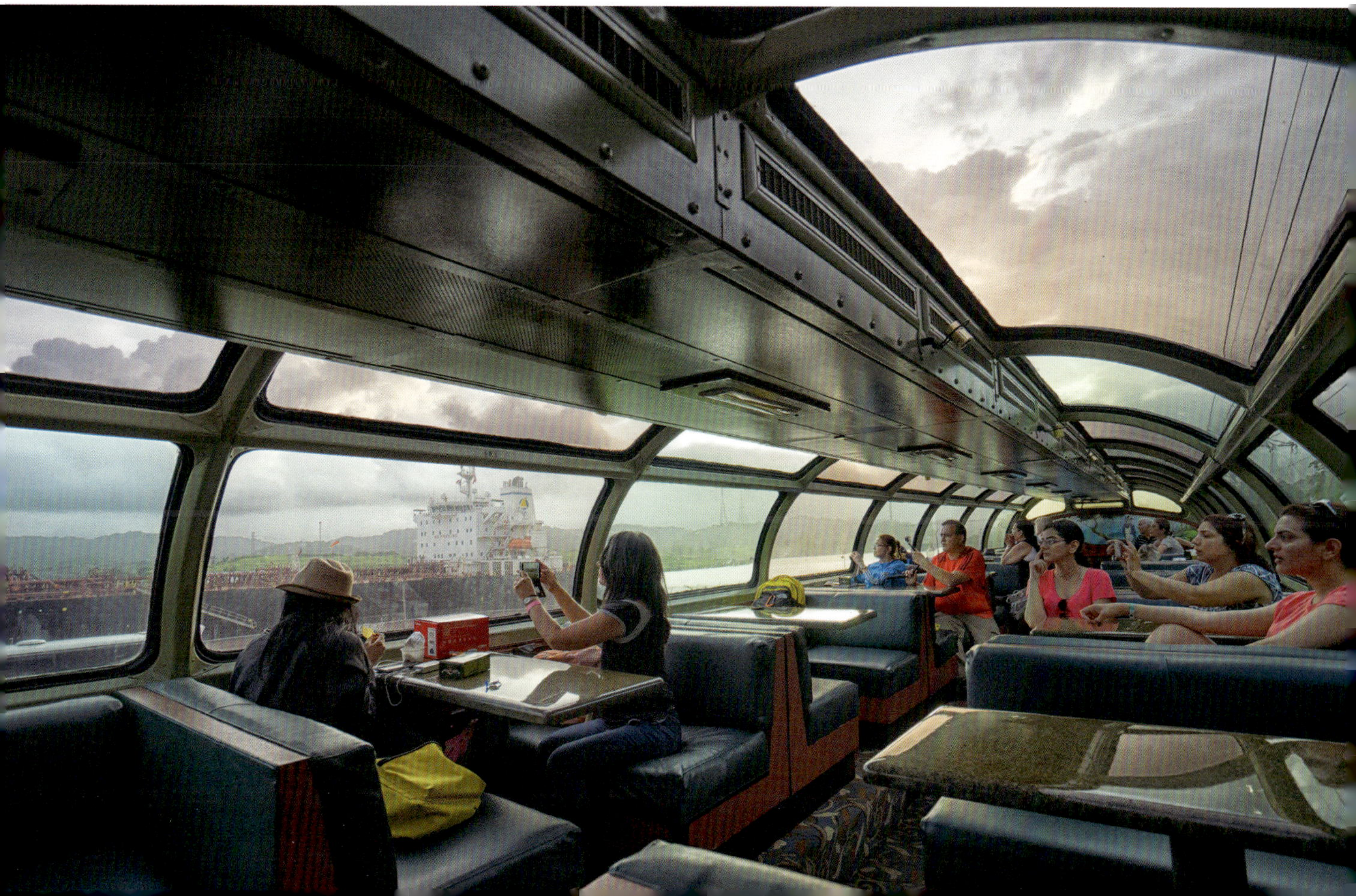

SEE CANADA'S BC FROM THE SKEENA

Propelling through the heart of British Columbia, Train 5, known colloquially as the 'Skeena', travels along the tracks of a historic early-20th-century railroad.

A diminutive middle-aged lady with a pink suitcase alighted in the town of Terrace leaving me as the only passenger left on board. For the final 90 miles (145km) of the journey alongside the Skeena River in western British Columbia (BC), I had the rather unique sensation of having a whole train to myself.

It was a cold, clear evening in March. Snowy mountains revealed their chilly countenance on the opposite side of the river as the spring light turned a honey yellow and began to fade. Rattling west towards Prince Rupert, I sank back into my seat, imagining for a moment that I was a wealthy earl on the Orient Express or a detective in a shadowy film noir.

Sporadic passengers had been getting on and off since Jasper, the previous day – tourists on day trips, a man weighed down with bags of shopping, hunters and fishers on outdoor adventures – but now it was just me and the attendant enjoying the train's rhythmic swaying.

Still referred to as the 'Skeena' (after the river), the Jasper-Prince Rupert train, officially known as train 5, cuts 721 miles (1160km) across the lightly populated mountain ranges and plateaus of central BC, making an overnight stop in the city of Prince George. While the line's history is pioneering and the scenery cinematic, the Skeena remains a community affair, serving a necklace of remote towns and settlements with sporadic flag-stops allowing locals to hail the train to get on and off.

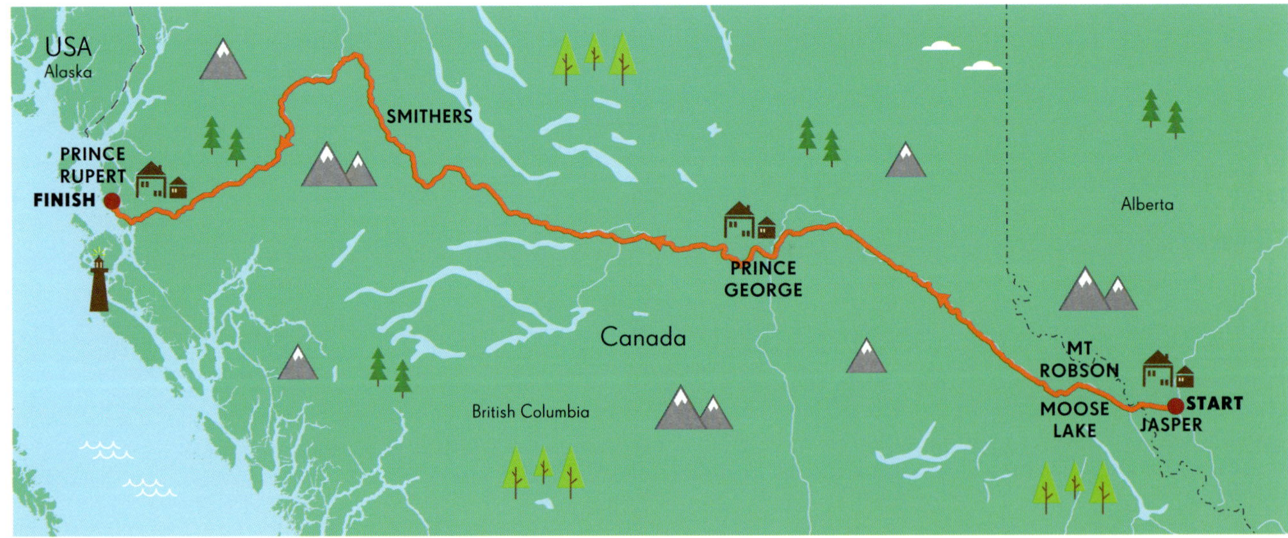

I was making the journey as part of a triangular tour of BC: a train ride from Vancouver to Jasper, the Skeena to Prince Rupert, a ferry south through the Inside Passage to Vancouver Island, and a series of buses and Ubers back to Vancouver. The two-day Jasper-Prince Rupert segment was a highlight. A product of Canada's early 20th-century railroad construction boom, the line was built between 1907 and 1914 by the Grand Trunk Pacific Railway (GTPR). Vying with the Canadian Northern Railway to become the nation's second transcontinental railroad, it was run privately for five years before being taken over by the Canadian government in 1919 when the GTPR defaulted on its loans.

Crossing the Rockies at Yellowhead Pass on the border of Alberta and BC, the CTPR tracks continue west to Prince Rupert on the Pacific coast while the old Canadian Northern route curls south to Vancouver.

I had climbed aboard the train in Jasper in brilliant sunshine praying for clear weather as we climbed through a muddle of snow-capped mountains to Yellowhead Pass. Just beyond the pass, the imposing hulk of 12,972ft (3954m) Mt Robson, the highest peak in the Canadian Rockies, revealed its rocky facade. As it's only fully visible on a handful of days each year, I was lucky to see the mountain's sheer southeast face encrusted with horizontal shafts of ice and framed by feathery clouds as the train skirted the north shore of Moose Lake.

This part of the ride is frequented mainly by day-trippers on organised tours who travel as far as the small forestry town of McBride, 50 miles (80km) west of Mt Robson, where an SUV-driving guide meets them and takes them back to Jasper. Thereafter, most of the train's passengers are locals rather than tourists, travelling between a string of isolated communities, many of them lonely stops where the train picks up 'hitchhikers'.

Sometime in the mid-afternoon we stopped for an elderly gentleman laden with shopping bags at a remote station and dropped him several miles down the line in the middle of nowhere. I watched as he trudged off into the snow like an arctic explorer heading into the unknown. He was a regular, the attendant told me, a rural dweller who used the train for his weekly shopping.

As we continued west, snow-covered farmland flashed by, interspersed with grey-blue lakes and vast tracts of coniferous forest, a fertile habitat for elk, moose and bears.

With darkness falling, we braked for what seemed like the umpteenth time just short of Prince George, our way blocked by a freight train in the station. Such is the fate of Canadian passenger services. Obliged to give way to the needs of freight,

Clockwise from left: Waterside in Prince Rupert; passing through forests between Jasper and Prince Rupert; VIA Rail's iconic stainless steel carriages. Previous page: Mt Robson's peak escapes the clouds, briefly.

they spend long periods of time parked idly on the sidelines and are perennially late.

Sensing a long wait, the attendant called me a taxi and, 20 minutes later, it pulled up alongside my carriage and took me along rutted backstreets to my overnight hotel.

The second day of travel was as lonesome as the first, a whirl of vintage stations, backcountry post offices and pinprick towns barely large enough to support a Tim Hortons cafe. The mountains grew taller as we pulled into Smithers and most of the passengers got off, leaving just me and the lady with the pink suitcase.

Prince Rupert is a port and wilderness gateway located around 30 miles (48km) south of the Alaskan border that was incorporated in 1910, four years before the railway opened. It was dark by the time I arrived with the lights of the town's industrial container facility emitting a supernatural glow.

I jumped down onto the deserted platform, the only remaining passenger, and found a train guard who was able to call me a cab to take me to my hotel. Attracting only around 150 passengers a week, the Skeena is one of the world's most understated and under-utilised trains but, jockeying between the Rockies and the deep fjords of British Columbia, it's also one of the most spectacular. **BS**

JASPER STATION

Jasper Town grew up around the Grand Trunk Pacific and Canadian Northern railways whose construction spurred the creation of Jasper National Park in 1907. When the two companies merged, authorities built a new station mixing 'parkitecture' (rustic National Park-style design) and the prevailing Arts and Crafts aesthetic. The handsome edifice, with gabled roof, stucco walls and cobblestone chimney, has since been declared a heritage building.

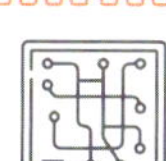

Start/Finish // Jasper/Prince Rupert
Distance // 721 miles (1160km)
Duration // 2 days
Ticket types // The train currently offers one ticket class, Economy, with comfortable reclining seats and access to a 'Park' car with curved windows for panoramic views. Takeout meals are available.
How to book // It's best to book a week or so in advance on the VIA Rail website (viarail.ca)
When to go // Longer days in the spring and summer allow for better views.
Things to know // You're required to book your own overnight accommodation in Prince George. There are several well-appointed hotels close to the station. The Hyatt Place is a stylish modern option with its own gym and restaurant.

Clockwise from top: Encounters with polar bears in Churchill; classic VIA Rail rolling stock is used on the Canadian; Hopewell Rocks Park in the Bay of Fundy – accessed via the Ocean.

MORE LIKE THIS
CANADIAN ODYSSEYS

CHURCHILL TO WINNIPEG

Canada's most northerly passenger train service cuts across the prairies and boreal forests of Manitoba and part of Saskatchewan, providing the only overland connection between isolated Churchill on the shores of Hudson Bay and the rest of the nation. The line as far as The Pas, 323 miles (520km) northwest of Winnipeg, was completed in 1908, while the extension to Churchill didn't open until 1929. The southern part of the route is dotted with heritage stations, many of them national historic sites, dating from the first two decades of the 20th century. Today, the train operates as one of VIA Rail's five 'Scenic Adventure Routes', running twice a week from the provincial capital to Churchill, the world's best viewing spot for polar bears, as well as the Northern Lights. Comfortable Sleeper Plus carriages are available for the two-night trip.

Start // Winnipeg
Finish // Churchill
Distance // 1054 miles (1697km)
Duration // 2 days

THE CANADIAN

Canada's most famous train is a monumental cross-continental classic that takes four days to ferry passengers between Vancouver and Toronto with stops in towns and cities along the way. The scenery is a conveyor belt of extraordinary views from the gothic-like splendour of the Rocky Mountains, via big sky prairies, to the lakes and escarpments of the Canadian Shield. Inaugurated in 1955, the veteran train still uses its original stainless-steel coaches with facilities that include a restaurant car, sleeper compartments and a more deluxe Prestige sleeper service. There are a couple of dome observation cars for wide-screen vistas and a posher 'Park' car with a signature bullet lounge that offers excellent views from the rear. Three meals a day are served, including a three-course dinner with wine. Three-hour stops in Winnipeg, Edmonton and Jasper (going west) allow time for plenty of leg-stretching and local exploration.

Start // Vancouver
Finish // Toronto
Distance // 2775 miles (4466km)
Duration // 4 days

THE OCEAN

Eastern Canada's emblematic Ocean has been running in some form or other since 1904, making it the oldest continuously operating passenger train in North America. The service departs three times a week and dips into three provinces starting in the cultural colossus of Montréal in Francophone Québec. As the city's skyscrapers slide into the distance, the train sets off alongside the St Lawrence River before turning south into New Brunswick where it crosses the Tantramar Marshes around the Bay of Fundy and cuts through the Cobequid Mountains to deposit passengers in historic Halifax, capital of Nova Scotia. With a journey time just shy of 24 hours, the Ocean offers private sleeper compartments, a restaurant car and a spacious lounge where passengers can spread out and admire the views.

Start // Montréal
Finish // Halifax
Distance // 836 miles (1345km)
Duration // 22hr

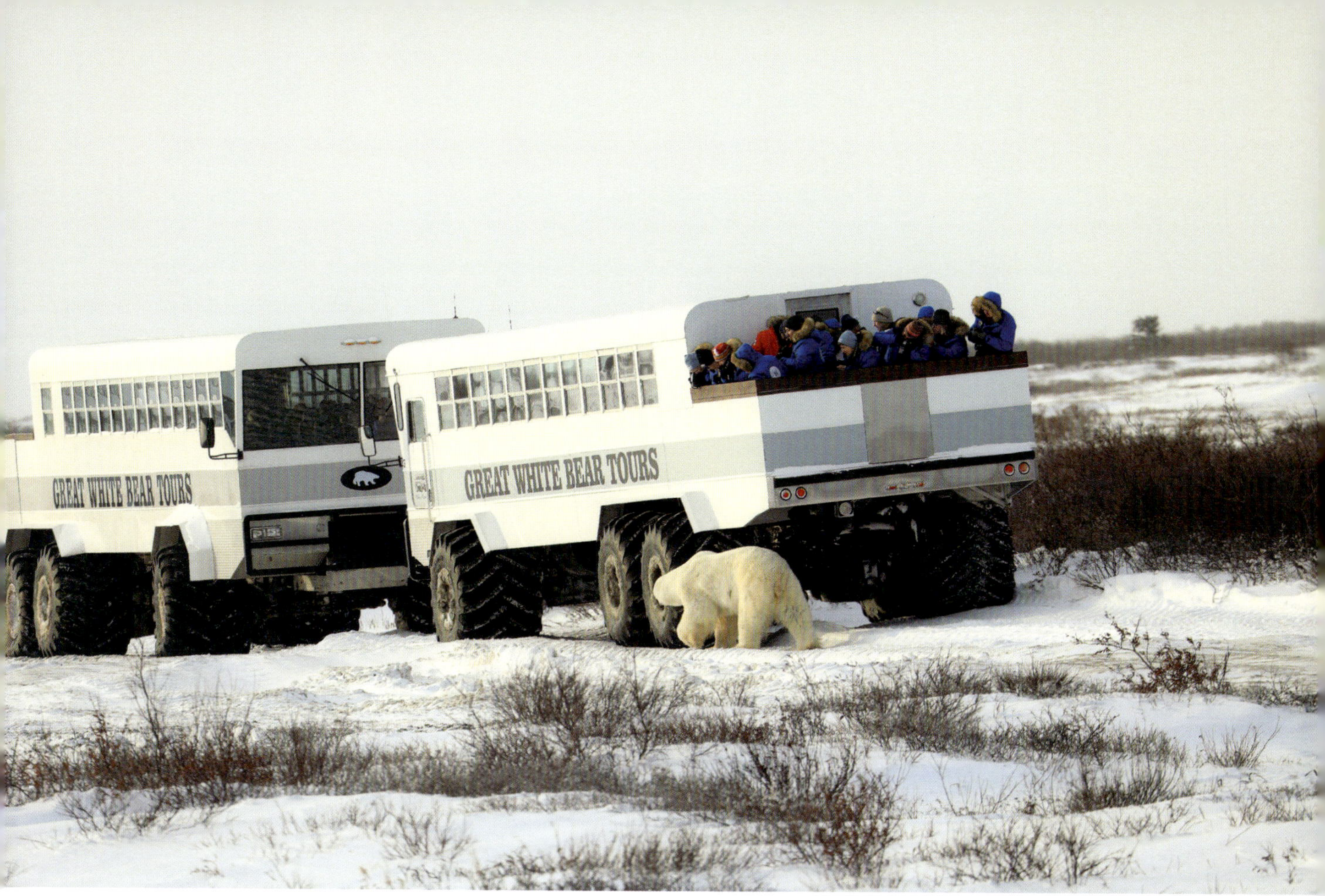
GREAT WHITE BEAR TOURS
GREAT WHITE BEAR TOURS

VIA

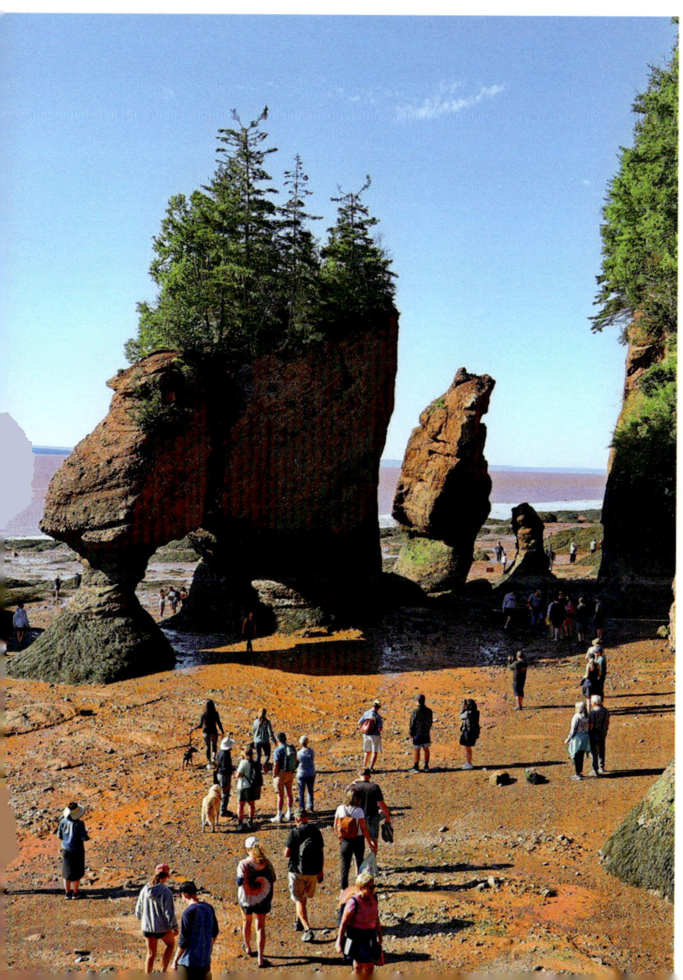

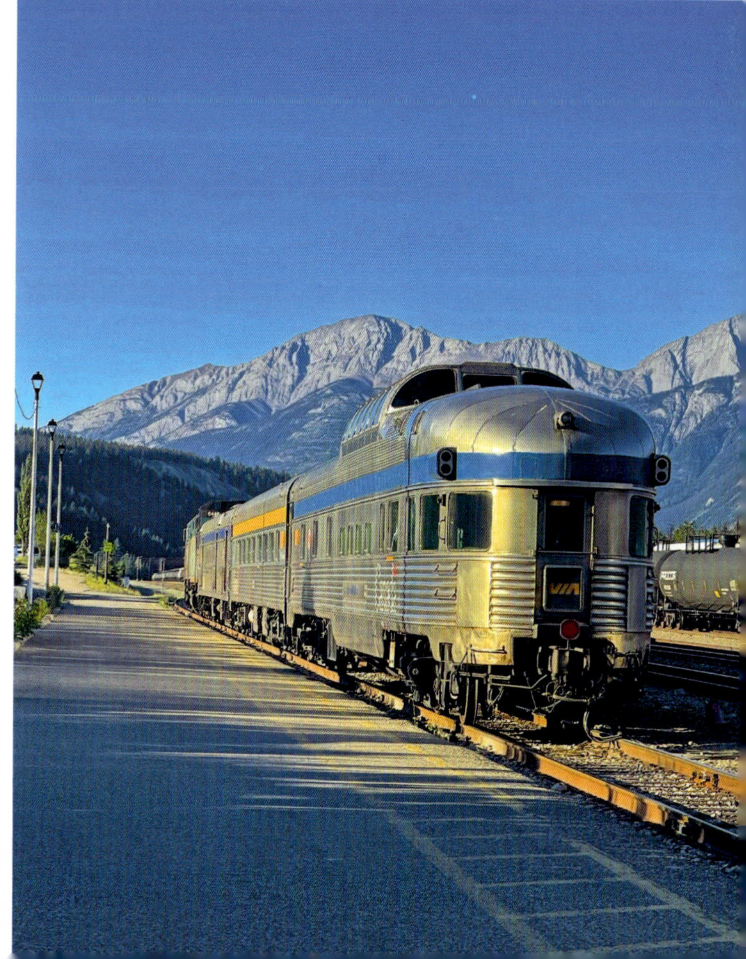

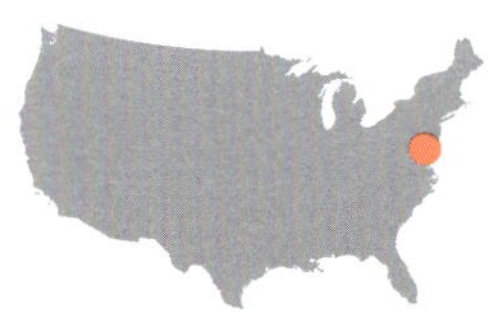

BOSTON TO DC ON AMTRAK RAILS

Amtrak's showpiece route between Boston and Washington, DC, is also the country's most environmentally friendly, promising a sustainable city-packed East Coast adventure.

The USA has a long road ahead before it catches up to Europe or Asia in terms of its rail infrastructure and services, but for travellers with *flygskam* (a Swedish word meaning 'flight shame') or those who hope to replicate an epic Interrail trip across the pond, the bounty of trains in the Northeast is a boon for public-transport-starved passengers.

Sure, the Northeast Regional doesn't sound anywhere near as romantic as many of Amtrak's other lines – Coast Starlight, Sunset Limited, Pacific Surfliner – but it guarantees a rail journey that's not possible anywhere else in the country: fast, frequent and environmentally aware. This route isn't Amtrak's most scenic, but it is by far the most popular: more than nine million passengers boarded the Northeast Regional in 2023.

It certainly feels busy when I board at South Station in Boston, with nearly every seat taken by suited business travellers clacking away on their laptops or sleepy college students juggling multiple laundry-stuffed suitcases on the way home to visit their parents. Unlike them, I am on a car-free odyssey along the eastern seaboard that could almost pass

HYATT
2837

for a European city-hopping train trip. I've spent several days in Boston soaking up the history of the American Revolution, walking the Freedom Trail and stuffing my face with cream-oozing cannoli from the old-school Italian bakeries outside Paul Revere's house (one if by land, two if by sea, three if by train?).

My next destination is New York City, about four hours away by rail. Taking the Northeast Regional train generates less than a fifth of the carbon emissions compared to driving or flying. Acela services – the only high-speed trains in the USA, reaching speeds up to 150mph (241km/h) – also make the journey, but I opt for the slower Northeast Regional. Acela tickets come at a price premium (they don't offer Coach seats, only Business and First) and shave off just 30 minutes for this leg of the journey.

I was astounded by and grateful for the hourly departures – the place where I grew up in Middle America sees only two Amtrak trains per day, one going east and one going west on the same line, with scheduled departures between the ungodly hours of midnight and 3am – not the most enjoyable time to be hanging out at a train station or anywhere besides bed. The Northeast Regional trains are clean and relatively quiet and gift me with far more legroom than I've ever seen on a plane. As I stare out the window, urban Boston dissolves into greenery before the scenery builds back up again. Before I know it, I'm in the Big Apple.

In NYC, Amtrak arrives not at the iconic Grand Central but rather at Moynihan Train Hall, a glass-ceilinged space opened in 2021 in a former postal mail-sorting office a couple of blocks west of the Empire State Building. It feels like it could be a

"It guarantees a rail journey that's not possible anywhere else in the country: fast, frequent and environmentally aware."

European train station in miniature. I tackle as many museums, restaurants, bars and breweries as a few days in the country's most populous city allows, before returning to Moynihan and boarding for Philadelphia.

The journey to the City of Brotherly Love is even shorter, just an hour and a half on another comfortable Northeast Regional train, and my eyes light up as I walk through Philly's 30th Street Station, dripping with art deco details. I go on another history bender: Independence Hall, the country's first capitol building and the place where the Founding Fathers debated and adopted the Declaration of Independence and the Constitution; the famously cracked Liberty Bell; the cutesy cobblestoned Elfreth's Alley. At a hostel, I chat with one of my temporary roommates who has been assigned the bunk next to mine about all the history I've witnessed that day. She, a fellow American woman, starts tearing up as she recounts her own visits to the same spots the day before.

Too soon, I make tracks again, this time for the country's capital, Washington, DC, a two-hour journey. Stepping off the train at Union Station makes for a fittingly grand welcome. I walk through the beaux-arts beauty wondering whether I've

STATION STUNNERS

Philadelphia and Baltimore have grand beaux-arts stations that are worth lingering in. Philly's 30th Street Station is a mix of neoclassical and art deco, with long geometric chandeliers dangling from the coffered ceiling. The huge clock and columns on the front of Baltimore Penn hint at delicious details inside, including Tiffany stained-glass ceiling domes.

From left: Inside Washington Union Station; an Acela service; Old State House in Boston; the Washington Monument. Previous page: New York City's downtown, near Moynihan Train Hall.

stumbled into an optical illusion or have accidentally entered an art museum. Nearly 100ft (30m) above my head, gilded coffered hexagons cover Union Station's toothpaste-white barrel-vaulted ceiling while 46 massive plaster statues of ancient Roman legionary soldiers stand guard in illuminated bays, extending a sense of protection to the travellers passing by under their feet.

Outside, in the blinding sunlight, I spy the dome of the US Capitol building peeking through the trees a short distance away, so I walk towards it. The Capitol bookends the eastern side of the National Mall, a grassy expanse punctuated with monuments, memorials and some of the country's best museums, ending at the colonnaded Lincoln Memorial and the Potomac River.

On this perfectly balmy day, I stroll along the lawn and go over this train journey in my mind. I've just visited a handful of world-class cities in as many days on public transport in one of the planet's most car-centric countries. The travel part of the experience wasn't as amazing as it could have been – Amtrak's trains aren't frequent enough, and the high-speed line is pricey and hardly saves any time – but it is gaining steam. The trains were busy, and Amtrak is breaking ridership records, which can only mean that better things are coming down the line. No, the train network here isn't as good as those in Europe or Asia, but it is uniquely American. **LK**

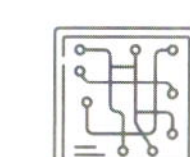

Start/Finish // South Station, Boston/Union Station, Washington, DC

Distance // 457 miles (735km)

Duration // 6hr 40min (Acela); 8hr 10min (Northeast Regional)

Ticket types // You can travel in Coach on Northeast Regional, but it's Business and First only on Acela.

How to book // On the Amtrak website (amtrak.com)

Things to know // In 2023, Amtrak introduced low-cost Night Owl fares between Washington, DC and New York City, later adding routes to Boston. Search for these cheap tickets on select Northeast Regional trains that depart between 7pm and 7am. Ticket prices increase with distance, so the shortest journeys (such as DC to Baltimore and Baltimore to Philadelphia) can cost as little as $10. Longer routes (New York City to DC and Boston to New York City) are priced at $25.

Opposite top: The New Mexico Rail Runner adorned with its roadrunner livery. Opposite below: Crowds on the Walkway Over the Hudson.

MORE LIKE THIS
DAY TRIPS BY TRAIN IN THE USA

NEW MEXICO RAIL RUNNER EXPRESS

New Mexico's Rail Runner connects the state's two most-visited cities and is named after the state bird (the roadrunner) – the door-closing warning sound is the unforgettable 'beep beep' of Road Runner from Looney Tunes cartoons. Before leaving Santa Fe, rail fans should stop by La Fonda on the Plaza, a historic adobe hotel that's one of the few surviving Harvey Houses – a chain of hotels, restaurants and lunch rooms that served passengers headed to the 'Wild West' on the Atchison, Topeka and Santa Fe Railway. For a more scenic Santa Fe train journey, see what's on the schedule at the separate Sky Railway, which runs themed trips in refurbished and open-air cars that might feature Native American dancing or a sunset serenade with live music.

Start // Santa Fe
Finish // Albuquerque
Distance // 97 miles (156km)
Duration // 1hr 30min

METRO-NORTH HUDSON LINE

Think you need a car to take a nature-filled day trip outside of New York City? Think again. Pack your hiking gear and use the Metro-North Hudson Line from Grand Central to escape – the line follows the Hudson River northward from the Big Apple. Take a countryside hike in Rockefeller State Park Preserve, a big bird-watching destination (get off at Tarrytown). Or walk along the Old Croton Aqueduct Trail, which follows a water-supply system built in 1842. Get off at Philipse Manor in Sleepy Hollow to tackle a shorter section of the 26-mile route, which also means you can visit Lyndhurst Mansion, an art-filled Gothic Revival country estate. At the end of the line in Poughkeepsie, stroll over the 212ft-high (66m) Walkway Over the Hudson, built for the railway in 1889 but now the country's longest pedestrian bridge.

Start // Grand Central Terminal, New York City
Finish // Poughkeepsie
Distance // 74 miles (119km)
Duration // 2hr

DOWNEASTER

If you want to extend your East Coast railway adventure from Boston, hop on the Downeaster and continue north to Maine. In summer, take a beachy day trip, alighting at Old Orchard Beach Station, where the rails nearly touch the sand. Further on, Portland is one of the hippest small towns in the country and is said to have the most craft beer breweries per capita. Journey all the way to Brunswick for art and culture. It's home to Bowdoin College, one of the oldest universities in the country and the alma mater of Henry Wadsworth Longfellow, Nathaniel Hawthorne and 19th-century US President Franklin Pierce. The campus has a small art gallery, and museums and historic homes are dotted around town.

Start // North Station, Boston, Massachusetts
Finish // Brunswick, Maine
Distance // 145 miles (233km)
Duration // 3hr 20min

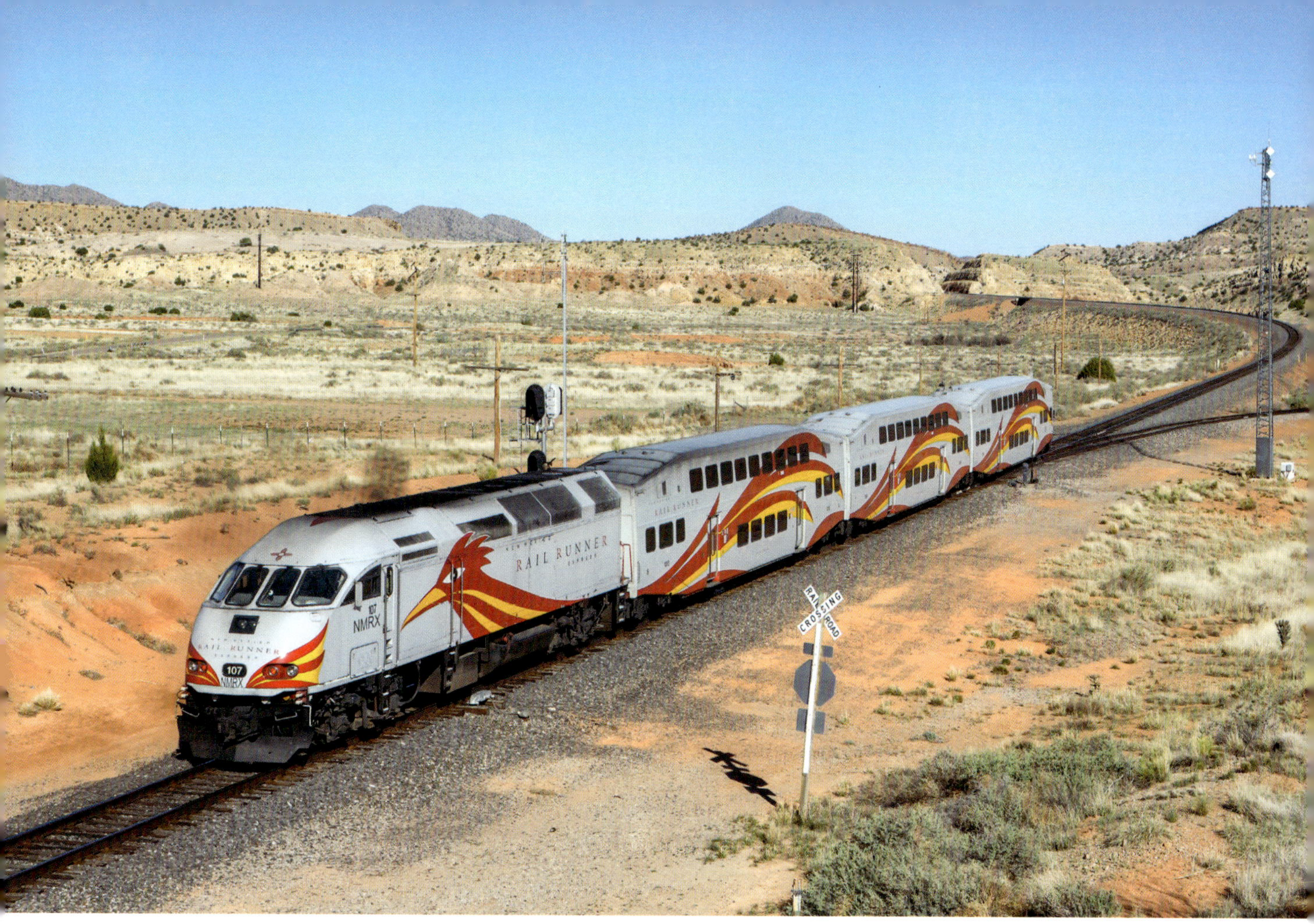
RAIL RUNNER
107
NMRX
RAIL ROAD
CROSSING

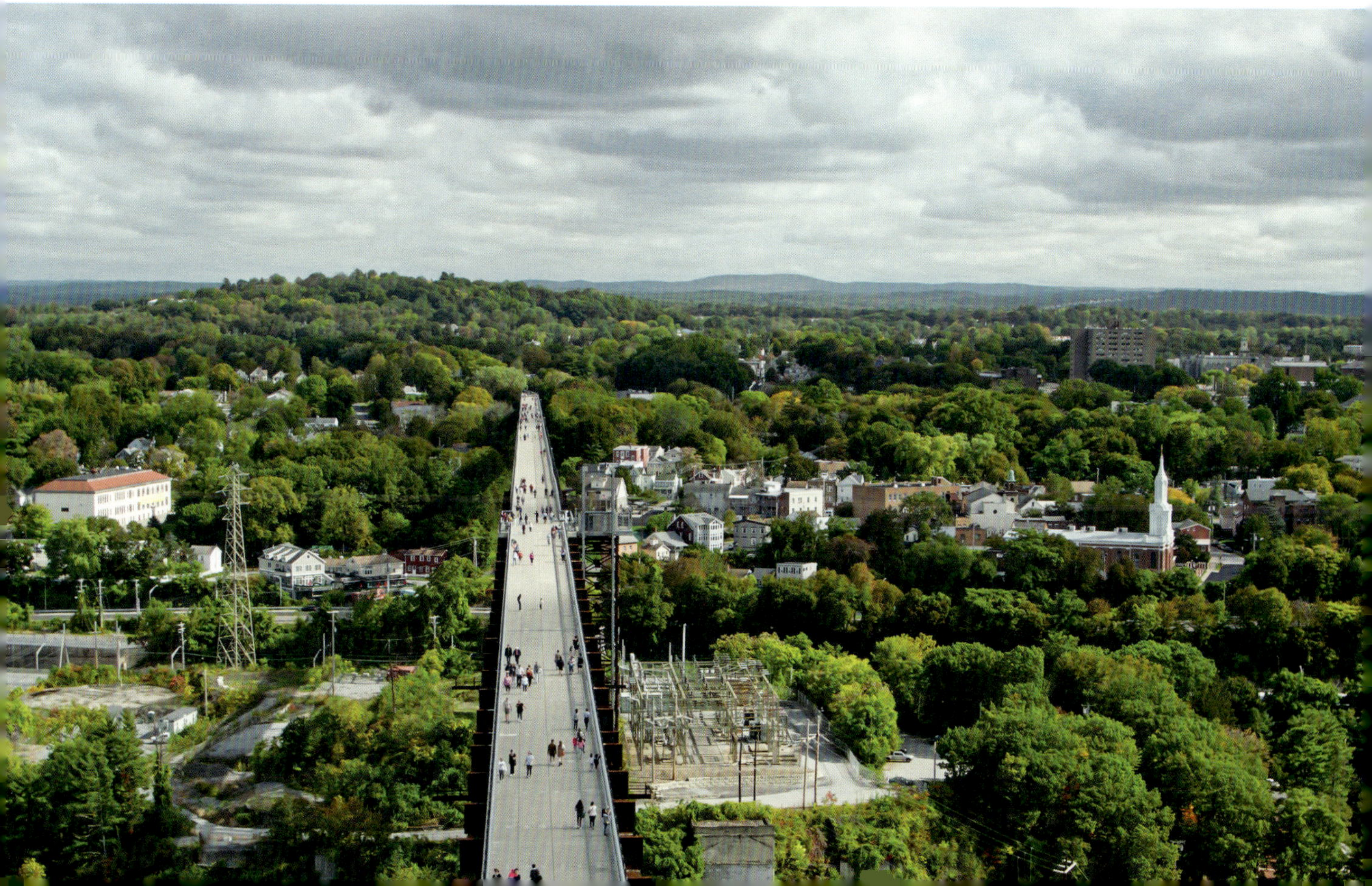

OVER GREEN MOUNTAINS ON THE SERRA VERDE EXPRESS

Defying challenging topography, Brazil's Serra Verde Express forges a spectacular path through Paraná state, offering intriguing glimpses of the country's endangered coastal rainforest.

There was a point on the Serra Verde Express when I felt as if I was floating in mid-air, transported momentarily from the carriage of a train into the fuselage of a plane. The sensation occurred as the train negotiated the Viaduto do Carvalho, a curved section of track raised on mortar pillars that clings precipitously to the side of a mountain in Brazil's Serra do Mar.

The mirage was sudden and fleeting. As we emerged from one of many tunnels that dot the line, the land on the left-hand side of the train fell away, leaving the impression that the carriage was flying above a forested valley ringed by verdant peaks. The feeling disappeared as quickly as it had arrived as we entered another tunnel.

In a country practically bereft of passenger trains, the Serra Verde Express is a welcome anomaly. Running several times weekly between the famously 'green' city of Curitiba and the small gastronomic hub of Morretes, 43.5 miles (70km) to the east, it styles itself as a heritage railway, with elegantly attired carriages furnished with leather seats, polished wood and the throwback charm of an Agatha Christie novel – without the murderous plot.

Considered an almost impossible feat of engineering when it was built between 1880 and 1885, the line was based on the plans of André and Antônio Rebouças, two brothers of African descent who worked as engineers in an era when Brazil still practised slavery. Their original idea was to build a 435-mile-long (700km) line from Iguaçu Falls to the coast but, due to

unfavourable costs and tricky logistics, a shorter 68-mile (110km) option was chosen, between Curitiba and Paranaguá, one of Brazil's main ports.

The biggest challenge for the line's 9000 construction workers was the terrain. Separating Curitiba from the coast is the Serra do Mar, a natural bulwark of deep-cut valleys and jungle-covered mountains. To crest them, the railway required not just a delicately balanced viaduct, but 14 tunnels and 30 bridges to be blasted and built along its course.

My journey began in Curitiba, a city celebrated for its groundbreaking rapid bus network and innovative approach to urban planning. The Serra Verde Express augments the green theme, carrying passengers east as far as Morretes, and freight – mostly soya and maize – all the way to Paranaguá.

I prebooked a return ticket, allowing me enough time in Morretes to sample the local cuisine, a meat stew called *barreado*, slow cooked in a medley of spices. For the outbound journey, I travelled Tourist Class while, on the return, I treated myself to a more expensive 'Imperial' carriage with vintage decor.

A loud and jovial crowd of mainly Brazilian vacationers had amassed in my seating area for the 9.15am departure. As it takes over three and a half hours to cover the relatively short distance, I quickly realised that this journey was more about scenery than speed. We chugged slowly out of Curitiba's eastern suburbs, the roads and buildings gradually giving way to trees and ferns as we entered the crinkled web of the Serra do Mar, a muddle of mountains and valleys overlain by Brazil's endangered Mata Atlántica (coastal rainforest).

While most railways tend towards straightness, the Serra Verde incorporates a wild number of curves and switchbacks into its route. Camera in hand, I had ample opportunities to lean out of the window and snap pictures of the brightly painted carriages wrapped around the bends in the track.

As the tunnels became more ubiquitous, I stuck my head back inside and captured the unfolding scenery through the glass instead. Thanks to helpful hints from the onboard guide, I was able to admire the steep forested walls of the Garganta do Diabo (a narrow gorge) and the waters of Véu da Noiva (bridal veil) falls that glittered like a flash of foam in the foliage.

Sporadic stations streaked by in various states of repair. Some lay in ruins, reclaimed by the jungle; others remained mostly intact. Somewhere around the halfway mark, the train began to navigate the most spectacular section of the trip. The vistas broadened as we crossed the 180ft-high (55m) São João Bridge, a lofty design marvel crafted out of Belgian steel in 1883, before negotiating the Carvalho viaduct. Soon afterwards, we began a

BARREADO

Morretes' culinary gift to the world is *barreado*, a dense meat stew thickened with manioc flour that's cooked in a clay pot over an open flame for 24 hours. In the town's restaurants, *barreado* comes to your table in its component parts, with pots of stew, manioc flour, rice, battered bananas and pickled peppers. If you're a beginner, the server will help you put it together.

From left: The Serra Verde Express' Imperial class; some of the motley carriages on the railway; Tangua Park in Curitiba; a street scene in Curitiba. Previous page: Passing through Atlantic rainforest.

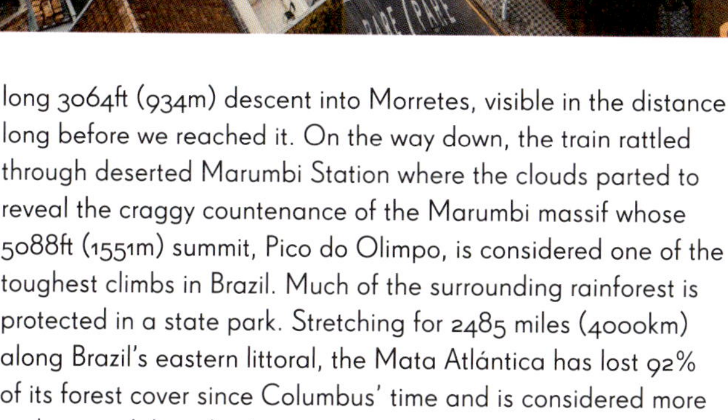

long 3064ft (934m) descent into Morretes, visible in the distance long before we reached it. On the way down, the train rattled through deserted Marumbi Station where the clouds parted to reveal the craggy countenance of the Marumbi massif whose 5088ft (1551m) summit, Pico do Olimpo, is considered one of the toughest climbs in Brazil. Much of the surrounding rainforest is protected in a state park. Stretching for 2485 miles (4000km) along Brazil's eastern littoral, the Mata Atlántica has lost 92% of its forest cover since Columbus' time and is considered more endangered than the Amazon.

The train schedule allowed for an ample three hours in Morretes, plenty of time to wander the handsome streets and sample a *barreado* lunch. I ordered the dish in Restaurante Casarão, beside the river, and watched as it was brought to my table in an elaborate ensemble of pots and dishes.

After the crowds and bustle of the outbound journey, I was expecting a tight squeeze on the way back. However, much to my surprise, I reboarded to discover that I had a whole Imperial carriage to myself – 1930s lampshades and obliging Brazilian attendant included. Sticking to the right-hand side of the train as we wheezed uphill back to Curitiba, I nursed a complimentary beer and reclined in my seat like a contented Hercule Poirot, summarising the day's events. **BS**

Start/Finish // Curitiba/Morretes
Distance // 43.5 miles (70km)
Duration // 3-4hr
Ticket types // There's a choice between Tourist, Boutique and plush Imperial classes.
How to book // It's best to book online several weeks in advance at serraverdeexpress.com.br.
When to go // Peak season is December to March; you'll find the train less busy during the shoulder months of November and April.
Things to know // You can opt to return to Curitiba from Morretes via bus or repeat the journey on the train. The views from the latter are best from the left-hand side on the outward journey and from the right-hand side on the return.

Opposite top: A train departs for Cristo Redentor on the Corcovado Railway. Opposite below: a Santa Teresa tram crosses the Arcos da Lapa aqueduct.

MORE LIKE THIS
BRAZIL BY TRAIN

VITÓRIA-MINAS RAILWAY

Brazil's longest and most reliable passenger train runs daily in both directions between the cities of Belo Horizonte in Minas Gerais state and Vitória in Espírito Santo on the Atlantic coast. Operated by Companhia Vale do Rio Doce, it was built in stages starting in 1904 with the final extension to Belo Horizonte opening in 1991. The original line was closely connected to the extraction of iron ore and the export of coffee from the interior. These days, it transports around 3000 passengers a day in modern carriages that include a restaurant car and two classes of service: Econômica and Executiva. The 13-hour journey incorporates 30 stations, passing through coastal rainforest and Brazilian cerrado (savannah), following the 530-mile (853km) Doce River for much of its course.

Start // Belo Horizonte
Finish // Vitória
Distance // 413 miles (664km)
Duration // 13hr

CORCOVADO RAILWAY

Since its completion in 1931, Rio de Janeiro's Cristo Redentor, the 98ft-high (30m) statue that stands arms outstretched atop the Corcovado hill, has been an enduring symbol of Brazil. The most popular way to reach it is by the red, narrow-gauge train that departs every 30 minutes from a station in the Rio neighbourhood of Cosme Velho. The Trem do Corcovado predates the statue by almost 50 years and was used to carry the component parts of the monument to the summit in the 1920s, where they were carefully reconstructed. The railway opened with steam-powered locomotives in 1884 before switching to electric in 1910. The modern trains, which are speedy by erstwhile standards, date from 2019. The short, intense journey climbs steeply through the forested Tijuca National Park, reaching inclines of up to 30% and calling at four stations on the way.

Start // Cosme Velho
Finish // Corcovado
Distance // 2.4 miles (3.8km)
Duration // 20min

SANTA TERESA TRAMWAY

This tramway's vintage golden-yellow cars are symbolic of Rio de Janeiro and its clattering wheels provide one of the city's most evocative soundtracks. The Bonde de Santa Teresa is the last surviving vestige of Rio's once extensive tram system that crossed the metropolis until the mid-20th century. Inaugurated in 1877 and originally pulled by mules, it ran uninterrupted until 2011, when a fatal accident led to a four-year closure. Back in business since 2015, with new cars fashioned in the old open-sided style, it continues to ply its familiar 3.7-mile (6km) route from downtown Rio to the cobbled hillside quarter of Santa Teresa, running over the double-arched Arcos da Lapa on the way, a former aqueduct that dates from the early 18th century. Passengers are treated to a broad panorama of Rio's urban tapestry, from striking street art and leafy residential streets to monkeys scampering across highwires.

Start // Largo da Carioca
Finish // Dois Irmãos
Distance // 3.7 miles (6km)
Duration // 20min

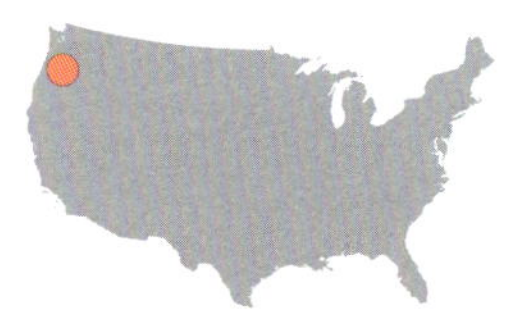

UNDER PACIFIC SKIES ON THE COAST STARLIGHT

A grand West Coast US adventure, taking passengers from the forests of Washington state to the golden shores of California.

No one rides America's railways, I was told. At least, no one American. They fly or drive from one state to the other, appalled at the idea of travelling on Amtrak. So it was with worry and excitement that I arrived one fresh fall morning at Seattle's glorious King Station to board the Coast Starlight to Los Angeles. This was a behemoth of a train, a silver double-decker taking centre stage in a scene reminiscent of the 1950s: inspectors checked names off clipboards and luggage was sent ahead to compartments. Unwilling to fork out the fare for a roomette, I'd bought a ticket in Coach Class and was delighted to find airline-style seating with plenty of room. I noticed that most passengers were leaving their luggage then disappearing down the aisle to the next carriage. Curious, I followed.

Outside, the Lumen Field Stadium passed by – we were already on the move through the grubbiness of the industrial hub of SoDo, warehouses looming and chimneys piping smoke. Departing just before 10am, the sleeper service takes 35 hours to descend the West Coast before terminating the follow evening at LA' s Union Station. It was set to be a long ride so I'd come equipped with an eye mask, ear plugs and blanket for the night.

As the door slid open to the adjoining carriage, I discovered the sightseer lounge, unique to the seven superliner services across Amtrak. With floor to ceiling windows and a domed roof providing panoramic views, the lounge was already filling up with passengers getting comfy in the outward-facing seats, packs of Bud Light at their feet. The sunshine was trapped in here, making it much warmer than my carriage, so I slipped into one of the seats and opened my book. But it was impossible to read. Every

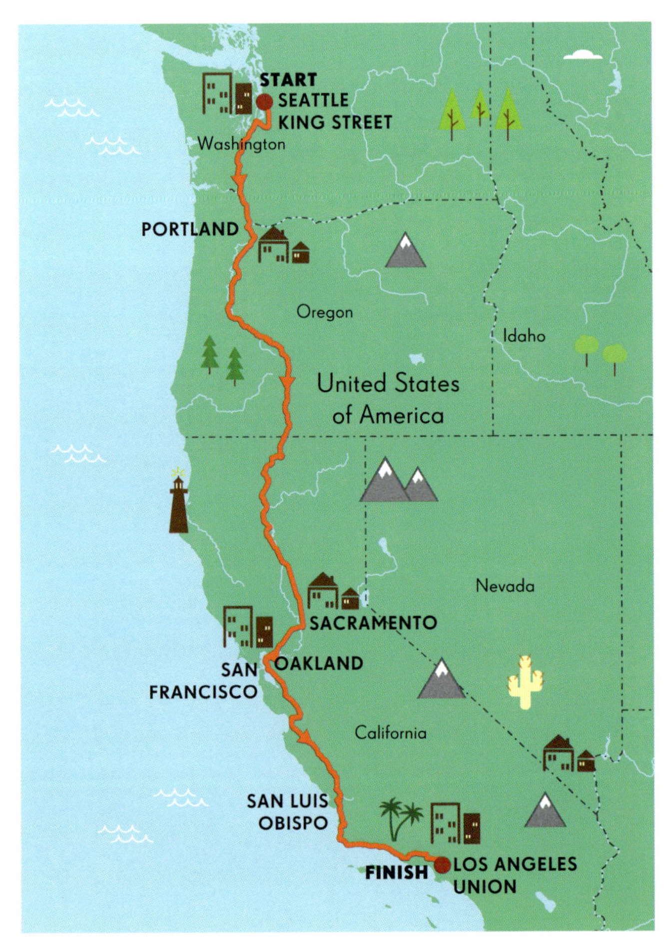

UNION
STATION

minute or two the train swerved through new suburbs, wooden houses lined up with barbecues in back yards or teens shooting hoops in the drive – a captivating distraction from my book.

The tannoy crackled and the train manager announced that he would be coming through to take sittings for lunch and dinner – I glanced round wondering with whom I might be seated. Amtrak dining cars are the heart of the action, where strangers are assigned tables at random. Some older passengers were knitting, puzzling over crosswords or reading, while younger ones sat at tables sharing Doritos and salsa. In one corner a guitarist in a checked shirt quietly strummed Simon & Garfunkel, while in another, a couple shared earphones, their feet tapping as the train thundered on past farmland and forest. The lounge was soon full. Two solo travellers had struck up a heated conversation about a scandal involving a senator, while two others bought rounds from the cafe and bonded over a mutual love of Nirvana. It was here, in this buzz of new friendships developing and old ones deepening that I felt at home.

By early evening the train was carving out a path through an evergreen expanse flushed with the glow of a disappearing sun. Our community had wound down to read, watch films or eat dinner, so I made my way towards the dining car where I was seated with two retirees who had boarded at Eugene. They were en route to visit their grandchildren in Oakland, California. In the past they'd always driven, but had decided for the first time in 20 years to take the sleeper train and 'be tourists in our own beautiful back yard'. Over flat iron steak with port wine sauce, we swapped travelling stories across a table dressed with starched white linen, the red stripes of sunset sweeping across our faces. They were sharing a roomette so cramped they could barely fit in at the same time, and as I settled into my own seat to sleep, I felt comforted that at a fifth

SCENIC HIGHLIGHT

Check with the train manager for the specific timing of the approach to San Luis Obispo, but around 3pm it's a good time to move to the tail end of the train. From here passengers can take in a view of the entire line of carriages as they form a horseshoe curve like a silver snake, before crossing the Stenner Creek Trestle. The area is a key spot for rail fans who loiter at the track's edge waiting to photograph the moment.

Clockwise from top: the Coast Starlight near San Luis Obispo; passing through scrubby hills; the Pacific in California; Seattle's King Street Station. Previous page: Portland's Union Station.

of the price, I was probably getting a better deal.

Giving my neck a twist and a crack, I woke to the warmth of first light over Sacramento's vineyards. Around me passengers were still asleep, using everything from coats to towels to stay warm in the chill of the carriage. Stepping carefully around socked feet, I returned to the dining car, a plate of hot French toast soon stacked before me. There was an air of magic about these moments, when others slept and the train continued to make its journey nonetheless, opening up the American landscape to whoever cared enough to wake up and witness it. Before long before the magnificence of the Pacific Ocean shimmered into view, a rich expanse of blue flecked with tiny white waves. From here on, it was a coastal ride of dreams, Californian sunshine bouncing above the train as it wound around clifftops, the water flashing in and out of view.

Over the last couple of hours, I got chatting to passengers who were too scared to fly, too unwell to drive and too lacking in annual leave to travel anywhere further than the West Coast. Americans clearly did use their trains, and those who didn't had no idea what they were missing. With a glass of chardonnay in hand, I watched foam fizzing on golden sands as surfers and swimmers dotted bays and walkers followed dogs down promenades flanked by palms. As the sky turned from red to pink, lights flickered on in passing towns, and the train got into its stride, whipping by one beach after another until it slowed into Los Angeles, a deep sonorous horn heralding the end of our mighty West Coast adventure. **MR**

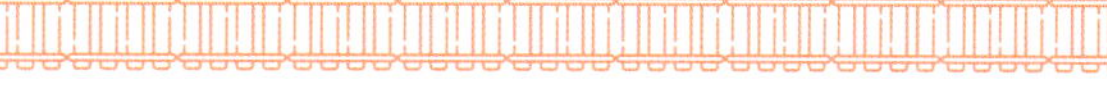

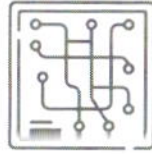

Start/Finish // King Street Station, Seattle/Union Station, Los Angeles

Distance // 1377 miles (2216km)

Duration // 35hr

Ticket types // Passengers can travel in upright seats in Coach Class or upgrade to a roomette where seats convert to berths, or a bedroom which has twice the space of a roomette and comes with an in-room sink, restroom and shower, plus the option to have meals delivered.

How to book // Online at amtrak.com

When to go // Fall (September to November) sees the landscape's colours range from mustard yellow to deep purple.

Things to know // Keep plenty of cash to hand: tipping is normal at every meal. Think about breaking up your journey into separate legs: many passengers visit microbreweries in Portland, wineries in Sacramento or surf spots in Santa Barbara.

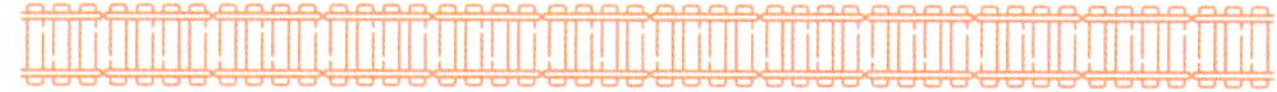

Opposite: A summer scene among the vineyards of Napa Valley.

MORE LIKE THIS
THREE CALIFORNIAN RAILWAYS

YOSEMITE MOUNTAIN SUGAR PINE RAILROAD

Yosemite Mountain Sugar Pine Railroad is an awfully long name for a very little railway. Nonetheless, thousands come to ride this hallowed narrow-gauge line, set by the southern threshold of the Yosemite National Park, technically within the territory of the Sierra National Forest. Dating to the 1960s, the YMSPRR is a modern recreation of an old timber line which was laid in the 1900s – these days it's people rather than logs being transported through the shadowy conifer forests, keeping eyes peeled for squirrels and birds in the canopy. The biggest beasts in this forest, however, are unquestionably the two vintage steam locomotives in the YMSPRR fleet – confusingly numbered 10 and 15 – two Ohio-built leviathans that are a century old but still working California's tracks.

Start/Finish // Fish Camp
Distance // 8 miles (13km) round trip
Duration // 1hr

NAPA VALLEY WINE TRAIN

Napa Valley is California's viticulture epicentre, with constellations of wineries taunting motorists who drive by, unable to imbibe so much as drop. Drunk driving laws don't apply, however, to passengers aboard the long-standing Napa Valley Wine Train – in business since the 1980s, shuttling back and forth between Napa itself and the town of St Helena, with the driver hitting the brakes at illustrious vineyards along the way so passengers can hop off and sample the vintages. There's a rich range of itineraries, spanning gourmet meals, murder mysteries and grape-treading experiences. Train aficionados are just as content as their wine-loving counterparts thanks to the plush Pullman-style coaches, hauled by vintage 1950s diesel engines through landscapes chequered with quivering vines.

Start // Napa
Finish // St Helena
Distance // 36 miles (58km)
Duration // Varies

THE SKUNK TRAIN

The Skunk Train supposedly earned its name because locals could smell oncoming engines before they could see them. These days rail enthusiasts from afar flock to this particular corner of Northern California to breathe in those heady fumes. The line more officially known as the California Western Railroad runs from the Pacific waves at Fort Bragg up to the city of Willits, 1312ft (400m) up in Mendocino County – the territory in between is largely composed of giant redwood groves that straddle the Noyo River Canyon. Daily departures are hauled by both steam and diesel locomotives and depart from both ends of the line. What marks the Skunk out as unusual, however, is the option of travelling on 'railbikes' – with riders pedalling their way over creeks and through sun-dappled woodlands. You're out in the open, meaning you get closer to the sights – and smells – of the landscape.

Start // Fort Bragg
Finish // Willits
Distance // Varies
Duration // Varies

TIERRA DEL FUEGO BY RAIL

The southernmost railway on Earth, the Tren del Fin del Mundo (End of the World Train) showcases Tierra del Fuego's turbulent history and dramatic landscapes.

After chugging across the ice-flecked Río Pipo towards a snow-streaked massif, the Tren del Fin del Mundo ground to a halt at a miniature station – where it was immediately besieged by an excitable gaggle of men and women dressed in yellow-and-blue-striped prison jumpsuits. As we gingerly disembarked from our carriages, they gesticulated wildly at us, pulling grotesque faces and bellowing at the top of their voices. One wielded a pickaxe, another waggled a meaty fist.

Yet the air of cartoon menace soon dissipated and the 'prisoners' – railway staff in mocked-up prison garb – were soon posing for photos, pretending to put each other in headlocks and gently ushering passengers in the direction of the souvenir stalls.

This surreal scene was a nod to the grisly history of Tierra del Fuego, the archipelago at the tip of South America, some 620 miles (1000km) north of Antarctica. Thanks to its isolation,

inhospitable climate and rugged terrain, the region – inhabited by Indigenous peoples such as the Yagán and Selk'nam for around 10,000 years – escaped colonisation until the late 19th and early 20th centuries.

During this period, the Argentine and Chilean governments both tried to secure their claims to Tierra del Fuego. Following in the wake of British Anglican missionaries, waves of South Americans and Europeans headed south, eager to make their fortunes in gold mining or sheep ranching. Their colonisation of the area devastated the Indigenous population, who were killed, displaced and suffered epidemics of diseases such as smallpox and measles. It has been described as a genocide.

In a bid to cement its control over the west of the region, the Argentine government founded a penal colony in the fledgling town of Ushuaia, on a wide bay facing the Beagle Channel, named after the ship that carried a young Charles Darwin on his groundbreaking voyage. As a result of the frigid climate and brutal treatment, the prison was soon dubbed the 'Siberia of the South', home to a motley collection of political prisoners, anarchist revolutionaries and notorious criminals. As Ushuaia expanded, the inmates were enlisted to build homes, infrastructure – and a narrow-gauge railway to transport timber from the surrounding forests. Working conditions on the latter could be horrific, yet as one prisoner wrote, unlike in his cold, cramped cell, 'At least I can breathe some air and see the sun.'

Launched in 1909, the Tren de los Presos (Prisoners' Train) eventually ran along a 13.6-mile (22km) line and played a vital role in the development of Ushuaia over the following decades. But it gradually ran out of steam and closed in 1952, its fate sealed by the closure of the prison in 1947 and, two years later, an earthquake that blocked a large section of the track. Four decades passed before the railway was finally revived as a 500mm-gauge heritage line in the mid-1990s, when it was rebranded as the Tren del Fin del Mundo. Today, replica steam trains run 365 days a year back and forth along a 4.3-mile (7km) section of the track, from Estación Fin del Mundo, 5 miles (8km) west of Ushuaia, to a station on the eastern edge of Parque Nacional Tierra del Fuego. Its presence here is important as this southernmost tip of South America is a place where railways are all but non-existent.

Despite its touristy veneer, the Tren del Fin del Mundo provides a fascinating insight into the history of Ushuaia – now a busy city of more than 80,000, thronged during the southern summer with passengers boarding cruises to Antarctica – and Tierra del Fuego as a whole. The scenery is also spectacular.

After leaving behind the cheerful faux convicts at Estación La Macarena, the train carried us west into the park, travelling through sphagnum peat bogs, southern beech trees carpeted with lichen and moss, crystalline waterfalls and saw-toothed mountains. There were also reminders of the labours of the long-departed prisoners, including an expanse of stumps

MUSEO DEL PRESIDIO

Ushuaia's old prison has been turned into an atmospheric museum, the Museo del Presidio. It tells the history of the penal colony and the development of the Tren de los Presos, illustrated with first-hand testimony and evocative photos. One wing has been kept in its original condition, providing a chilling glimpse into the harsh conditions the prisoners endured. There's also a maritime museum (the Museo Marítimo) onsite.

Clockwise from top: Ushuaia; a Garratt engine hauls into the platform; 'prisoners' greet passengers. Previous page: A steam service in winter; a glacier outside Ushuaia.

known as the 'tree cemetery', the remnants of a woodland chopped down for firewood, and the remains of a sawmill.

As we sipped coffee and nibbled crumbly dulce de leche-filled biscuits known as *alfajores*, the onboard narration – delivered in the hyperbolic style of a boxing announcer – alternated with tango classics. There were tales of Ushuaia's early days; anecdotes about inmates such as Cayetano Santos Godino, a teenager serial killer nicknamed the 'Petiso Orejudo' (Big-Eared Short Man); and a brief account of a misguided idea of the Argentine authorities to introduce Canadian beavers to Tierra del Fuego in the 1940s – the planned fur industry failed to take off and the rodents proliferated in the absence of local predators, spreading across the archipelago and damaging great swathes of its forests.

After 45 minutes, I got off at a station inside Parque Nacional Tierra del Fuego, a haven for hiking and birdwatching wedged between the Andes and the Beagle Channel. A trail took me through a woodland studded with *Cyttaria hariotii*, an orange, golfball-shaped fungus that was once an important food source for the area's original inhabitants, and echoing with the taps of crimson-headed Magellanic woodpeckers. Passing a series of ancient middens – grassy mounds of discarded mollusc shells left behind by Yagán families over millennia – I eventually emerged onto a deserted pebble beach snaking west towards the Chilean border.

The channel ahead was framed by frosted peaks and squadrons of petrels and oystercatchers zipped above the surface. It was perfectly quiet until the faint sound of a steam engine whistle drifted over on the afternoon breeze – the Tren del Fin del Mundo setting off on its return journey. **SM**

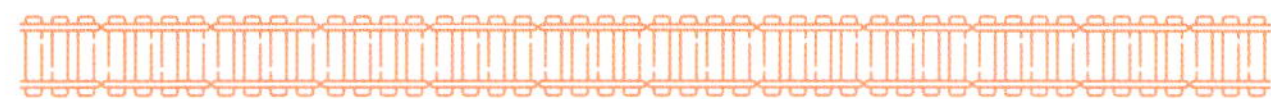

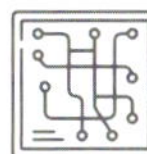

Start/Finish // Estación Fin del Mundo/ Estación Parque Nacional
Distance // 4.3 miles (7km)
Duration // Around 45min one way
Ticket types // There are 2-3 daily services throughout the year and three classes: Tourist (carriages with three seats per row); Premium (more comfortable carriages and a one-course meal); and VIP (a fancier carriage and a three-course meal).
How to book // Buy tickets at trendelfindelmundo.com.ar or in Estación Fin del Mundo.
When to go // Visit in October and November for spring flowers; March and April for autumn colours; and July to September for snowy winter scenes. Summer (December to February) provides some good conditions, but also plenty of tourists.
Things to know // It's wise to book tickets in advance during the summer and peak winter month (July).
More info // turismoushuaia.com

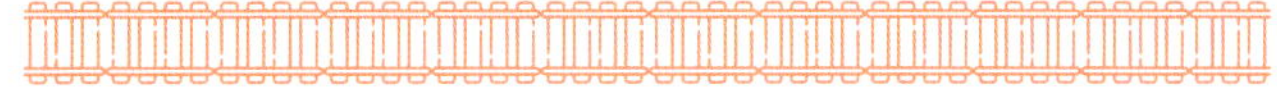

Clockwise from top: High times on the Tren a las Nubes; a railway line through Uyuni's salt flats; waterways in the resort of Tigre.

MORE LIKE THIS
ANDEAN LINES AND RIVER RIDES

TREN A LAS NUBES, ARGENTINA

One of the highest railways in the world, the Tren a las Nubes (Train to the Clouds) cuts through northwest Argentina, an otherworldly region of mountains, volcanoes and rugged rock formations known as the puna. Launched in the late 1940s to connect isolated mining hubs, the line is an engineering marvel that takes in gravity-defying viaducts, bridges and tunnels. Relaunched as a tourist line in the 1970s, it currently runs between the town of San Antonio de los Cobres and the lofty Polvorilla Viaduct. At 13,845ft (4220m), the latter is the literal and figurative high point of the route – so much so that staff are on hand with oxygen cannisters, though the mesmerising landscapes and precipitous drops are just as likely to take your breath away.
Start/Finish // San Antonio de los Cobres
Distance // 27.2 miles (44km)
Duration // 2hr 45min

TREN DE LA COSTA, ARGENTINA

A tourist service launched in 1995, the Tren de la Costa (Train of the Coast) glides through the leafy suburbs of northern Buenos Aires to the faded resort of Tigre on the edge of the labyrinthine waterways of the Paraná Delta, the second largest river system in South America. Travelling a route built at the end of the 19th century, a time when Tigre was a playground for the rich and famous, it's best treated as a hop-on, hop-off service. The stations en route have been meticulously refurbished – or, in some cases, built from scratch – and given their own distinct themes and characters. Estación San Isidro has a modern feel with restaurants, bars, shops and cinemas close at hand, while the British-style Estación Barrancas is home to an antiques market. Estación Borges – named after the legendary Argentine writer Jorge Luis Borges – offers up an artistic cafe and a collection of sculptures.
Start // Maipú Station
Finish // Delta Station, Buenos Aires
Distance // 9.6 miles (15.5 km)
Duration // 25min

EXPRESO DEL SUR, BOLIVIA

Following a 19th-century line built to carry Bolivia's abundant mineral reserves to Pacific ports, the Expreso del Sur (Southern Express) barrels across the altiplano, a stark plateau between two branches of the Andes sitting, on average, more than 12,000ft (3750m) above sea level. After departing the tin-mining city of Oruro, the train traces the dusty shoreline of Lake Poopó – once the size of Luxembourg before almost entirely evaporating in the mid-2010s – and then skirts the shimmering white, pancake-flat expanse of the Salar de Uyuni, the world's biggest salt flat. Later it travels through the cactus-dotted badlands of the Cordillera de Chiches where Butch Cassidy and the Sundance Kid met their match in a shootout with the Bolivian army in 1908. The finish comes in the town of Villazón, right on the border with Argentina.
Start // Oruro
Finish // Villazón
Distance // 373 miles (600km)
Duration // 19hr

GO FOR GOLD ON THE WHITE PASS AND YUKON ROUTE

Alpine landscapes, a mountain pass frontier and vestiges of the Klondike gold rush provide a fascinating backdrop to this narrow-gauge heritage railway linking Alaska and the Yukon.

Plenty of people, at some point in their lives, find themselves running for a train. But my 33-mile (53km) dash to catch the White Pass and Yukon Route (WPYR) before 3.15pm on a muggy afternoon in late June was trickier than most.

I was trying to complete the legendary Chilkoot Trail in a day, the historic route hiked by thousands of stampeders on their way to the Klondike gold fields in 1897-8. The trail begins near Skagway in Alaska, crosses 3759ft (1146m) Chilkoot Pass and terminates at a middle-of-nowhere train station beside Bennett Lake in British Columbia. From there, the only way back to civilisation is by expensive floatplane or by booking a ride on the WPYR. The caveat with the latter option? There's only one train a day, in mid-afternoon, meaning I had had to start my hike at 5am and scamper across the mountains at a swift pace.

The WPYR is a vintage narrow-gauge railway that runs in both directions between Carcross in the Yukon and Skagway in Alaska, with a brief international border crossing in British Columbia. Passengers are accommodated in elegant 19th-century parlour carriages pulled by muscular diesel locomotives dating from the 1950s and 1960s.

The line was conceived in 1898 at the height of the Klondike gold rush with the aim of opening Canada's mineral rich interior to ambitious prospectors. By the time the last spike was hammered into the ground in 1900, though, the rush had lost its sparkle, and the railway ended up becoming both a conduit for less glamorous mining interests and a transport artery for adventurous travellers looking to penetrate the country's wild interior.

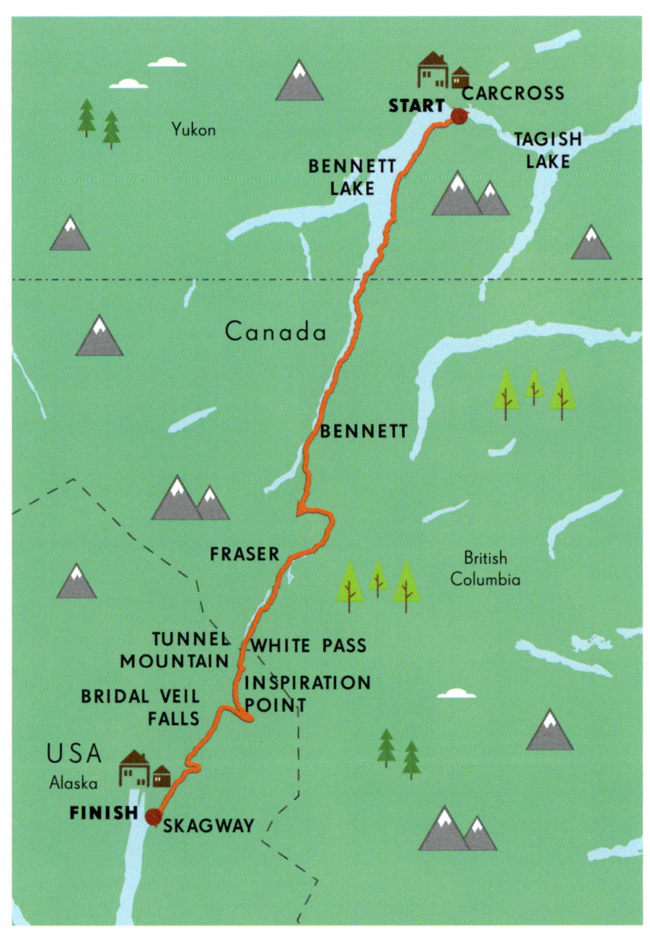

White Pass
White Pass

From the cruise port at Skagway, the line meanders up the side of a steep-sided valley on a 4% grade to reach 2877ft (873m) White Pass in a little over 20 miles (32km). There, it crosses the US-Canadian border on a high alpine plateau scattered with small lakes and speckled with snow well into the summer.

After eight decades of up and down fortunes, the railroad closed for economic reasons in 1982 but re-opened six years later after cruise ship operators successfully pushed to have it turned into a heritage railway targeting Alaska's growing deluge of cruise passengers. Today, the WPYR functions primarily as a tourist line between Carcross and Skagway, with buses connecting to an old station terminal in Whitehorse.

I've twice ridden the route, first on a standard tourist package between Carcross and Skagway, and then using the so-called 'hikers' shuttle' that picks up exhausted backpackers fresh off the Chilkoot Trail at Bennett Lake before whisking them back to Skagway.

The steep, weather-beaten 33-mile (53km) trail is normally hiked over three days, but in the spirit of the Klondikers of yore, I had decided to 'run' it in one. By the time I jogged into off-the-road-grid Bennett Station, I was sore, tired and in need of refreshment. Arriving 45 minutes early, I had ample time to stretch, inhale a couple of power bars and take a quick look inside Bennett's reconfigured station, preserved

"The railway ended up becoming a transport artery for adventurous travellers looking to penetrate the country's wild interior..."

as a local railway museum, before the train pulled in bang on time. I scrambled aboard, a dishevelled runner joining a carriage full of relaxed, fresh-faced tourists.

From Bennett Lake, the line curves southwest, with subalpine firs gradually giving way to blustery tundra. The real fun starts soon after the tiny Canadian border community of Fraser as the train enters Alaska and begins its descent into Skagway. Looking out the window I watched as we quickly lost altitude, paralleling the still visible 'Trail of 98', one of two walking routes that were available to Klondike-bound prospectors. The winding path leading up to White Pass was marginally less steep than the nearby Chilkoot Trail, meaning horses could be used, although thousands of them perished in the cold, muddy conditions.

On booking my ticket I had pre-ordered a boxed lunch and the cold snack arrived at my seat, courtesy of a smartly attired attendant, as we emerged from a narrow tunnel soon after crossing the international border. As I devoured a chunky sandwich, I caught sight of the skeletal form of the disused 18A cantilever bridge, a spectacular steel structure built in 1900, but abandoned in 1969 when the line was re-routed nearby. Still nobly spanning a deep ravine, it was once the highest steel cantilever bridge in the world.

Stoked with my post-hike endorphins, I found the views doubly dramatic as the line curled around the mountainside on a narrow ledge that had been blasted from the rock face with the cliff falling away sharply on the right-hand side. We passed Dead Horse Gulch, Inspiration Point and Tunnel Mountain as I looked across the valley at the sparkling flow of Bridal Veil Falls, and strained to spot the houses of Skagway beside icy blue Taiya Inlet below. With my late lunch over, I relocated to the carriage's outdoor platform to breathe in the mountain air and get some better photos.

At Denver, a lonesome flag-stop, we passed a red trackside caboose converted into an overnight cabin for hikers heading to the nearby Denver Glacier. Soon after, the forest became lusher, with deciduous trees interspersing with firs as we joined the Skagway River for the final section into the former gold rush settlement. As the town drew near, we passed a cemetery, a campground and finally arrived at the port-side station, overlooked by the original 1898 ticket depot. Revived by my wonderfully scenic journey, my legs felt just about ready to walk again. **BS**

KLONDIKE GOLD RUSH

The Klondike gold rush was ignited in August 1896 when three tenacious prospectors found placer gold in a tributary of the Klondike River in the Yukon, Canada. The discovery fuelled a mining frenzy that prompted over 35,000 stampeders to descend on Dawson City seeking their fortune. Of those, only a paltry couple of hundred became rich as a result.

From top: Bennett station in Canada; Skagway station in Alaska; the landscape close to the border. Previous page: A diesel service emerges from a tunnel.

Start/Finish // Carcross/Skagway
Distance // 67 miles (108km)
Duration // 4hr 45min
Ticket types // There's only one class on the service.
How to book // It's best to buy tickets several weeks in advance of travel on the WPYR website (wpyr.com).
When to go // Trains run in spring and summer only, from late-May to mid-September.
Things to know // Various packages can be organised as day excursions starting in either Carcross, Bennett and Fraser in Canada, or Skagway in Alaska, with a bus or train return. All riders will need to travel with a valid passport because of the international border crossing. There are two additional flag-stops at Glacier and Denver, both on the Alaskan side.

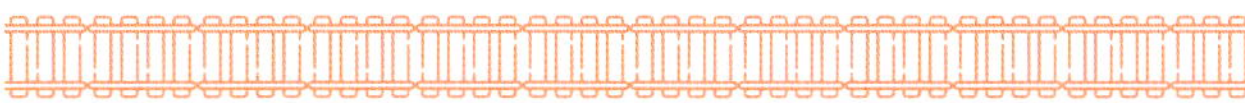

Opposite: Sunset seen from an Alaska Railroad GoldStar dome coach.

MORE LIKE THIS
ALASKAN ADVENTURES

COASTAL CLASSIC

The southern part of the state-run Alaska Railroad system extends from Anchorage around the steep-sided shores of Turnagain Arm, before pitching south across the Kenai Peninsula to terminate in the diminutive port town of Seward. Turnagain Arm is an elongated waterway that experiences the largest tide fluctuations in the US. The line parallels its north shore with mountains up to 6000ft (1829m) rising high on both sides, the Chugach range to the north and the Kenai ranges to the south. Beyond Portage, at the head of waterway, the tracks veer away from the road into an isolated landscape of wide rivers and glistening glaciers before descending into Resurrection Bay and Seward. The relatively luxurious train has two classes, Adventure and GoldStar, with the latter offering a full-service dining car, outdoor viewing platform, onboard guide and carriages with glass dome ceilings.
Start // Anchorage
Finish // Seward
Distance // 100 miles (177km)
Duration // 4hr 30min

GLACIER DISCOVERY

This tourist-oriented train runs along a similar route to the Coastal Classic but incorporates an interesting diversion through the 2.5-mile-long (4km) Anton Anderson Memorial Tunnel to the Cold War citadel of Whittier. It then rejoins the Coastal Classic route as far as Grandview, stopping at the Spencer Glacier whistle-stop where passengers can disembark for a bracing hike to a viewpoint with time to re-catch the train on its return journey. Whittier is another potential stopover, with the schedule allowing passengers a generous six hours to enjoy whale-watching, hiking and exploring an erstwhile military base developed during WWII. Other stops include Portage Lake, site of a tumbling glacier, and Girdwood, home to Alaska's largest ski area.
Start // Anchorage
Finish // Grandview
Distance // 104 miles (167km)
Duration // 6hr 30min

HURRICANE TURN

A flag-stop train that utilises the same tracks as Alaska's Denali Star, the Hurricane Turn is a radically different service to its intercity cousin. The flexible schedule lists no trackside stations – instead, passengers can get on and off where they like. To stop the oncoming train, just wave something white – a cloth, a t-shirt, a towel – anywhere along the route. The service sets out from Talkeetna, 115 miles (185km) north of Anchorage, and rattles through the remote Indian River Valley as far as Hurricane Gulch where it turns around and returns by the same route. It's primarily used by fishers, wilderness hikers, Alaskans accessing their backcountry cabins and curious tourists just along for the ride. The icy hulk of Denali, North America's tallest mountain, is visible on clear days. The 'Turn' is the last genuine flag-stop service in the US and runs year-round. Unlike other Alaska Railroad trains, it has no dining service, so bring your own snacks.
Start // Talkeetna
Finish // Hurricane
Distance // 58 miles (93km)
Duration // 2hr 30min

ASIA

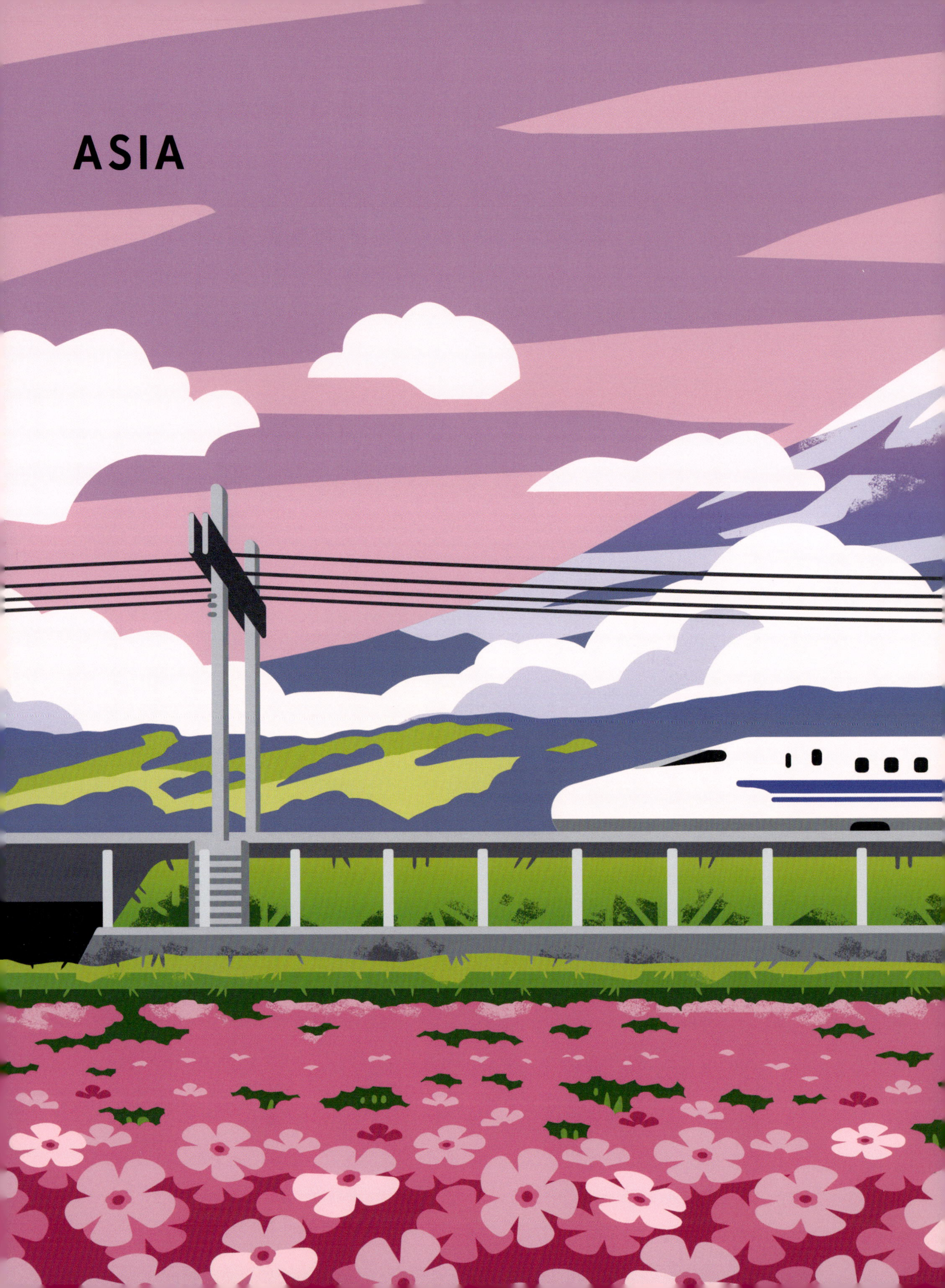

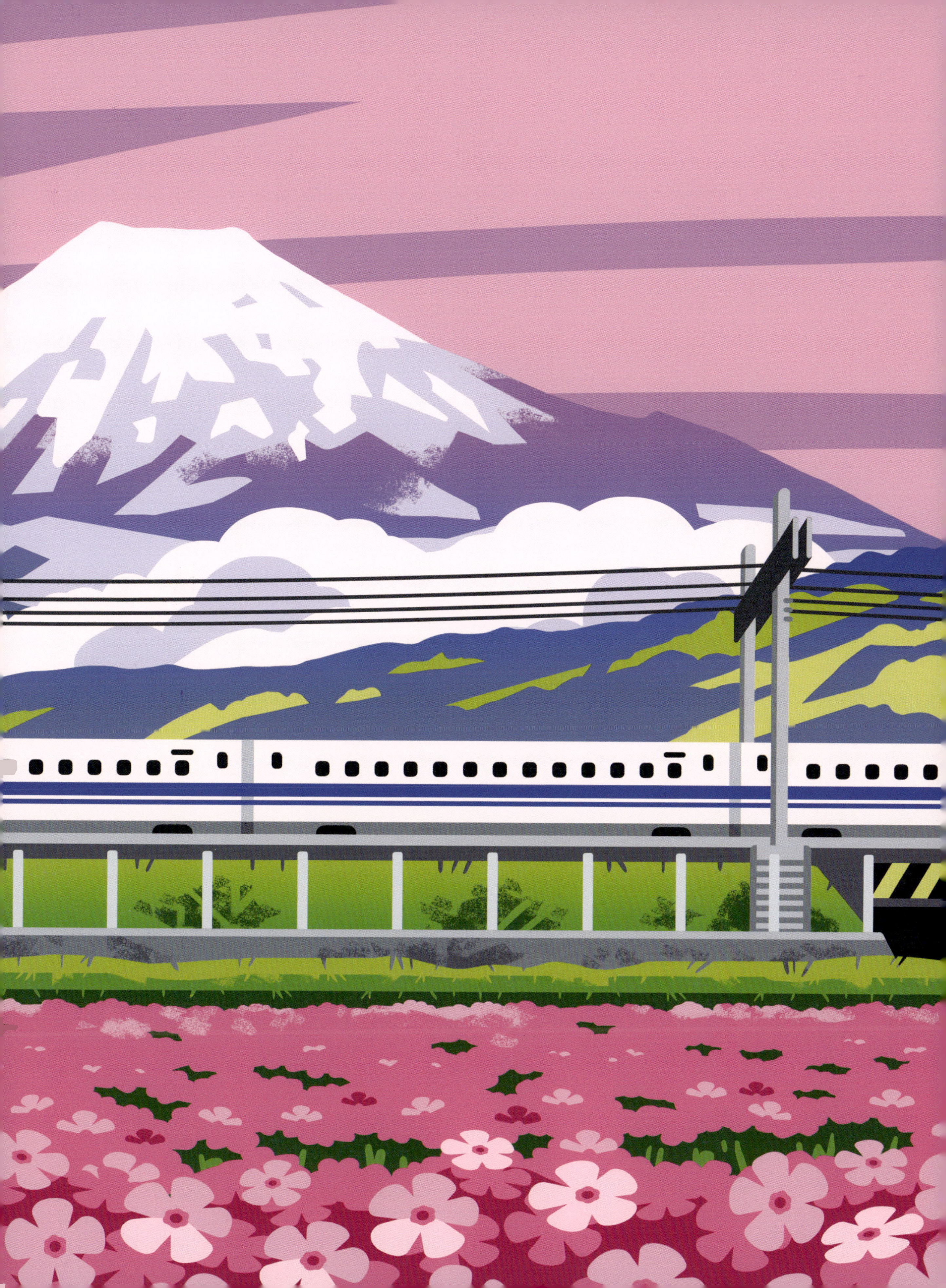

SMALL IS BEAUTIFUL ON THE DARJEELING HIMALAYAN

Tiny railcars pulled through the foothills of India's eastern Himalayas by an engine that looks like a child's toy – could any rail enthusiast ask for more?

For rail lovers, a trip to India brings both joy and sadness – joy for the epic train trips that connect every corner of this continent-sized country, but sadness at being a generation too late to ride India's thundering WP-class steam locomotives. The last mainline steam service in India ground to a halt in the Punjab in 1995, but a few nostalgic steamers still chug through the foothills of the Himalaya, including the charmingly pocket-sized Darjeeling Himalayan Railway.

Twisting uphill from New Jalpaiguri Junction (NJP) like a python with indigestion, this legendary mountain line was hacked through the jungle by British and Indian engineers between 1879 and 1881, completing 55 miles (88km) of steep climbs, vertiginous turns and 360-degree loops beside the Darjeeling road.

En route, you'll rattle past monkey-stalked forests, peridot-green tea gardens, bustling village schools, pagoda-topped Buddhist monasteries, plunging valleys, snow-crowned peaks and convoys of pick-up trucks that pass almost close enough to touch. Or you may just look out over swirling mist – the temperamental Himalayan weather is an important factor in deciding when to ride this route!

The line from NJP to Darjeeling was originally serviced using British-built B-Class steam engines, but today, the daily NJP–Darjeeling Passenger train is hauled by diesel – quieter but less charming, exhaling chemical fumes in place of the fireplace-whiff of steam. However, loco lovers can still experience the sensory immersion of steam travel on 'joyrides' between Darjeeling and Ghum.

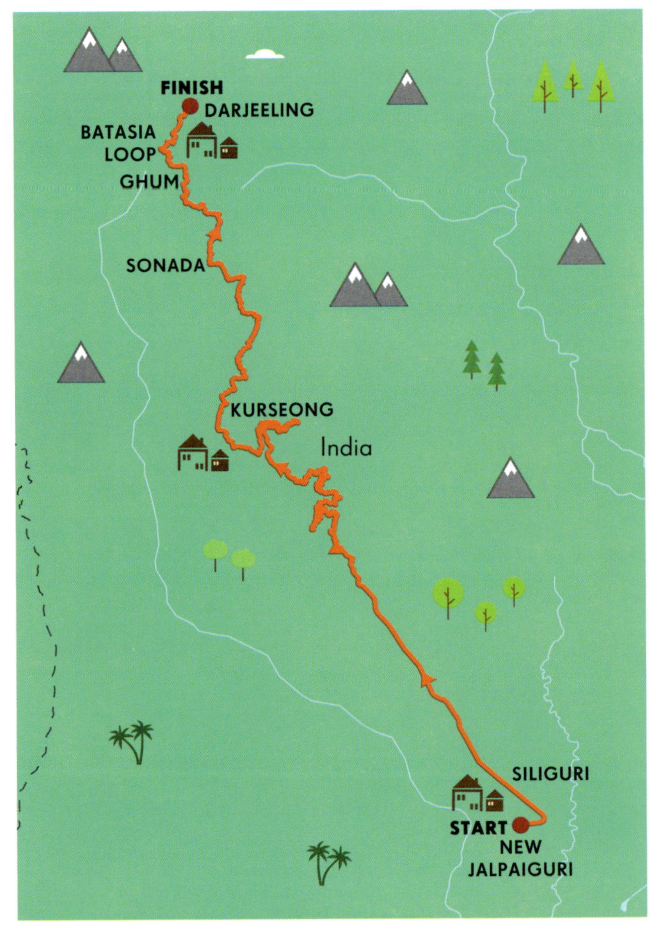

Don't dismiss the diesel-pulled trains entirely. The 52541 from NJP to Darjeeling connects with the overnight Darjeeling Mail from Kolkata, offering a epic sense of mission as you rumble from the onetime capital of British India to the green and pleasant hill station where those heat-addled colonials once came to cool off in a wistful facsimile of home.

It's a slow journey though, my goodness! The trip from NJP to Darjeeling involves seven hours in a scaled-down seat, clattering over tracks not much wider than your shoulders. I shared my cramped carriage with railway enthusiasts and holidaying families from across India. 'We came all the way from Chennai,' announced one youngster enthusiastically. 'That's half the length of India!'

Climbing (slowly) above lowland tea gardens and busy Bengali townships, I fell into conversation with a loquacious computer programmer from Kolkata who was a font of knowledge about the Darjeeling Himalayan Railway – 'Did you know this line has 500 bridges?' was one tidbit that stuck in my memory.

Initially, all eyes were glued to the windows, as the views opened up to reveal distant ridges, and closed in on tarmac and shopfronts where the rails tracked the Darjeeling road. But as time wore on, the novelty started to wane. Siblings started squabbling and the inevitable calls of 'When will we be there mummy?' began.

Popping in my earphones to dampen the clamour, I settled in to contemplate the remarkable feats of engineering required to build the Himalayan Railway. As well as endless bridges, the line completes 177 road crossings and three full loops as it coils uphill from 374ft (114m) to 6801ft (2073m). Five times, we juddered to a stop before climbing particularly steep sections in reverse, with the engine pushing the carriages uphill like a mechanical Sisyphus.

Despite the fug of diesel fumes, reaching Darjeeling's miniature station was a delight, not least for the sense of liberation after a day in a compact carriage. From the art deco terminus, an endearingly chaotic jumble of buildings – some historic and elegant, others modern and ungainly – straggled in all directions, melting into forested hills. My pockets weren't quite deep enough for a suite at the British-built Windamere Hotel, but I could stretch to a circulation-restoring cup of Darjeeling tea at the 130-year-old Glenary's bakery – served the proper way, milk-free and unsweetened.

I wasn't going to leave without a joyride on a steam train, of course. A day later, after an early morning wander through the tangle of fluttering Buddhist prayer flags atop Observatory Hill, I tramped back downhill to Darjeeling station, where a Thomas the Tank Engine–style steam engine sat panting on the platform.

GETTING TO DARJEELING

Although it stands on the site of an ancient Tibetan Buddhist shrine, Darjeeling was a British creation, built on land seized from Sikkim and Nepal in the 19th century. Originally, the only way in was on foot, but Hill Cart Rd was constructed in 1862, allowing slow, uncomfortable transfers by bullock cart. Things improved dramatically with the arrival of the railway in 1881 – some 8000 passengers were carried in the first year alone.

Clockwise from top: A diesel service near Ghum; approaching Darjeeling station; the statue of Tenzing Norgay at Darjeeling. Previous page: Near Ghum.

Darjeeling and Ghum are just 3.7 miles (6km) apart, but it takes nearly two hours to complete the return trip. You won't mind, though; huge windows in the observation cars plant you right amid the scenery and you can disembark at some of the most dramatic sections for a quick leg-stretch.

Below the stacked-up houses of Darjeeling, the train chuffed to a halt at the Batasia Loop, where the line completes a 360-degree spiral to gain elevation. There was time enough to read the plaque dedicated to soldiers killed in the 1814–16 Anglo-Nepalese War and take some photos of hazy Himalayan views. I could just about make out 28,209ft (8598m) Khangchendzonga, the world's third-highest peak, among banks of clouds that looked like mountains themselves.

Then, with a flurry of activity from the drivers and firemen who tended to the engine, we were off again. By the time we reached Ghum, the highest point on the line at 7218ft (2200m), swirling grey mist had closed in around the tracks (indeed, 'Gloom' might have been a better name). But before we crept back to Darjeeling, the town's small museum provided shelter from the damp and a cornucopia of Darjeeling Himalayan Railway facts.

Two rides on the Darjeeling Himalayan Railway was enough, though. After a busy few days touring Darjeeling's temples and monasteries – and the ice-axe-stuffed Himalayan Mountaineering Institute, where Tenzing Norgay was director from 1954 to 1976 – I exited Darjeeling by road, zooming down to the valley floor in just two and a half hours. **JB**

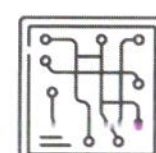

Start/Finish // New Jalpaiguri/Darjeeling
Distance // 55 miles (88km)
Duration // 7hr-8hr
Ticket types // Chair Car (small, padded seats, divided by a narrow aisle); First Class (comfy, airline-style seats).
How to book // Book tickets for the trip from NJP to Darjeeling online from Indian Railways (irctc.co.in). Joyride tickets can be booked at Darjeeling Station (ideally a day or two ahead).
When to go // October to November and February to March, for dry skies, moderate temperatures and clear views of Khangchendzonga.
Things to know // Himalayan views are best in the morning – take in the sunrise from Observatory Hill and you'll have plenty of time to make the 9.25am joyride.
More info // Darjeeling Himalayan Railway (dhr.in.net); West Bengal Tourism (wbtourism.gov.in)

Opposite: Trundling up to the summit of Snaefell in an old school electric railcar.

MORE LIKE THIS NARROW-GAUGE MOUNTAIN RAILWAYS

MARIAZELLERBAHN, AUSTRIA

While it stands well east of the hills where Julie Andrews frolicked in *The Sound of Music*, a similarly bucolic vibe pervades in the Alpine town of Mariazell, reached by one of Europe's most delightful narrow-gauge lines. The Mariazellerbahn (Mariazell Railway) was constructed in 1898 to whisk pilgrims uphill from the Lower Austrian capital of St Pölten to the revered Mariazell Basilica. Special, four-axled steam locomotives were constructed to haul the passenger cars, one of which is still in service today, pulling special tourist trains on fixed dates from May to December. During summer and at Easter, weekend services use a century-old electric engine; at other times, modern electric trains take over duties. Whichever train you take, expect uplifting – perhaps even song-inspiring – views over forest- or snow-covered summits and Alpine villages.

Start // St Pölten
Finish // Mariazell
Distance // 57 miles (91km)
Duration // 2hr 30min

SNAEFELL MOUNTAIN RAILWAY, ISLE OF MAN

The Isle of Man is a bit of an oddity: place names are Gaelic and Nordic, rats are called 'longtails', cats have no tails, and the island maintains its own system of government, allied to but independent from the United Kingdom. It's also the setting for the endearingly teensy Snaefell Mountain Railway, rumbling uphill from Laxey to the 2036ft (621m) summit of Snaefell, the highest point on the island. Running on narrow 3ft 6in (1m) tracks, the boxy, wood-lined railcars have been powered by electricity since 1895. In fact, there's just a single carriage per service, with no attached engine; railcars are propelled uphill by vintage electric motors, providing a surprisingly quiet ride that complements the soul-lifting vistas of mountains, sea and sky.

Start // Laxey
Finish // Snaefell Summit
Distance // 5.5 miles (8.9km)
Duration // 30min

KUKUSHKA, GEORGIA

There's something a little Wes Andersen about the Borjomi–Bakuriani Railway – aka the Kukushka (the Cuckoo). Constructed in 1897, when Georgia was a vassal state of Tsarist Russia, this mountain climbing narrow-gauge railway included some prestigious names on its engineering team. Gustave Eiffel designed the bridge crossing the Tsemistskhali River, and the steam engines that operated the original service were produced by Henry Kirke Porter, later US congressman for Pittsburgh. Today, the dainty red-and-cream carriages of the Kukushka are hauled by a nostalgic, electric 'crocodile' engine (named for its elongated snout) produced by the Škoda works in Czechoslovakia in the 1960s. The two-hour ride to the ski resort of Bakuriani is an evocative piece of time travel, particularly in winter, when snow cloaks the forested mountainsides that envelop the line for most of its route.

Start // Borjomi
Finish // Bakuriani
Distance // 23 miles (37km)
Duration // 2hr 30min

SNAEFELL MOUNTAIN RAILWAY

LIVING HISTORY ON THAILAND'S DEATH RAILWAY

The Death Railway is Thailand's most famous trainline, winding through scenic jungle-clad hills and by rushing rivers while revealing its tragic WWII history.

It would have been hard to imagine a more cheery scene as our train rattled along the Wang Pho Viaduct.

Passengers gasped as we rolled over the trestles, with sheer cliffs teetering to one side and the murky current of the Khwae Noi River eddying beneath us. Picnics were eaten, photos taken. People leaned out the windows, closed their eyes and felt the humid jungle air against their skin. It was a line with a holiday mood – such that you might be forgiven for forgetting the brutal circumstances under which the viaduct, indeed this entire railway, came into being. This is the dissonance passengers on the Death Railway must come to terms with – a lively ride through beautiful landscapes, paid for by the lives of countless civilians and prisoners of war.

My journey had begun some hours earlier, at Bangkok's Thonburi Station – a small terminus, with the feel of a country station accidentally misplaced in the centre of an Asian megacity.

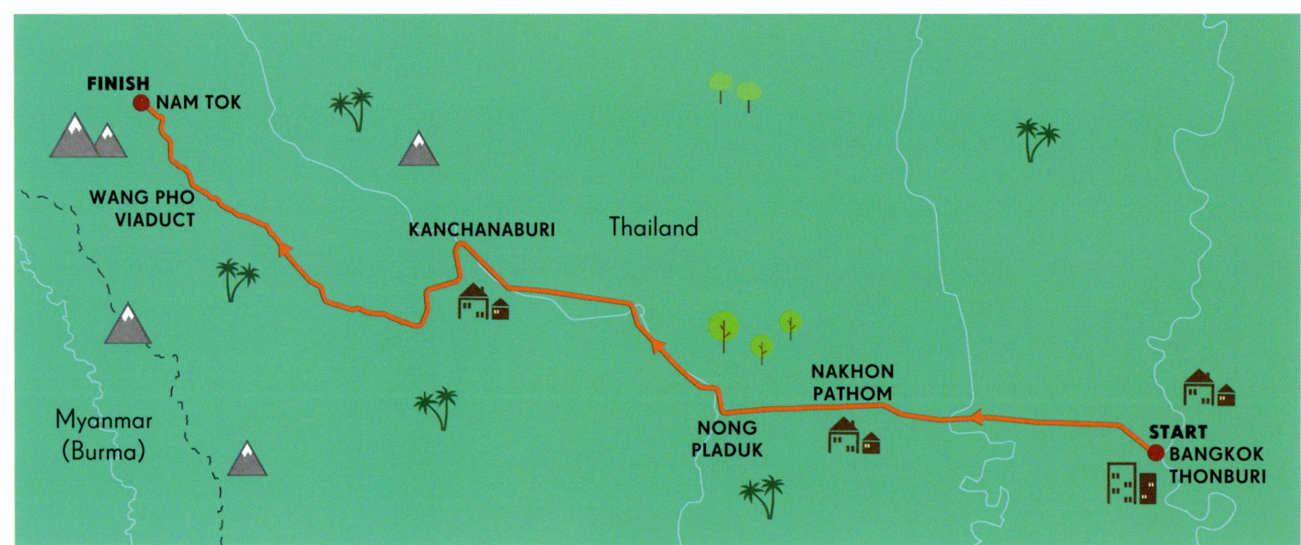

Similarly, my Kanchanaburi-bound train was a charmingly rustic affair – the diesel-hauled carriages soon slipping out of the Bangkok sprawl and onward into the hinterland. Only at the junction of Nong Pladuk did we technically cross onto the line once known as the Burma Railway but now more commonly referred to as the Death Railway.

The story of the line is a well-known one: it has featured in Hollywood films such as *The Bridge on the River Kwai*, and loomed large in memoirs like Eric Lomax's *The Railway Man* and novels like Richard Flanagan's outstanding *The Narrow Road to the Deep North*. It had its genesis in WWII, when Thailand's Japanese occupiers sought to build a railway to supply their frontlines against the British Empire in Burma, now Myanmar. The border country between Thailand and Burma was no easy territory for a railway engineer, consisting of steeply contoured jungle carved up by fast-flowing rivers. The Japanese settled on forced labour as a way to hack a path through the trees – bringing in civilians from across Asia, and captured Allied servicemen (largely British, Dutch and Australian soldiers).

Conditions for railway workers were brutal – forced to chip away at the rocks while being lashed with bamboo, succumbing to starvation and tropical disease. Around 100,000 perished. For many visitors, a ride on the Death Railway is akin to a trip to Flanders or the D-Day Landing Beaches – a chance to commemorate and to learn more about this chapter of 20th-century history. Most foreign tourists, however, only ride the dramatic westernmost part of the railway; far fewer ride these first miles

"A ride on the Death Railway is akin to a trip to Flanders or the D-Day Landing Beaches – a chance to commemorate…"

where it remains a decidedly local operation. My train trundled past rice paddies and stilt houses, slowing deferentially beside temples, stopping intermittently at tidy stations adorned with Thai flags. Fellow travellers included monks and school children. For such a troubled line, it was strangely peaceful.

That changed by the time we arrived in Kanchanaburi town – a busy staging post for tourists hoping to get to the national parks, monasteries and floating hotels in the eponymous province beyond. Eight decades ago, Kanchanaburi was the strategic hub for Japanese forces marshalling construction of the Burma Railway – a past writ large in a number of landmarks. I got off my train to visit the Thailand-Burma Railway Centre which tells the story of the POWs' onward journey from Kanchanaburi to remote work camps, and is full of dioramas and video testimonies. The town's greatest attraction, however, is the iron span over the Kwae Noi River, billed as the real-life 'Bridge on the River Kwai' from David Lean's 1957 film. The truth is more complicated. The actual bridge was indeed a strategic target for Allied bombers looking to disrupt Japanese supplies in the last years of the war, but Lean's film took its cue from a work of fiction. Those looking for the bridge famously detonated by Alec Guinness in the final scenes of the movie can

BEYOND KANCHANABURI

The Death Railway serves as a way to reach the attractions of Kanchanaburi province. From Kanchanaburi town, it's an hour's bus ride north to the cascades of Erawan National Park. Beyond is Sangklaburi and its extraordinary Mon Bridge – a wooden footbridge that is among the longest of its kind in the world. Here the old railway route is submerged under a modern reservoir.

From left: The Wang Pho viaduct beside the Kwae Noi; a locomotive on the viaduct; the bridge at Kanchanaburi. Previous page: Buddhist monks on the line just north of Kanchanaburi.

see the foundations by making a detour to Kitulgala – over two thousand miles away in Sri Lanka.

My train crept over the fabled span, dispersing the pedestrians that wander back and forth when the thrice daily trains aren't running. After this point, the railway was at its most radiant. We swerved among bamboo groves, stands of laurel and mighty fig trees, past smallholdings full of mango and papaya, with the scent of frangipani slipping through open windows. Soon the line was flush to the current of the Kwae Noi, soaring over the Wang Pho Viaduct with limestone caves lurking below. Until 1947 the line ran over the border into Myanmar – today services hit the brakes in the little village of Nam Tok, where you'll find a rusting steam engine, a few coffee and snack stands and a little waterfall. Though this is more or less the end of the modern route, you can still find ghostly remains of the Death Railway in the forests nearby – old cuttings, tumbledown embankments. One of them, Hellfire Pass, is open to tourists, a deep gash in the Tenasserim Hills which railway workers worked 18-hour shifts to excavate.

I boarded a return train back to Kanchanaburi, joining the great river on its downstream procession. As we moved along I reflected on this railway's legacy, a complex one, forged through pain and suffering. Unlike a memorial or a museum, the Death Railway is a living relic of the last world war – still in motion 80 years on – and riding it today means that its tragic story stays alive. **OS**

Start/Finish // Bangkok Thonburi Station/Nam Tok
Distance // 130 miles (210km)
Duration // 4hr 20min
Ticket types // Trains are split between Second and Third Class carriages – both are comfortable, but you get air-con in Second. There's also a dedicated tourist service running on weekends – it makes one more stop past Nam Tok at the little waterfalls at Sai Yok.
How to book // Online on the Thailand State Railway website for travel at peak times like public holidays and weekends (dticket.railway.co.th).
Things to know // The luxurious Eastern and Oriental Express train used to travel the Death Railway as part of its Bangkok to Singapore itinerary – sadly this was not the case at the time of writing. Check the Belmond website to see if it returns (belmond.com).

Opposite top: Rice terraces in the hills near Chiang Mai. Opposite below: A service on the wilfully eccentric Mae Klong railway.

MORE LIKE THIS
BEYOND BANGKOK BY RAIL

BANGKOK TO CHIANG MAI SLEEPER

The Bangkok-Chiang Mai rail artery is a busy one, linking Thailand's capital with its second city. Many choose to take the overnight sleeper service – a useful train that in its northern stages is also a quietly scenic one. You'll likely be settling into your bunk as the train rolls out of Bangkok and into the lowland plains where for much of the journey the route shadows the Chao Phraya River and its tributaries. The following morning is when the view shifts up a gear – expect misty dawns as services climb the green hills on approach to Chiang Mai itself. Sleepers in Thailand broadly divide between private First Class compartments and more open Second Class bunks, with curtains for privacy. Bear in mind, trains for Chiang Mai now depart the new Bangkok Krung Thep Aphiwat Central Terminal Station (aka KTW).
Start // Bangkok
Finish // Chiang Mai
Distance // 462 miles (744km)
Duration // 12hr 25min

BANGKOK TO NONG KHAI SLEEPER

Nong Khai represents another frontier of the Thai railway network, sat at the furthest end of the Northeastern Line on the border with Laos. To get there, board a train at Bangkok KTW which will head north as far as the evocative ruins of Ayutthaya before branching eastward and coming close to the famous Khao Yai National Park. You then reach Thailand's third city, officially known as Nakhon Ratchasima, but familiar to most as Khorat. Here again the line turns north on the final leg to Nong Khai, where the Mekong River marks the international boundary. This need not be the end of the trip however – while some sleeper services terminate at Nong Khai, others continue across the friendship bridge into Laos, bound for the capital, Vientiane.
Start // Bangkok
Finish // Nong Khai
Distance // 388 miles (624km)
Duration // 10hr 30min

MAE KLONG RAILWAY

Thailand has many options for long-distance rail travel – the Mae Klong Railway is emphatically not one of them. This 40-mile-long (64km) line began as a private operation, transporting fresh seafood from the ports of Samut Sakhon and Samut Songkhram to Bangkok's markets (with a ferry halfway). Long since absorbed into the state railways, it now transports human beings, many of whom start their journey at Bangkok's tiny Wongwian Yai Station, which has just a single platform and a single set of rails. The route slices through the city, rattling over canals and past back yards, saving the best for last as it approaches Mae Klong Seafood Market, where stalls placed on the tracks are quickly put away and awnings are retracted to allow the train to barge past.
Start // Bangkok
Finish // Mae Klong
Distance // 40 miles (64km)
Duration // 2hr, with a ferry midway

SRT
1234

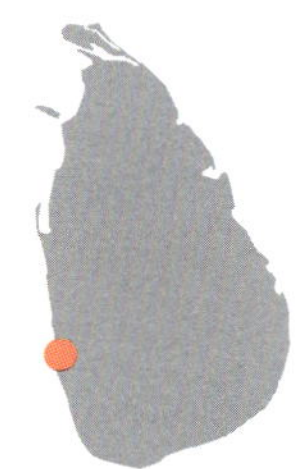

TEA OFF ON SRI LANKA'S MAIN LINE

Adventure brews at Colombo Fort Station, where trains depart for tea plantations and the lush green heart of Sri Lanka.

My day in Colombo began with a cup of tea. So too, as a matter of fact, did the story of the railway I had come here to ride.

Sri Lanka's Main Line has its origins in the days of British colonial rule over the island. Across the empire, railways were a means of exploiting and pillaging natural resources such as iron ore and coal. Here, in Ceylon (as Sri Lanka was then known), it was something more delicate – tea and coffee, whisked to waiting ships and then to breakfast tables across the world. But there was a challenge for engineers – coffee and tea mostly grew at the lofty elevations of the island's Central Highlands. Any railway exporting these crops would have to wind its way skywards from the heat of the ports into the cool mountains of the interior.

Brewing for over a century, Sri Lanka's Main Line still makes for a spectacular railway ride, winding from sea level to almost 6562ft (2000m), puttering past rice paddies, beneath jungle canopies and through endless tea plantations. It

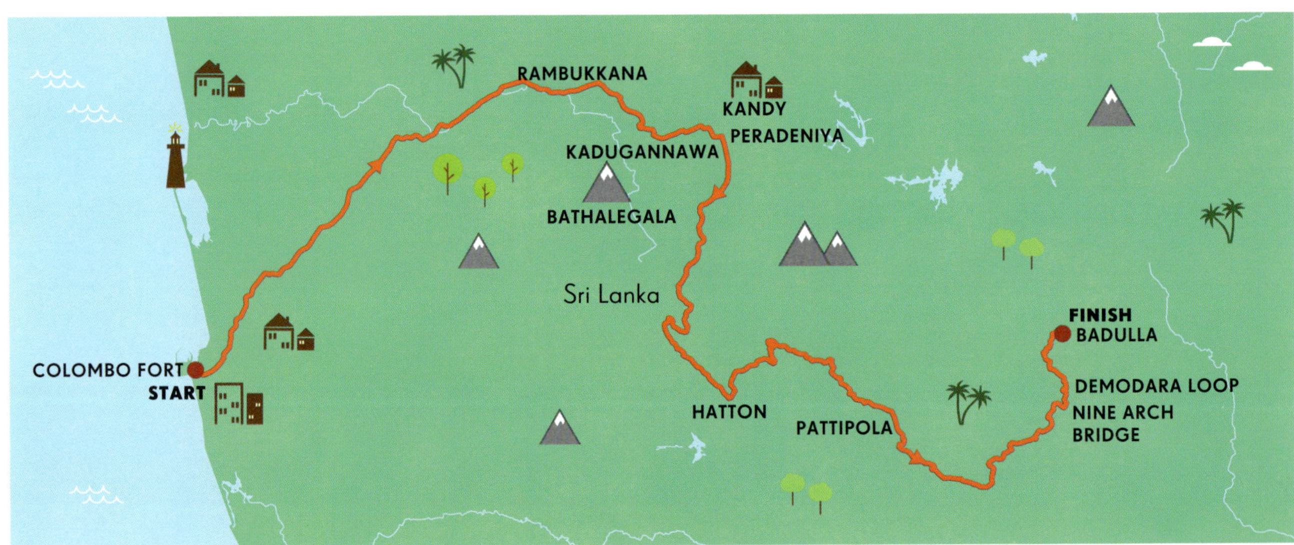

is indeed a journey analogous to a cup of tea – bracing, refreshing – not something to be downed in one like an espresso, but to be sipped and savoured so you can appreciate all its richness and depth.

I was mindful of this as I navigated the bustle of Colombo Fort Station – an instantly likable terminus built by the British in 1917 and said to be partly modelled on Manchester Piccadilly Station. It would be a long day on board, so I had loaded up on supplies from food stalls – samosas and vegetable rotis – before heading to the platform. At the rear of my Badulla-bound service was a scarlet carriage enticingly marked 'observation car' – firmly pitched at tourists, with panoramic windows and air-con. But – all passengers come to realise – free air-con eventually comes as standard in every class, as the thick humid air around Colombo turns to cool mountain breezes with every yard of ascent.

First our train clattered northeast along the coastal plain, tracing the route of the island's original railway, completed in 1865. Settlements thinned out as we passed palm groves, rice paddies and tidy country stations with potted plants arranged on the platforms. Buddhas watched from lineside temples. Girder bridges bellowed as we rolled over sluggish rivers. Beyond the town of Rambukkana the inclines began in earnest: our red train started climbing up a single track to the heavens. It sliced through cuttings, clung to the precipices of a steep escarpment. Soon there was a hazy panorama out to the Indian Ocean and to the sentinel peak of Bathalegala – known in English as Bible Rock, because it looks rather like the good book propped on a lectern. Sri Lanka abounds in holy places, but for trainspotters there is nowhere more sacred than the National Railway Museum at our next stop, Kadugannawa. Engines from decades past watched on as their modern successor chugged past, continuing the long-standing service of Highland stations.

Not all Main Line trains go to Badulla. At Peradeniya's curious triangular station we reached a junction: services bound for Kandy fork north here, with many passengers making a pilgrimage to the Temple of the Sacred Tooth (believed to house one of the Buddha's teeth). My train however made its own pilgrimage south into tea country proper – with every contour, from the trackside to the horizon, swathed in quivering leaves. Here and there were tea-pickers with tarpaulin bags tied to their backs – picking is back-breakingly hard work, often done for poor pay. By now the mercury had dropped: mist coiled in the valleys below, and drizzle snuck through open windows to mop the brows of all aboard. We passed waterfalls, whose ribbons of whitewater punctuated those endless shades of green. After hours stewing in our own sweat, everyone was instantly refreshed.

More stops followed. Some got off at Hatton, the station serving the sacred, cone-shaped mountain of Adam's Peak. Others disembarked at Nanuoya to travel on to Nuwara Eliya, where colonists built a Tudor-style hill station to cure their homesickness in a climate not wholly dissimilar to Britain.

The highest point of the line came at Pattipola, perched at a breathtaking 6224ft (1897m). By then the train had travelled some 141 miles (227km) from Colombo – and over a mile vertically into the clouds. From here we began a slow and incremental descent. Dusk came, and bonfire smoke perfumed the air. The lights of Highland villages twinkled out in the gloaming. The train rolled on. The engineers of the Main Line saved some of their best work for last in the form of Nine Arches Bridge – a stone span where the railway takes flight over a jungle ravine. It serves as an aperitif for the Demodara loops, where the line twists around itself, the engineer supposedly inspired by the tying action of a turban. The train hauls into Badulla over 10 hours after leaving Colombo – a long day of rail travel by any measure, but it almost comes too soon.

It should be noted that a favourite – but ill-advised and dangerous – pastime on this last section of the Main Line is for passengers to hang out of open doors, clinging to the handrails. It's a trend that has grown in an age of Instagram – but it has a long history. Feeling the Highland air against your skin, and inhaling the rich, earthy after-rain scent of the tea plantations, is nothing if not intoxicating. **OS**

NINE ARCHES BRIDGE

Completed in 1919, Nine Arches Bridge – sometimes known as 'The Bridge in the Sky' – is the most famous railway landmark in Sri Lanka, measuring some 299ft (91m) in length. It owes its current form to WWI when the British had planned to construct it using steel, but, with metals needed for the war effort, local engineers built the bridge using rocks and cement instead.

Opposite top: A service crosses Nine Arches Bridge. Opposite below: The Jamiul Alfar Mosque in Colombo. Previous page: Winding through the tea plantations of the Highlands.

Start/Finish // Fort Station, Colombo/Badulla
Distance // 181 miles (291km)
Duration // 10hr
Ticket types // Daytime trains present four options: a First Class observation coach (seats face backwards, and a large rear window looks to the retreating track); ordinary First Class seats (with air-con); unreserved Second and Third Class (no air-con). Note that more comfortable blue Chinese-built trains have replaced the classic red Sri Lankan ones on most departures.
How to book // Second and Third Class tickets can only be purchased on the day; First Class can be pre booked at seatreservation.railway.gov.lk
Things to know // Sleepers travel this Main Line route – though you obviously won't get to appreciate the scenery at night.

Clockwise from top: Galle Lighthouse is Sri Lanka's oldest; monks at Anuradhapura; boats on the beach by the Bay of Bengal at Trincomalee.

MORE LIKE THIS
THREE MORE RAILWAY JOURNEYS FROM COLOMBO

THE COASTAL LINE

The second oldest line in Sri Lanka also ranks number two in terms of scenery, with trains departing Colombo bound for the historic port of Galle in the southwest. The starting point is Maradana Station, a venerable whitewashed building crowned by a clock tower. In almost no time trains barge out of the city centre to flirt with the Indian Ocean – close enough to be flecked by spray. Coastal views are the abiding memory of the line as it plunges south, passing fishing fleets, palm-shaded beaches and rolling waves with a few interludes inland too. For some, it's a commuter line connecting Colombo to its suburbs, but many tourists are headed for Galle's modernist station and the Dutch colonial architecture that lies beyond. It's a deeply popular trip, though it has a tragic recent history – you'll find memorials to the 2004 tsunami up and down this shore.
Start // Maradana Station, Colombo
Finish // Galle
Distance // 72 miles (116km)
Duration // 2hr 10min

COLOMBO TO TRINCOMALEE

The ride from Colombo to Trincomalee is Sri Lanka's great coast-to-coast odyssey, connecting the Laccadive Sea to the country's eastern shore. It's less celebrated than the Coastal and Main Line journeys, with few ascents or seaside forays to speak of, but it does let you take in rustic island scenery, while also unlocking the attractions of the interior. Among the stops is little Habarana, where many passengers change for a tuk tuk or local bus to see elephant herds in nearby national parks. Some venture a little further on to famous Sigiriya, a monolithic rock topped with an ancient fortress. With the end of the line comes the port of Trincomalee – gateway to some of the country's best beaches. Before you seek them out, take a stroll from the station to the town's rocky peninsula, graced by a beautiful Hindu temple.
Start // Fort Station, Colombo
Finish // Trincomalee
Distance // 183 miles (295km)
Duration // 7hr 35min

COLOMBO-JAFFNA

Off limits for many years due to conflict in the north, it's now very easy to make a rail trip from Colombo to Jaffna, where you're somewhat off the tourism circuit (and almost within touching distance of India). Trains follow the same route as those bound for Trincomalee as far as Maho Junction, before heading north and passing by Anuradhapura – one of the country's great archaeological complexes, with dagobas (stupas), tumbledown temples and a sacred tree. At Vavuniya you cross an unofficial border between the island's majority Sinhalese and Tamil populations. After trundling over the Elephant Pass causeway you arrive in Jaffna itself, where you can immerse yourself in Tamil culture, visit magnificent temples and strike out to the archipelago of islands beyond.
Start // Fort Station, Colombo
Finish // Jaffna
Distance // 247 miles (398 km)
Duration // 6hr 54min

0973

TŌHOKU SHINKANSEN: FAST RAILS TO THE DEEP NORTH

Ride this classic high-speed line into Japan's deep north, to where the island of Hokkaido beckons just over the Tsugaru Strait.

Journeys into the north have a certain resonance in Japan. In his great poem, *The Narrow Road to the Deep North*, the 17th-century poet Matsuo Bashō wrote he had 'been tempted for a long time by the cloud-moving wind, and filled with a strong desire to wander'. Feeling restless, he found himself pacing the pathways of Tōhoku – the more remote northern end of Honshu, Japan's main island – covering some 1500 miles (2414km) on foot, meditating on the nature of travel along the way.

Today it's easier to travel to this region thanks to the Tōhoku Shinkansen – trains take minutes to cross the distances that Bashō laboured over for months. This ultra-fast artery has, for forty decades, served as a means of escape into a land of crater lakes, historic towns and rustic onsen (hot springs) concealed in snowy mountain forests. Its story continues in the 21st century with the ongoing construction of the Hokkaido Shinkansen – trains departing the Tōhoku Shinkansen line disappear beneath the Tsugaru Strait bound for the island of Hokkaido beyond. The Hokkaido Shinkansen is scheduled to arrive at the island capital, Sapporo, in 2030. But there's no reason to wait until the extension is complete.

It was a sleek E5-series Shinkansen that swept onto my platform at Tokyo's Marunouchi Station. I watched the choreographed ballet of people boarding the train: passengers lined up at little gates, shuffling on board to a symphony of jingles, finding their seats in the monastic silence of the carriages. Soon we were gliding out of Tokyo, the track passing the neon signage of video game district Akihabara and almost brushing beside the trees in Ueno Park. Then we were powering north, grey cityscapes slowly shifting to green landscapes as the train reached speeds of 200mph (322km/h).

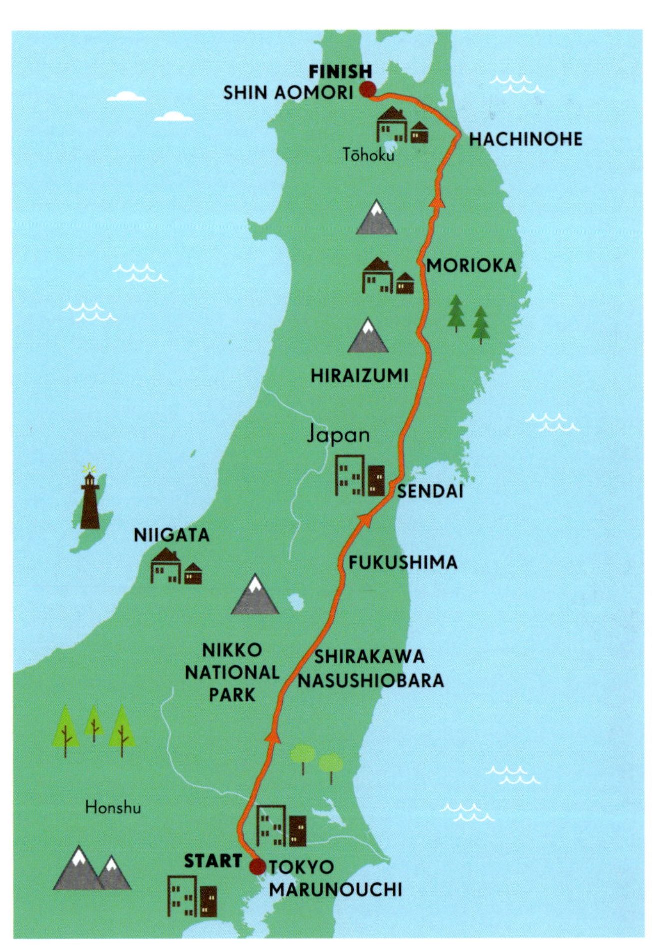

MUFG
三菱東京UFJ銀行

The Shinkansen makes for an exhilarating kind of travel, but also a disorientating one as the views out of the window are frustratingly fleeting. The foreground is a mad blur – dizzying velocity makes it impossible to pick things out. Buildings are a blip, rivers a silver flash. Instead it's the horizon on which your gaze must fix itself – more distant features like the mountains and the sea, which linger a little longer and give a sense of the country through which you're passing.

Among these were the foothills of the Nikko National Park, rising out of the left-hand window as we approached the station at Nasushiobara, famed for its onsen and suspended bridges. There was a blink-and-you'll-miss-it glimpse of the Edo-era Komine Castle as we slowed at Shirakawa. Here, we were closely shadowing Bashō's route to the deep north. He once wrote of one local scene: 'The chestnut by the eaves / In magnificent bloom / Passes unnoticed / By men of this world'. Even today, this part of the country remains one of Japan's more unexplored corners, and I felt far from Tokyo as we sped through Fukushima's quiet green interior.

Set around a crescent bay, Sendai is a big metropolis known as the city of trees on account of its leafy thoroughfares. I got only a brief impression of these as we paused momentarily in its vast station before my train continued, impatient to clock up the miles.

Shinkansen lines are generally arrow-straight – they soar over bridges and pass through interminable tunnels, making no concessions to the topography through which they travel. For much of the journey we were on elevated track beds, the line almost placed on a pedestal, rising regally over the landscape. The names of the trains that travel this line are grandly poetic too: the fastest is the Hayabusa (meaning peregrine falcon), followed by the Hayate (powerful wind) and the Yamabiko (mountain echo). These trains are freighted with meaning. In the 1960s the Shinkansen was the proud symbol of a country that had risen from the ashes of the war. They continue to serve as

WHAT'S IN A NAME?

Shinkansen lines are seen as a modern innovation – and still evolving with the development of the revolutionary Chūō Shinkansen, which levitates on magnets – but few realise they have a long history. While the Tōkaidō Shinkansen was first unveiled in the 1960s, the first plans for high-speed rail were actually drafted in the 1930s under the name *dangan ressha* – which translates as 'bullet train'. The name stuck among English language users, and almost a century on, Shinkansen are still widely called 'bullet trains.'

Clockwise from top: Tokyo's Shibuya Crossing; the Yamadera valley in winter; eating a bento box on board; the classic E5 trains which operate along the line. Previous page: passing cherry blossoms in the capital.

21st-century totems, and being Japan's longest Shinkansen line, the Tōhoku route is one of the most revered.

The deep past is not forgotten in this modern wonder though. We speed by Hiraizumi – a city that thrived in the 11th and the 12th centuries, conceived as a living paradise and rivalling Kyoto in its grandeur. Today little of it remains. Bashō stopped here, meditated on its 'Summer grass, all that remains of warrior dreams', and then turned westward to the Sea of Japan, whose coastline he traced southward out of the Tōhoku region. Our line briefly rendezvoused with the Pacific in the port of Hachinohe – part of a coastline that suffered in the 2011 tsunami – before closing on its final terminus at Shin Aomori. This is a gateway to some of Honshu's most sublime scenery – the great volcanic lake of Towada is close by, as are the wind-lashed cliffs of the Shimokita Peninsula. It has an eerie, end-of-the-world feel. For some it is also a portal to the afterlife: the sacred site of Mt Osore is where people come to commune with the dead.

Since 2016, however, this furthest nook of Honshu has been a portal to another realm, with the opening of the Seikan Tunnel for Shinkansen trains. Rail users now travel direct from Tokyo to Hokkaido at thundering speeds. On this island, visitors can see an entirely different side to Japan: wild, sparsely inhabited, home to the indigenous Ainu people – one of Japan's few minorities. It was tantalisingly close. Instead I disembarked my E5 Shinkansen at Shin Aomori Station to wander the winter forests of Tōhoku at a more sedate speed. As Bashō wrote: 'Every day is a journey, and the journey itself is my home'. **OS**

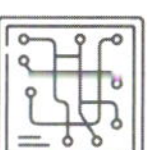

Start/Finish // Marunouchi Station, Tokyo/Shin Aomori
Distance // 419 miles (674 km)
Duration // 3hr 20min
Ticket types // Most Shinkansen broadly divide between Ordinary Class and Green Class – essentially First Class. On certain trains working the Tōhoku Shinkansen you'll come across Gran Class, an even swankier tier – airline-style seats have an at-seat drinks and snack service.
How to book // Buy Tōhoku Shinkansen tickets from an agency – baolau.com is among the most intuitive to use.
Things to know // Traditionally, visitors to Japan purchased the excellent-value Japan Rail Pass, giving seven days or more of unlimited train travel across the network, with only a few trains excluded. Recently, the pass has become more expensive but still represents a worthwhile investment if travelling on the Tōhoku Shinkansen, and especially if venturing beyond Sendai.

Opposite top: The Yamagata Shinkansen technically counts as a Mini-Shinkansen route. Opposite below: An attendant on board a Hokkaido Shinkansen service.

MORE LIKE THIS
EXTENSIONS TO THE TŌHOKU SHINKANSEN

HOKKAIDO SHINKANSEN

When it's completed around 2030, some 225 miles (362km) of track will make up the Hokkaido Shinkansen, running from Shin Aomori to Sapporo. For now, however, it's about half that length, and the tracks ends at Shin-Hakodate-Hokuto Station on Hokkaido's Oshima Peninsula. It's a fascinating ride, albeit a rather gloomy one. Soon after rolling out of Aomori you enter the Seikan Tunnel, its entrance guarded by a little shrine. The line continues underground as far as Cape Tappi, and then plunges under the Tsugaru Strait, dividing Honshu from its northern neighbour, via the world's longest underwater tunnel – it comes as a small surprise when you reemerge into bright sunlight on Hokkaido. There are yet more tunnels before you finally draw into Shin-Hakodate-Hokuto Station, from where you'll need to catch a connecting train to get to the port of Hakodate proper, famed for its seafront vistas.

Start // Shin Aomori
Finish // Shin-Hakodate-Hokuto Station
Distance // 103 miles (167km)
Duration // 1hr

AKITA MINI-SHINKANSEN

When is a Shinkansen not a Shinkansen? When it's a Mini-Shinkansen of course. An example being the Akita route, where Tōhoku Shinkansen trains head off the main artery to travel a branch line at more sedate speeds of 80mph (129km/h), with more twists and turns in the track and chances to appreciate the scenery too. The Akita Mini-Shinkansen forks off at Morioka, coming close to the shores of Lake Towada – the caldera of an active volcano – with charming onsen along the shores. The loveliest stop on the ride is Kakunodate with a station designed like a samurai's residence in tribute to the old houses in the cherry tree-lined streets beyond. The terminus is the workaday city of Akita, set beside the Sea of Japan, well off the beaten tourism path.

Start // Morioka
Finish // Akita
Distance // 79 miles (127km)
Duration // 1hr 30min

YAMAGATA SHINKANSEN

The second of the Tōhoku Shinkansen's Mini-Shinkansen branch lines, the Yamagata Shinkansen departs from Fukushima to veer westwards, roughly parallel but some way south of its sibling the Akita route. The first big stop is Yonezawa, famed for the quality of its wagyu beef and its 17th-century castle. Next comes the city that gives the line its name, Yamagata, an industrial hub known for its potteries. It's set in the shadow of the mountainside temples of Yamadera – another favoured haunt of Matsuo Bashō. The line terminates at little Shinjō – here you're not far from Dewa Sanzan's trinity of sacred peaks, said to represent birth, death and rebirth.

Start // Fukushima
Finish // Shinjō
Distance // 91 miles (146km)
Duration // 2hr 5min

LIVE THE HIGH LIFE ON THE TOY TRAIN TO SHIMLA

Spiral up the forested slopes of the Himalayan foothills to the cool climes of a secret summer getaway, on a rickety and rolling piece of history on wheels.

A stranger's elbow pressing lightly into my ribs, I leaned out of the open window as the Himalayan Queen sprang to life. A latecomer was on the platform, pleading to get on to no avail. He jumped back as the train let out a deep and determined hoot and began to snake out of Kalka Station, whistles and applause breaking out on board. It was the weekend of a spring harvest festival and the carriages were fully booked by multi-generational Indian families and a group of students, backpacks on laps, their suitcases rolling around the aisles. As we picked up pace, a merry thud sounded from the wheels and I settled in for the five-hour ride, my neighbour's elbow still in my side. Enjoying the clamour and camaraderie, I glanced round with amusement at the ear muffs and balaclavas – even in April the idea of travelling to cooler climes was enough to send Indians into winter mode.

The country is home to a handful of mountain railways, known lovingly as 'toy trains', and one that had piqued my interest in particular was the Kalka-Shimla, a regular passenger service from the town of Kalka in the foothills of the Shivalik mountain range to the city of Shimla. I'd heard that with its mock-Tudor buildings Shimla looked as English as Stratford-upon-Avon, though scattered along the ridges of the southwestern Himalaya, and I was curious to witness it for myself. British colonists had laid the foundations for the railway in 1898, and five years later the narrow-gauge steam railway was inaugurated by Lord Curzon. The intention was to ease the journey for the British from the centre of rule in Delhi to Shimla, where they fled in summer to escape the heat.

Still hooting to alert trackside idlers – of whom there were

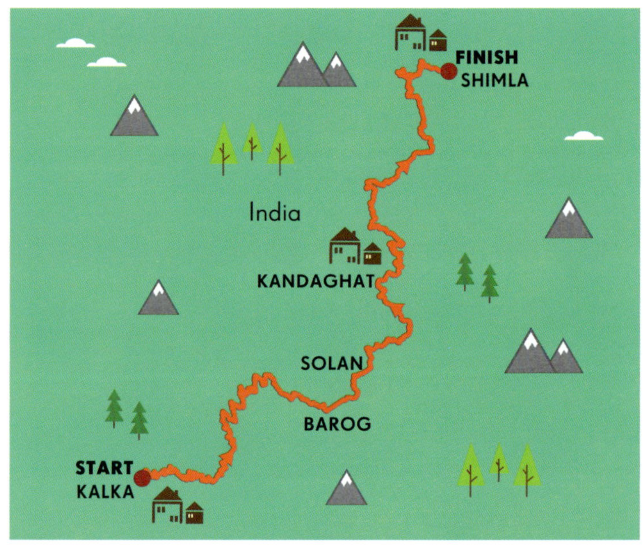

many – the train clacked along through oaks, maples and willows trailing their fingers along the ground. From time to time, I'd spot single sandals lying beside the tracks as we wobbled through cuttings as high as the carriage, palms fronds flicking at my face. Wondering how they got there, I pulled my head back in as we entered a tunnel, emerging to where the cliffside fell away, a stomach-turning drop beneath us. We soon hissed to a halt and passengers jumped down onto the tracks, with little care for what might be coming in the other direction. Some slid down the undergrowth to take pictures in the trees, while others mooched around the shack selling tea and bread pakora – triangles of deep-fried bread battered in chickpea flour. With few signs as to when we'd set off again, I stepped around the netted rock face, the stains of monsoon waterfalls still damp to the touch.

The horn rang out and I reboarded to find my companion had moved to stand in the open doorway, his bouffant hair now billowing in the wind as we twisted above stepped hillsides, the shriek of wild birds echoing around the valleys. By now passengers had settled into routines, the rail fans hanging from doorways, students playing cards across the seats and others sitting quietly by the windows, content in their own company. After a couple of hours we were approaching the tunnel at Barog, a highlight of the journey and one with a legend attached. Typical for Indian train travel, one of the students turned sideways, pulled his foot into his lap, and began to tell me all about it. Numbered 33, the longest tunnel on the railway was named after Colonel Barog, an engineer whose first name no one knew. Tasked with constructing the 3753ft (1144m) tunnel, the colonel ordered his men to dig from each end – only to discover that they didn't meet in the middle. In fury, the British government allegedly fined Barog one rupee, but, tormented by the humiliation, the engineer shot himself. He was buried near the tunnel and since his death there had been a number of sightings of his spirit chatting to local villagers. My companion pointed as we approached the station, pleased by my appalled reaction. It took more than two minutes to pass through the darkness, a dank smell accompanying the roar as we rattled on.

"I'd heard that with its mock-Tudor buildings Shimla looked as English as Stratford-upon-Avon, though scattered along the ridges of the southwestern Himalaya..."

TREAT YOURSELF TO AN UPGRADE

For passengers who want to travel in style, there is an alternative service: the Shivalik Deluxe Express runs the same route as the Himalayan Queen, and while more expensive, this train is fitted with wall-to-wall carpeted carriages and upholstered seats. There's more space for luggage and the ticket includes hot drinks and vegetable cutlet sandwiches.

From left: Colonial architecture at Shimla's Scandal Point; the train climbing through the hills. Previous page: Houses cling to the steep slopes around Shimla.

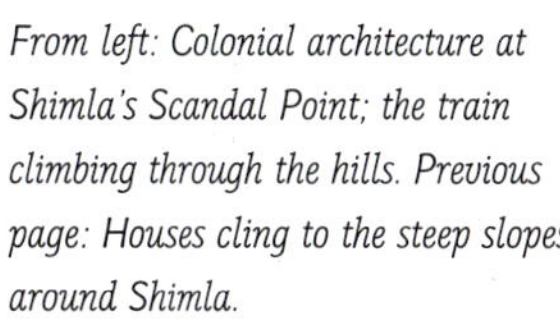

On the other side, the altitude was increasing with each turn, the tip of my nose now cold, the scent of pine strong and clean. Bright stations sailed by, pink-roofed with signature yellow signs, and during the last hour of travel passengers began jumping off to go home. I'd assumed that everyone on board was a tourist but many were disembarking to visit family while newcomers hopped onto the side for a ride uphill that would save them a tedious walk. Glancing back, I saw a labourer clinging to the carriage and it now dawned on me how the single sandals had come to litter the tracks. Corkscrewing up the final stretch, dangerous drops on either side, the train pulled in and out of short tunnels and between pine trees growing sideways, their branches dusting the roof. Houses piled up the slopes, their pink and orange walls soft in the late afternoon light. Walkers stood back from the track, cyclists pedalled hard, and then the ground levelled out, the haze of mountains now below. Shimla rose into view between the branches, the clear black and white lines of mock-Tudor housing stark against a perfect blue sky. With a wail of brakes, the train slowed into the little station and shuddered to a halt, and our fabulous five-hour ride was rounded off with one final burst of applause. **MR**

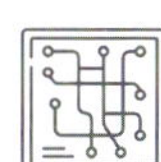

Start/Finish // Kalka/Shimla
Distance // 58 miles (94km)
Duration // 4hr 50min
Ticket Types // As well as regular services and the Shivalik Deluxe, look out for the Kalka-Shimla Special. Recently introduced by Indian Railways, it offers passengers the chance to travel in Vistadome carriages which have glass roofs. The train makes five stops so passengers can hop on and off en route.
How to Book // Visit indiarailinfo.com for timings of the different services running the route and book tickets at 12go.asia.
When to go // Winter is stunning, with snow on the ground, but trains are often unable to run and taken out of service. Travel in spring or post-monsoon when the trees are in bloom and waterfalls tumble down the cliffs.

Opposite top: eyeing an opportunity on the Nilgiri Mountain Railway. Opposite below: A station on the Kangra Valley Railway.

MORE LIKE THIS
THREE INDIAN HILL RAILWAYS

MATHERAN HILL RAILWAY

Buried deep within the jungled crags of the Sahyadri Hills, 50 miles (80km) east of Mumbai, Matheran is a tiny, fully pedestrianised town accessible only on foot, on horse or by rumbling uphill for three hours on a narrow-gauge railway. Built in 1907, the little cream train still runs twice a day in each direction, following tight twists of a red clay track bed at a speed of 5mph (8km/h). With plenty of time to take in the scenery, passengers sit six to a compartment in carriages resembling those of a fairground ride, winding around jungle glistening with dew and alive with the sound of langur monkeys bounding from one branch to the next. Towards the summit, the train makes a stop for passengers to jump off and take photographs of the panoramic views before drawing into Matheran where newlyweds hold hands and eat ice cream and families picnic by Charlotte Lake.

Start // Neral Junction
Finish // Matheran
Distance // 12.5 miles (20km)
Duration // 2hr 40min

NILGIRI MOUNTAIN RAILWAY

The only rack railway in India, this magical route in the south of the country takes passengers from the Tamil Nadu town of Mettupalayam up to the hill resort of Udagamandalam, better known as Ooty. Running on a single track, the metre-gauge railway is the steepest in Asia, covering 29 miles (46km) in just under five hours, steam puffing from its comical blue engine as it pulls wooden carriages through the dampness of tea plantations, the medicinal smell of eucalyptus heavy on the air. Having featured in many a Hindi movie, the ride is often accompanied by Bollywood singalongs and plenty of whoops and cheers.

Start // Mettupalayam
Finish // Udagamandalam
Distance // 29 miles (46km)
Duration // 4hr 45min

KANGRA VALLEY RAILWAY

Ask anyone in the area and they'll tell you that they remember skipping school to ride the Kangra Valley Railway as a kid – usually without a ticket – such is the thrill of this train that runs from Nurpur Road in Punjab to Joginder Nagar in Himachal Pradesh. Built in 1929 and originally running from Pathankot, the journey now starts at Nurpur Road after monsoon rains caused a bridge across the Chakki River to collapse a few years ago. Over a long six hours, the train rolls through farmland, crossing olive-green bodies of water filled with buffalo, fans whirring overhead. Perched in open doorways, passengers dangle over viaducts, watching women beating laundry on the rocks and kids playing makeshift games of cricket.

Start // Nurpur Road
Finish // Joginder Nagar
Distance // 75 miles (121km)
Duration // 6hr

पालमपुर हिमाचल
PALAMPUR HIMACHAL
धरती माता करे पुकार, आसपास का करो सुधार।
स्वच्छता अपनाओ समाज में खुशियाँ लाओ।
स्वच्छता की ज्योती जलाओ देश को सुन्दर बनाओ।
आओ मिलकर करें ये काम स्वच्छता का चलाएं अभियान।
साफ सफाई है अपना नारा सहयोग आपका प्रयत्न हमारा।
बेटी बचाओ बेटी पढ़ाओ और देश का मान बढ़ाओ।
जल ही जीवन है इसको व्यर्थ न बहायें।
बोलिए आप है किसके संग।
हम सबका एक ही सपना, स्वच्छ भारत हो अपना।
स्टेशन को साफ सुथरा रखने में रेलवे की सहायता करें।

SOUTHEAST ASIAN LUXURY: THE E&O EXPRESS

This 'rail cruise' aboard a delightful train explores the culture and landscapes of Southeast Asia, while serving up fine food in interiors of utmost elegance.

Nobody would describe Singapore's Woodlands Checkpoint as a romantic railway station recalling the splendours of train travel's golden age. Frankly, this 1990s station resembles an airport in decor and atmosphere. In 2011 it replaced the island-city's historic Tanjong Pagar Station as the terminus for international services, a symbol of the brisk efficiency for which Singapore is famous. But no matter, because this is the starting point for the Eastern & Oriental Express (E&O), a 'rail cruise' offered by Belmond, which operates other famous trains including the Venice Simplon Orient Express.

This sleeper service echoes the luxury of that famous European train, though with a distinctive Asian style. On my E&O journey I was welcomed by my carriage's steward, who presented me with a lemongrass drink and explained the features of my compartment (which the rail company refers to as a cabin, though in truth that's a maritime term). It's an elegant, impressive space, with timber panelling, rich upholstery in a burgundy shade, and lamps which have a hint of art nouveau style. Overall, it's very tasteful, evoking the past without going over the top.

Before the pandemic, the E&O threaded the Malay Peninsula from Singapore to Bangkok, with off-train excursions in Thailand and Malaysia. While preparations are underway to return the train to Thai rails, the current signature tour, 'Essence of Malaysia', has a tighter focus. Starting in Singapore, it heads north through southern Malaysia towards Kuala Lumpur, with passengers enjoying afternoon tea as the cityscape gives way to the tropical greenery of the peninsula. This is the perfect

EASTERN & ORIENTAL EXPRESS

opportunity to relax in one of the onboard common areas with their wood-panelled corridors and soft furnishings, and bars supplied with comfortable sofas.

A major highlight of this train is the food, an expertly balanced choice of European and Asian cuisines served in beautifully outfitted dining cars. When I travelled, one dinner menu had main course options of roast duck breast on a fricassee of Asian vegetables or green curry with fish. Desserts were colourful and inventive, with the likes of a lychee mousse roll or mango parfait with papaya jelly on offer.

On the current Essence of Malaysia itinerary, the menu is presided over by chef André Chiang, presenting his up-to-date interpretation of Southeast Asian cooking in the two restaurant carriages, named Adisorn and Malaya. Their design seeks to reflect the passing landscape, borrowing from the distinctive shades of tea plantations and jungle foliage.

The done thing aboard this train is to dress for dinner, so I carefully packed a jacket and tie among the more prosaic contents of my backpack. Although it sounds a hassle, in the end it's well worth making the effort to dress up like everyone else. As with most long-distance train journeys, this three-day trip is a social affair, sparking lively conversations between passengers from across the globe. This convivial vibe adds to the pleasure of the journey, in my experience; in fact I preferred the on-train time to time spent on excursions.

"As with most long-distance train journeys, this three-day trip is a social affair, sparking lively conversations between passengers from across the globe."

On the morning of day two we're well beyond Kuala Lumpur and passing rural villages and rice paddies in western Malaysia. After lunch, passengers step off the train at Alor Setar for the first outing of this ride – a boat trip to the island of Langkawi to experience the offshore Pulau Payar Marine Park. This protected marine zone is full of vivid sea life, including parrot fish, angel fish, moray eels and groupers. An array of options now come into play: passengers receive a fancy picnic hamper and can decide how to spend their time before the return to the train. Among the choices are wellness experiences including massage, meditation and tai chi; or more active alternatives such as paddle boarding, snorkelling and taking an island walk. It's a taste of leafy tropical paradise – but with a bar and barbecue included.

Back on the train, there's music from local entertainers in the bar car, which contains, believe it or not, a piano. During my time on board I embarrassed myself by singing along badly with the pianist's best efforts – you only live once (and probably only ride this train once).

THE TAJ MAHAL OF STATIONS

When the Eastern & Oriental Express passes through historic Kuala Lumpur Station, cast your eye over the architecture. Opened in 1910, it was designed in an alluring combination of styles. Rather than drawing on local Malay designs, however, it has an unlikely Indian-style 'Raj' look, a blend of Western and Mughal decor. It's an echo of the British Empire at its wackiest.

From left: Palatial rooms on the E&O Express; E&O carriages were originally used as a sleeper train in New Zealand; the hills of Peninsular Malaysia seen from the train. Previous page: the dapper Observation Car.

On day three of the itinerary, the action moves south to Butterworth, the train's next stop. The destination of the morning is another island, Penang, where, yet again, there's a range of activities. The tastiest is an exploration of the local Peranakan cooking culture via a visit to a spice shop and local grocery stores to buy herbs and vegetables. You then get the opportunity to combine them in the form of traditional dishes (under instruction, of course). An alternative culture-focused tour sees passengers head to Georgetown's Old Quarter to visit temples, a contemporary art studio, and an opera and puppet house. Or if you'd rather do your own thing, you can explore the town with a map, a trishaw and a driver.

Upon reboarding the Eastern & Oriental Express, lunch is served before passengers enjoy a leisurely afternoon in motion. This was a good time to visit the open-sided observation car with its views of the passing countryside and no windows to spoil photography with errant reflections.

There's a final fancy dinner on my last night on board, followed the next morning by our last breakfast, enjoyed in your compartment or the dining car as the train travels through the southern Malaysian state of Johor and crosses the strait to Singapore. That's journey's end, back where you started – though with much fine dining and memorable excursions under your belt. **TR**

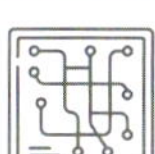

Start/Finish // Woodlands Checkpoint, Singapore
Distance // 1000 miles (1600km)
Duration // 3 days
Ticket types // There's a number of accommodation options on the E&O, all very plush with en suite. Pullman Cabin is the standard, with bunk beds; State Cabin is more spacious, with twin beds at floor level; or splurge on the Presidential Suite which includes a spacious compartment, luxury toiletries, a spa treatment and free-flowing champagne. Tickets include food, some drinks and excursions. The route is also served by regular intercity trains, see ktmb.com.my.
How to book // belmond.com
When to go // November to March is the best time to visit, avoiding the wet season.
Things to know // Passengers are expected to dress formally for dinner – pack accordingly.
More info // visitsingapore.com, malaysia.travel

Opposite: The Venice Simplon Orient Express passes through Austria's Brenner Pass.

MORE LIKE THIS
THREE MORE ORIENT EXPRESSES

VENICE SIMPLON ORIENT EXPRESS

This is the world's most famous train, partly because of its appearance in such novels as Agatha Christie's *Murder on the Orient Express*. The original service ran across several different routes from Paris to Istanbul, commencing in 1883. Its retirement inspired a yearning for the heyday of rail, prompting the launch of the Venice Simplon Orient Express as a luxury service in 1982. Compartments are glamorous, fitted out with polished woodwork and elegant lamps. Passengers dress up for dinner as the onboard meals are a big part of the appeal, enjoyed in the train's three spectacular dining cars and bar car. The scenery of Switzerland is a highlight of the journey, as is its grand finale – arrival at Venice's Santa Lucia Station on the edge of the Grand Canal.
Start // Paris
Finish // Venice
Distance // 690 miles (1110km)
Duration // 1 day

LA DOLCE VITA ORIENT EXPRESS

The chance discovery of several original Orient Express carriages in eastern Poland has allowed hotel company Accor to craft its own 21st-century version of the train, dubbed La Dolce Vita Orient Express. With a focus on luxurious rail journeys across Italy, the beautifully refitted compartments feature carpeted floors and timber ceilings, along with private bathrooms. The bar car and dining car are similarly stylish, the latter's walls decorated with a glossy lacquer. Meals are served to tables set with vintage silverware and Italian crockery, and accompanied by regional wines. There are a number of itineraries available, most starting in Rome, including the triangular Coast to Coast route linking Rome, Venice and Portofino, and longer trips crossing from the mainland to Sicily.
Start // Rome
Finish // various destinations
Distance // Varies
Duration // Varies

BRITISH PULLMAN

When American George Pullman invented the luxury sleeper car in 1865, he was onto a winner. His company operated a vast empire of Pullman Cars in the USA well into the 20th century, and the name made its way across the Atlantic to become a respected brand in the UK. The British Pullman retains the glamour of its predecessors, with carriages containing pairs of comfortable armchairs facing dining tables in open-plan interiors. Some carriages served as parts of such famous trains as the Golden Arrow boat train and the upmarket Brighton Belle, and one carriage's interior has been redesigned by filmmaker Wes Anderson. The train offers a range of excursions through the year, including a regular champagne afternoon tea from London through Kent and back, and the occasional 'moving murder mystery' at which lunch comes with a heaping side dish of clues.
Start/Finish // Victoria Station, London
Distance // Varies
Duration // Varies

DES WAGONS LITS ET DES GRANDS EXPRESS EUROPEENS

MARVELLOUS MAHARASHTRA ABOARD THE DECCAN QUEEN

A relaxing ride from bustling Mumbai to laid-back Pune, the Deccan Queen takes you through green swathes of Maharashtra's untouched countryside, enjoyed with endless cups of chai.

It starts, as train journeys in India usually do, with chai. Before the train has pulled out of the station in Mumbai, and before the conductor has made his rounds, the caterer weaves along the aisle, aluminium kettle in one hand, paper cups and sugar expertly grasped in the other. The tea and air-conditioning are soothing, offering a welcome change after the heat and chaos of the city's Chhatrapati Shivaji Maharaj Terminus (CSMT) – which most Mumbaikars still call 'VT', short for 'Victoria Terminus'. A grand Gothic Revival structure that opened in 1887, the station sees an estimated three million daily passengers. Today I'm one of them, heading to Pune.

Of course, you can drive between Mumbai and Pune, and the train journey is identical time-wise. However, people tend to opt for the Deccan Queen (named after its destination Pune – dubbed the queen of the Deccan region) out of a fondness for rail travel. The service is known for its punctuality, leaving

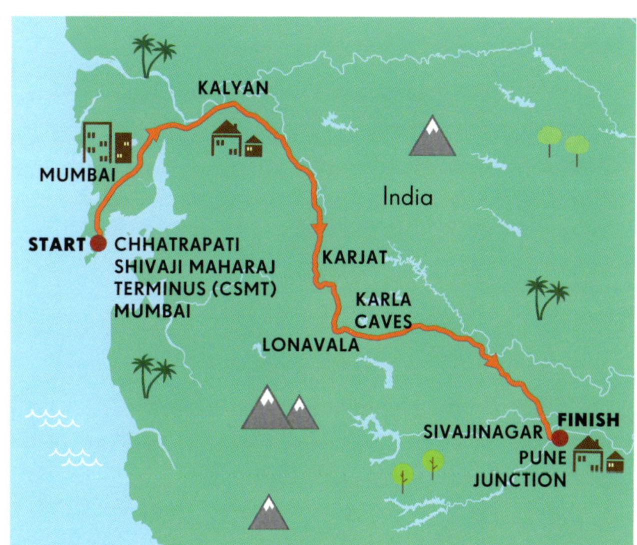

at 5.10pm on the nose and holding a record for 'right-time start and arrival', according to authorities on such matters. The short, fuss-free journey has a quiet air of magic about it. The greens are greener, the countryside is dotted with briefly glimpsed mini waterfalls and fat raindrops splash against wide glass windows – in India, this weather provides a good excuse to drink chai (and eat fried food) in excess.

In under an hour, the last of Mumbai's concrete-crammed suburbs are replaced with green hills rushing past the windows. Seats in the Vistadome compartment – which has large windows, skylights and a viewing deck – are swivelled outwards to face the countryside. Inevitably, the idyllic scenery melds with the hum of the train and the chatter of passengers to provide the perfect backdrop for introspection. Generally, this route sees a mix of people beyond office workers headed home after a day's work, clacking away on laptops, earphones in. Typically, you'll spot young families with toddlers, couples (old and young) looking to get away from the city and large groups of men and women headed away for stag dos and girls' trips.

Mumbaikars who can afford it head to smaller hill station towns during the monsoon between June and September. Two of these towns are en route to Pune: Karjat and Lonavala. Plus, the region between Mumbai and Pune has an abundance of Buddhist cave complexes, including the underrated but impressive Karla Caves, which date back to at least the 2nd century.

Before long, the caterer reappears waving paper-wrapped bun-omelette and *vada pav* – the Mumbai street food composed of a battered, deep-fried potato patty (*vada*), an assortment of chutneys and crunchy savouries sandwiched between two soft buns (*pav*). It's worth noting here that catering staff on Indian trains are skilled salesmen. This one talks up the hotness and freshness of his snacks, the coolness of his drinks and the invigorating qualities of his chai – but I've already eaten so decline.

Since June 1930, this route has been celebrated for its food. When it started, it was dubbed India's first 'deluxe' train, with a dining car and a ladies' compartment. Since then, the Deccan Queen has seen many upgrades including four air-conditioned standard compartments, the Vistadome compartment and a new dining car. Despite the food quality being so-so (experienced travellers say quality has dropped), this remains the only dining car across Indian Railways trains.

Nowadays, a growing number of customers opt to order food to station platforms while the train has stopped en route. Typically, a couple of hours before your journey, you'll receive an email from the e-Catering wing of Indian Railways asking if you'd like to order anything from a handful of restaurants directly to your seat – a service available at three of five stations for the Deccan Queen. Menu options are wildly

CHHATRAPATI SHIVAJI MAHARAJ TERMINUS

The first passenger train service in India ran from a station in Bori Bunder, Bombay, in 1853. It would later become the Victoria Terminus in 1888, before being renamed after Chhatrapati Shivaji Maharaj, founder of the 17th-century Maratha Empire, in 1996. The magnificent station is home to a quaint but enriching museum featuring miniature models, stone-carved lions and tarnished silver memorabilia from days of yore.

Clockwise from top: The Chhatrapati Shivaji Maharaj Terminus; the Gateway of India; a flower market in Mumbai. Previous page: The Taj Mahal Palace hotel in Mumbai; the Deccan Queen speeding through countryside.

varied and include everything from Domino's Pizza to local biryani chain, Behrouz Biryani.

The Deccan Queen journey peaks an hour and a half outside Mumbai as it rolls into its first stop at Karjat. The viewing deck in front of the Vistadome is empty as tufts of bubblegum pink candy floss clouds mist their way down into the valley. A third of the compartment empties and no one gets on at this station.

Although the train runs daily now, when it first began, it travelled between Bombay and Poona (as the two cities were then known) as a 'weekend special service' and was reserved solely for white colonists off to see horse races. The train ran 'Race Specials' on weekends and race days, offering passengers a discount. It was only later, when Indians were allowed to travel on this route (in 1943, four years before the country gained independence) that sufficient demand for a daily service came about.

At Lonavala, forty minutes later, the journey winds down as the sky darkens. What's left of my ride from this point on feels swift, in part because the sun has set and there are no hills to gaze on. By the time our train pulls into Pune Junction (there's one more stop in Pune, at Sivajinagar), it's easy to see why locals love this scenic and fuss-free journey.

As well as being the first super-fast train and the first long-distance electric-hauled service, the Deccan Queen is a part of the city's fabric. So much so, that Pune even celebrates the train's birthday every June 1st.

To me, this journey is seductive because of how well it lends itself to spontaneity. An instant escape from Mumbai's din to Pune, charming and quiet. **AS**

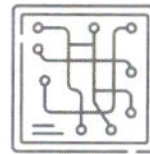

Start/Finish // Mumbai/Pune
Distance // 120 miles (192km)
Duration // 3hr 15min
Ticket types // There are three ticket options: Vistadome with air-con; Standard chair car; and more basic Second Sitting.
How to book // Online at irctc.co.in but note that the website is difficult to navigate. Most people visiting India tend to buy a local SIM for more reliable connectivity when booking or buy through third-party websites such as 12go.asia.
When to go // For the greenest views of the countryside, travel during the monsoon (mid-June to late August).
Things to know // Leaving Mumbai, you'll pass mounds of rubbish and several tarpaulin-tent settlements. This is a sad reality of travelling here. However, you can help by researching several NGOs that focus on waste management and homelessness and avoiding single-use plastic wherever possible.

Opposite top: Grabbing a bite to eat while riding the rails in Maharashtra. Opposite below: A view of the coastline near Palolem in Goa.

MORE LIKE THIS
INDIAN MAINLINE TRAIN RIDES

JAN SHATABDI EXPRESS

This stunning ride along the palm-fringed Konkan coast meanders through more remote parts of both Maharashtra and Goa states. The train comes with a Vistadome carriage as well as standard chair compartments. Meals are simple and unfussy; the menu features steamed classics such as *upma* (porridge), *poha* (rice snack) and bun-omelette. Highlights on board include LCD screens, wi-fi and swivelling chairs – but it's the view from your window that will really draw you in on this journey, as you zip past cascading waterfalls along the Western Ghats, through luxuriant forest cover and over several crossings including the Zuari Bridge.
Start // CSMT, Mumbai
Finish // Magaon, Goa
Distance // 470 miles (755km)
Duration // 11hr 30min

RAMESWARAM EXPRESS

With a total of 21 stops, this journey is for those who appreciate slow travel. This 'express' train runs daily and the highlights of the trip are the popular spots it winds through, most notably over parts of the Kaveri River flowing through Tamil Nadu and the iconic Pamban Bridge. The bridge connects the spiritual town of Rameswaram (Pamban Island) with the Indian peninsula. Expect to encounter an eclectic mix of people, ranging from solo domestic tourists and spiritual travellers to large groups of families and school children. As you whoosh over the bridge, the warm waters of the Palk Strait, which separates Tamil Nadu from Sri Lanka, are all that's visible.
Start // Chennai Egmore (sometimes referred to as Chennai Elumbur), Chennai
Finish // Mandapam (12 miles/20km outside Rameswaram)
Distance // 403 miles (648km)
Duration // 12hr (overnight)

GOA EXPRESS

Winding through a vast expanse of India, this is a well-loved train journey. Most people opt to start in Delhi and end in Goa, but there's something to be said about easing into this trip, enjoying the Goan *susegad* (quiet/chill/all is fine) atmosphere first. It's also usually less crowded in this direction. The train makes its way through several states, including Maharashtra and Karnataka, and stops in the regal towns of Gwalior and Agra (home to the epic Taj Mahal). The portion of the journey from Goa through Maharashtra is particularly stunning, with a combination of rocky hillscapes, untamed forests and the huge Dudhsagar Falls (1017ft/310m), tucked into Braganza Ghats. One thing to note is that the sleeper coaches are very crowded (there are only two), so if you can afford it, pay for an air-conditioned First or Second Class ticket.
Start // Vasco da Gama, Goa
Finish // Hazrat Nizamuddin, Delhi
Distance // 1372 miles (2208km)
Duration // 3 days/2 nights

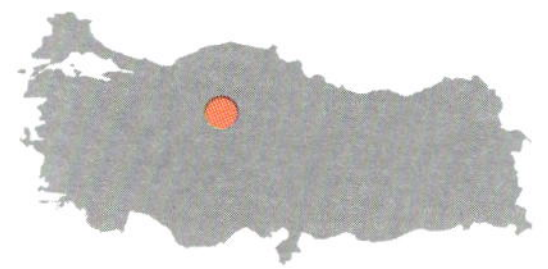

INTO EASTERN ANATOLIA ON THE DOGU EXPRESS

This slow night train is Türkiye's flagship sleeper, trundling through rugged mountains from the capital Ankara to the eastern city of Kars.

When riding the 26-hour Dogu Express from Ankara to far eastern Türkiye, the unique rules of the route soon become clear.

First, you must bring flashing fairy lights, and place them around your cabin window. Second, non-vegetarians must join in the mass kebab-eating session in the dining car (more on this later). Third, before departure you must yank a metal 'Doğu Ekspresi' sign from the side of a carriage, then pose for a photo with it.

This is the scene when I arrive at Ankara's main train station: reams of grinning passengers holding the signs at jaunty angles, before boarding and shunting fairy light plugs into carriage wall sockets. Much of this, of course, is for social media, and I can't blame my fellow travellers for gloating. Since videos of the Dogu Express' mountainous and stirring scenery got big online around the mid-2010s, sleeper berth tickets for the service have consistently sold out.

Previously, riding the 'Doğu Ekspresi' (Eastern Express) wasn't something many people crowed about. The train dates back to the 1930s, and for most of its lifetime it's been a largely functional affair, connecting villages in the middle and east of the country to urban centres.

A berth in a four-person cabin for the entire route still costs just 900 lira, thanks to the government subsidising tickets, making for an affordable way for people in the countryside to access cities such as Sivas, Erzurum, Ankara and Kayseri. The latter can serve as a gateway to the ancient hillside cave dwellings of Cappadocia, but no stops on the route could be described as tourist hot spots – many are just tiny hillside platforms at the end of dirt roads. Until recently you were more likely to bump into a crate of live chickens than a high-end Nikon camera on the train.

Not that the Dogu Express is now full of vacuous travel influencers. When dragging my wheelie suitcase to my cabin I meet two students taping fairy lights to their window, lighting a candle and getting ready to read Agatha Christie's *Murder on the Orient Express*. They tell me – via Google Translate – that they are best friends, and planned the journey as a chance to catch up with each other.

I too booked the trip for the journey rather than destination, and thus am travelling the entire route in one go to Kars, near Türkiye's borders with Georgia and Armenia. It's winter, so it gets dark soon after the train leaves Ankara in the early evening, but I make out stray dogs ambling through thick snow as we chug through the outskirts of the capital.

I'm travelling with a female friend and we have a four-person cabin to ourselves – if you book as a mixed-gender group your

"Until recently you were more likely to bump into a crate of live chickens than a high-end Nikon camera on the train."

cabin gets blocked out to prevent strangers of different genders sleeping in close proximity. My friend and I agree that it's a shame to have berths on such a popular route go to waste. We also agree that it's a sweet deal to have a private compartment free from smelly feet that are not our own.

We head to the dining car, which has the chatty atmosphere of a college canteen on the first day of term. We share a table with Ender, a medical student taking the train to Erzurum because it's so much cheaper than flying and he's not earning a doctor's salary quite yet. He's using the long journey to pore over diagrams of kidneys on his tablet.

You know that person who's always the firework of the party, forcing people to play Twister? Here that person is a bespectacled, curly-haired man named Metin, who makes friends with every table group within minutes. He explains that he's from Antalya, on Türkiye's south coast, and is riding the Dogu Express for a snowy solo experience. When the train briefly stops, he runs onto the platform and deliberately face-plants into the snow. He returns to the dining car covered in white powder, absorbing applause from tea-sipping passengers. I like Metin, and I hope every Dogu Express dining car has one.

The next day's sunlight finally allows some view-watching, and insight into how travel vloggers helped make this line a hot ticket for both international and domestic tourists. We sporadically plunge into darkness as the train enters tunnels cut into the mountains, emerging to pass the Euphrates River running south to Syria and Iraq.

The dining car manager asks me if I want a kebab from Erzurum – an interaction comprised of smiling and making chewing gestures, due to my own Turkish language ability level. Of course I want a kebab from Erzurum. He makes the call, takes my cash and an hour later 66 hot lamb kebabs are waiting for us on Erzurum's train platform. So 65 fellow passengers and I kick through the snow to grab them from the stall, then chomp in unison back aboard. The succulent meat helps ease the frustration of the train by now running many hours late due to engineering issues.

The journey to Kars ends up taking 35 hours, rather than the scheduled 26. But the Dogu Express is not a train you take for its swiftness. From Kars I visit the Ani ruins, the ancient, long-abandoned Armenian ghost city right by the border, which is patrolled by Russian soldiers. I plan a trip north into Georgia, and the woodland hot springs in the small Caucasus country's spa town Borjomi.

But really, I'm more excited about planning my return journey westward. I've booked another ride on the Dogu Express to take me back to Ankara, and this time I'm bringing fairy lights. **JF**

THE POSH OPTION

A 'touristic' version of the Dogu Express has operated since 2019, usually running December to March. All its passengers get to sleep in a two-person cabin. Instead of around 50 short stops, the train makes two or three long stops, halting for excursions for a few hours each time. It stops in İliç and Erzurum when going east, and in Erzincan, Divriği and Sivas on the westbound service.

Clockwise from top: The Turkish capital Ankara; the Dogu Express outside Kars; a statue of Ataturk in Ankara; a locomotive in snow. Previous page: The train near Erzincan.

Start/Finish // Ankara/Kars
Distance // 814 miles (1310km)
Duration // Around 26hr each way.
Ticket types // The three classes are: Seats; Sleeper in four-berth cabins; and private two-berth cabins.
How to book // Buy from Turkish State Railway's E-Bilet app or ebilet.tcddtasimacilik.gov.tr. English-speaking tour company Amber Travel (ambertravel.com) offers ticket-buying services.
Things to know // Tickets are government-subsidised and cheap (from 400 Turkish lira per seat for the whole route). Berths usually sell out when tickets go on sale 30 days before departure, but often become available again later due to cancellations.
When to go // The train runs daily in each direction all year, and is comfortable whatever the season.

Opposite top: Istanbul's Blue Mosque with the Bosphorus beyond. Opposite below: The Armenian Cathedral Church of the Holy Cross on Akdamar Island in Van Lake.

MORE LIKE THIS
TURKISH TRAINS TO TRY

VANGOLU EXPRESS

Like the Dogu Express, the Vangolu Express night train travels from Ankara to deep eastern Türkiye, and its berths sell out just as quickly. Tourists are rarer on this route than on the Dogu Express, though, so if you're not Turkish prepare to be thoroughly quizzed by chatty children about your favourite soccer team. As the train approaches Lake Van, Türkiye's largest, it passes vast fields dotted with stone ruins, and you might spot wild goats traversing hills beside the track. After arriving in Tatvan you can take a two-hour bus ride to the city of Van, hugging the lake's shore as you go. The city has its own cat breed: the handsome Van cats, known for long white hair and having one yellow and one blue eye. Visit them in Van Cat House at Van Yüzüncü Yıl University.

Start // Ankara
Finish // Tatvan
Distance // 774 miles (1246km)
Duration // Around 26hr each way

GUNEY KURTALAN EXPRESS

Another slow night train travelling east from Ankara, the Guney Kurtalan Express has the same vibe (plus the same engine, carriage and ticket pricing style) as the Dogu Express and Vangolu Express. This 27-hour route is notable for stopping at Diyarbakır, the Kurdish-majority city not far from the country's borders with Syria and Iraq. Parts of Diyarbakır's old city walls are derelict, largely due to conflict between Turkish forces and Kurdish militants in the mid-2000s, while other sections house cafes. Reports of Kurdish oppression are still common in the city, but it is safe for tourists. Diyarbakır's old quarter is full of markets, antique shops and top-grade, low-seated kebab joints. Rıdvan Kuday Gallery (ridvankudaygallery.com), housed in a residential area far from the old centre, showcases contemporary Kurdish art.

Start // Ankara
Finish // Kurtalan
Distance // 753 miles (1212km)
Duration // Around 27hr each way

ISTANBUL-ANKARA HST

If you're taking the Dogu Express, Vangolu Express or Guney Kurtalan Express, all of which start at Ankara's main train station, you can visit Istanbul first then take the high-speed connection to the capital from Istanbul's Söğütlüçeşme Station. Part of Türkiye's recently launched high-speed rail project, this slick service, featuring hot drinks delivered to your seat, is in gleaming contrast to the ambling slow night trains to the east. Many trains run this route every day, making it an easy option to use to connect the Dogu Express, which leaves Ankara in the early evening. Like the sleeper trains, these services often sell out, so book at least a few days in advance.

Start // Istanbul
Finish // Ankara
Distance // 345 miles (555km)
Duration // Around 4hr 20min

THE MAHARAJAS' EXPRESS: ARISTOCRAT OF INDIAN RAILS

A week-long tour of India aboard the ultra-luxe Maharajas' Express takes in ornate temples, steaming jungles and no small amount of adventure.

No matter how raucous an Indian train station is already, the arrival of the Maharajas' Express only brings more chaos. The country's premier luxury train demands actual red carpets be rolled out for its guests, and that bands loudly play them off the train. During my seven-day Indian Splendour itinerary from New Delhi to Mumbai, the music was then followed by people pelting us with flower petals, hanging garlands round our necks and daubing bindis on our foreheads. Flabbergasted locals reached for their phones to record these scenes, in case we passengers happened to be famous.

A colossal burgundy and gold monster too long for most local stations, the Maharajas' Express is designed to garner attention, whether it's moving or stationary, and especially when guests disembark. Subtlety is not at all the aim, but what it does offer is a regal order in a country of much unpredictability. Each night is spent sleeping on the train and each day passengers are shepherded onto buses for organised excursions at each of the stops. There's very little scope for things to go wrong. It seemed like a perfect way to introduce my mother to India for the first time.

Our week-long itinerary offered a kind of tourism tasting menu. Most days we had two guide-led excursions before retreating to the opulence of the train to move on. The whole journey took us from Delhi to Agra and the Taj Mahal, then on to Ranthambore National Park and the pink city of Jaipur. Having completed this 'Golden Triangle', we continued to Bikaner, the blue city of Jodhpur, and beautiful Udaipur with its calm lakes and floating palaces, finally ending with a near-24-hour uninterrupted journey to Mumbai.

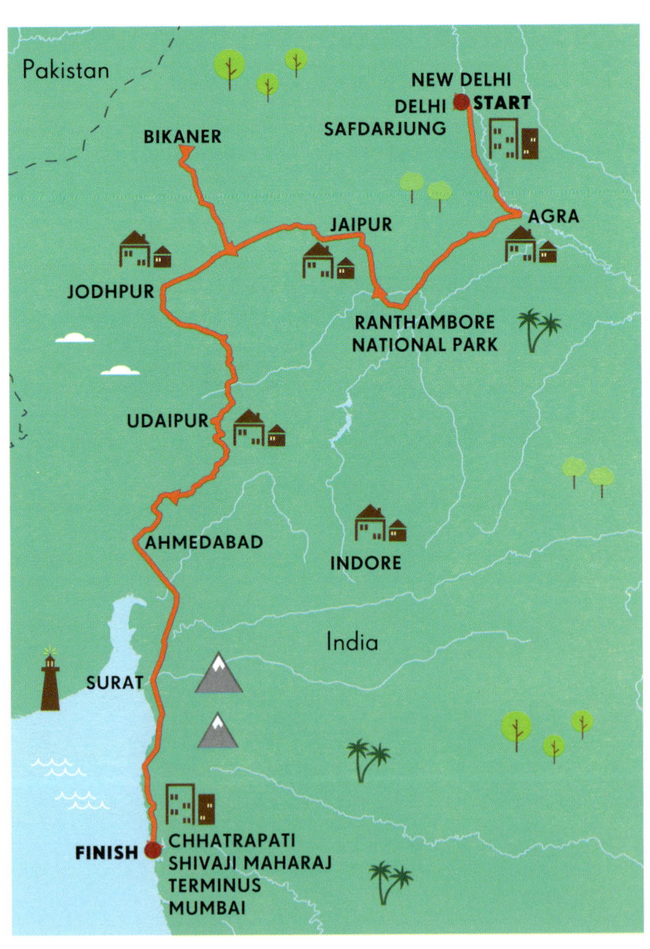

In the end, the trip boiled down to a series of memorable vignettes: the electric thrill of listening to the jungle alarm of monkeys and deer as a Bengal tiger lurked nearby in Ranthambore; the simple perfection of the Taj Mahal gilded by the late afternoon sun; those shimmering white island palaces in Udaipur; a puppet show in the grounds of the Khaas Bagh Hotel in Jodhpur, fireworks then exploding in the night sky just for us. None of it seemed completely real, and when I think back on the trip now, the memory that is clearest is that of my mother's face, locked in a state of near-permanent astonishment.

Each of the carriages (the number goes up and down depending on bookings) are named after jewels. Ours was Manik, meaning ruby. They all came with a butler. Ours was Yogendra, meaning God of Yoga, who was certainly very flexible and permanently on-call should we encounter even a minor inconvenience.

On the roadside in Jaipur, famous for its jewel merchants, hawkers loudly tried to sell us gems which may or may not have been precious but were apparently a great deal all the same. Among these were rubies.

'So, they're literally *manik* street preachers?' I asked, a little too delighted with myself.

'Sorry I don't understand,' replied Yogendra. But he had nothing to apologise for, and neither did I.

Despite the ludicrously attentive level of service, not all the carriages were full. Still, in the 14 years since the train first took to the tracks, it was busier than ever, thanks in part to British newsreader Sir Trevor McDonald who took this same journey in 2019, a trip which was then made into the rather grandly titled *Trevor McDonald's Indian Train Adventure*. As extraordinary as the places en route are, the whole point of the Maharajas' Express is to eliminate the chance of anything going wrong – the wing of the Indian government that owns the train wants reliability and safety above all.

> *"A colossal burgundy and gold monster too long for most local stations, the Maharajas' Express is designed to garner attention..."*

Ten of the guests I spoke to cited the former news anchor's documentary as a particular reason for booking. A little over half of the passengers were British, though others had travelled from Canada, Singapore, Russia, France and Australia. Wherever we'd come from, we were afforded the same royal level of service, meaning we were never once without a drink, or more food than a sensible person could ever really desire.

There were occasions on board when it felt like we were living in some kind of hyperbaric chamber, far removed from life just beyond our windows.

THE RAT PACK

An optional side tour from the main route will take you to the Karni Mata Temple outside Bikaner. This 500-year-old site of worship has become famous thanks to the 20,000-strong population of holy rats living inside. The rodents are cared for by temple workers, while worshippers come – barefoot – to be among them, all the while hoping to see one of the rare and particularly revered white rats.

From left: A platform scene unfolds beside the Maharajas' Express; luxurious onboard catering. Previous page: The city of Jodhpur seen from Mehrangarh Fort.

'At what point does all of this become inappropriate?' my mother asked, waving a golden fork around at breakfast.

The large, one-way window next to our tables allowed us to watch with curiosity the daily scenes outside, while locals could only see their own reflections. Some people used these mirrors to come and check how they were looking. Others, unaware there was a group of passengers just a few yards away, continued about their business, whether that was playing with children or chastising stray dogs. Often, I was reminded of a quote from Paul Theroux's *The Great Railway Bazaar*: 'The newcomer cannot believe he has been plunged into such intimacy so soon.'

We ate off the Maharajas' Express a few times, too, mostly at carefully selected palace hotels and at one spectacular open-air desert retreat just outside Bikaner. The rest of the meals were expertly prepared by the improbably named Chef John Stone and his team in the ungenerous confines of the train's kitchen, which divided its two bars and two restaurants and was never not a hive of feverish activity.

Each mealtime there was a choice between European and Indian dishes and the latter were always superior. Mum made sure to order the Indian dessert every time, and when I'd ask if she was enjoying it, she'd say it was 'interesting'. Rather like the whole experience. **JL**

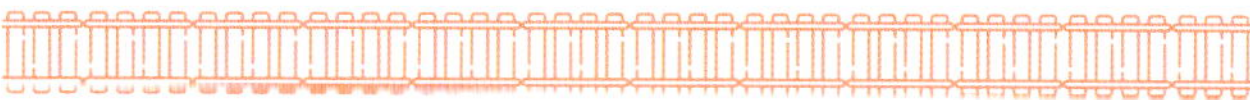

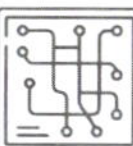

Start/Finish // Delhi Safdarjung/Chhatrapati Shivaji Maharaj Terminus Mumbai
Distance // 1692 miles (2723km)
Duration // 7 days, 6 nights
Ticket types // There are four classes of compartment on the Maharajas' Express: Deluxe Cabins; Suites; Junior Suites; and the Presidential Suite. All are expensive. The train uses India's main train lines, though it often operates out of smaller stations, allowing organisers to tailor the boarding and disembarking processes.
How to book // Book online at the-maharajas.com
When to go // The Indian Splendour itinerary runs between October and March.

Opposite top: After dark on the Palace on Wheels. Opposite below: Padam Talao – a lake in Ranthambore National Park.

MORE LIKE THIS
INDIAN LUXURY TRAINS

GOLDEN CHARIOT

Specialising in tours of southern India, the Golden Chariot runs a trio of itineraries between October and March. Its Pride of Karnataka route starts in Bengaluru before making a short journey west to Mysore, home of a famously grand palace. Construction began in the late 1800s, and while the Mysore Palace may not be particularly ancient, it is undeniably ornate and one of the most photogenic in the country. There's much deeper history to be found at the Hindu and Jain temples in Halebid, some of which have been standing for almost 1000 years. Later in the itinerary are visits to coffee plantations and luxury hotels, plus a cultural immersion in the colourful state of Goa – in Margao there's a crash course in Portugal's colonial history in India, many remnants of which are still visible today. The route concludes back where it started.
Start/Finish // Bengaluru
Distance // 958 miles (1542km)
Duration // 6 days

PALACE ON WHEELS

The oldest of India's cruise trains has been in operation for over 40 years. Offering just one, seven-night itinerary, the Palace on Wheels takes in many of India's most famous and popular destinations. Starting and ending in New Delhi, its route first visits the pink city of Jaipur and its spectacular hilltop Amber Fort. Ranthambore National Park comes next, and while various species of deer and monkey may well be spotted during a jeep safari, the real prize here is the chance of seeing a mighty Bengal tiger. Tranquil Udaipur, the City of Lakes, comes next, followed by Jaisalmer where a camel safari and dinner at the Gorbandh Palace await. The week aboard finishes with a tour of the Blue City of Jodhpur, and – just before returning to Delhi – a chance to visit Agra and the ever-gorgeous Taj Mahal.
Start/Finish // New Delhi
Distance // 1850 miles (2977km)
Duration // 8 days

DECCAN ODYSSEY

Like its nominal rivals, the Deccan Odyssey begins many of its tours in the Indian capital, New Delhi. It similarly visits Ranthambore National Park, Jaipur and Agra, too. However, from there its dedicated seven-night Cultural Odyssey changes track and heads to the historic fort at Gwalior. Looking out from the top of an imposing cliff, this stronghold has functioned as a palace and fortress for over 1000 years. Khajuraho is next, home to the UNESCO World Heritage Site that is the Chandela Temple complex. This spectacular network of ruins was lost for centuries before its rediscovery in the 19th century. While the temples here have a sort of haunted feel, the train's final stop at Varanasi feels much more alive – even for non-religious visitors, the holy city on the banks of the mighty Ganges River can have a powerfully spiritual effect.
Start/Finish // New Delhi
Distance // 1526 miles (2456km)
Duration // 8 days

FRIENDS REUNITED ON THE REUNIFICATION EXPRESS

Vietnam's most famous train trip is the perfect symbol for a once-divided nation, now reunited by a railway line spanning the length of the country.

Sometimes a train ride is more than just a journey. In the case of the Reunification Express – linking Hanoi to Ho Chi Minh City (HCMC) over 1072 miles (1726km) of sun-scorched, monsoon-drenched tracks – it's a philosophical statement. The French built this epic stretch of railway as an engine for imperial plunder, but at the end of the American War, it became a vital conduit for reconciliation.

It was a train I had always wanted to ride, after bumping into war photographer Tim Page in a bookshop in Cambodia. His reminiscences about 1970s Vietnam made me long to discover more about the tangled, troubled story of Indochina – and the snaking railway line that reunited former foes from North and South.

In fact, the Reunification Express is not one train, but a collection of long-distance services following the originally French-built North–South Railway. Arriving in Hanoi from China via the border crossing at Dong Dang, I had the perfect opportunity to experience the full length of this epic railway odyssey.

Many travellers barrel through, completing the Hanoi–HCMC run in a day and a half, but my dream itinerary involved stops in imperial Hue (for the food and architecture) and Danang and Nha Trang (for wartime history and chillout time on the sand).

Heading to Hanoi Railway Station at dawn to catch the morning train to Hue, I passed through a city still waking up. Enterprising traders set up stalls by the roadside, nightshift workers pootled home on Honda Dream scooters and groups of dancers executed slow-motion pirouettes in the city's parks. The station was refreshingly uncrowded too, apart from squadrons of train guards in outsized, military-style caps; I had no problem finding my train and berth, in a neat compartment lined with wood-effect Formica.

The cheapest way to ride the Reunification Express is in a 'Hard Seat' – part of a communist-era system that splits rail travel into Hard and Soft classes – but I wasn't sure my butt bones could handle 14 hours on a wooden bench. I was drawn instead to a 'Soft Sleeper' berth, with comfy bedding, access to a Western-style loo and air-conditioning that wasn't strictly needed this far north but would become increasingly desirable as we rolled south.

The toothpaste-striped loco rolled out of Hanoi more or less on time, picking up speed as we cleared the suburbs. Hanging up the bag of *bánh mì* sandwiches I'd purchased for the journey, I made acquaintance with the passengers sharing the compartment, which mostly involved polite nods and smiles and confirming that I was getting off in Hue.

Outside Hanoi, the landscape became increasingly lush and green – a mix of rice paddies and farmland, patches of forest, and expanding modern townships such as Vinh, once a major depot supplying the Ho Chi Minh Trail. I settled back to watch the long miles slip by, pausing for *bánh mì* breaks and circulation-stimulating strolls along the carriage.

My first stop in Hue passed in a blur of imperial tombs, royal palaces and Perfume River pagodas (plus delicious *bánh khoái* pancakes and *bún bò* noodle soup). While the scars of the American War lingered, modern-day Hue was looking to the future, with tall apartment buildings, neon shopfronts and home-produced electric cars.

For the short trip to Danang, I opted for the non-air-con Hard Seat class to minimise the chances of condensation obscuring views of this most scenic part of the route, where the railway tracks hug the coast beside the mountainous Hai Van Pass. The scenery opened up to reveal sweeping vistas of curving beaches and foliage-framed bays dropping into a bottle-blue South China Sea.

Danang was once notorious for its US air base, but the beachfront has now been reclaimed by upscale Vietnamese apartments and resorts. To remind myself of Vietnam's rich past, I took a bus over to Hoi An, joining crowds of backpackers goggling at dragon-topped Chinese assembly halls and Vietnamese-style pagodas.

A day later, I boarded the Super Express for Nha Trang, trading the *bánh mì* for hot-and-sour shrimp-flavoured instant noodles, rehydrated using the hot-water dispenser at the end of the carriage. I passed the journey leafing through *The Sorrow of War*, a profoundly human exploration of conflict by Vietnamese novelist Bao Ninh.

Danang's modern-age bling was mirrored in Nha Trang, but here the beachfront high-rises were backed up by some serious history. I made special trips to the still-venerated, 12th-century

STRATEGIC RAIL TRACKS

Laid in 1899, the North–South Railway was the route to power in Indochina. Under the French and Japanese, the railway faced sabotage by Viet Minh rebels before being split into North and South sections in 1954. During the American War, the railway became a supply line, and a target – 1334 bridges and 27 tunnels had to be reconstructed before full service could resume in 1976.

From left: A Vietnamese Railways attendant; a Chinese-built locomotive; Hoi An at dusk; the entry to a tomb in Hue. Previous page: A train passes Hai Van Pass.

Cham-era Po Nagar towers, and the Long Son pagoda, backing on to an ivory-white Buddha statue commemorating the Buddhist monks who immolated themselves in protest at the US-backed South Vietnamese government in 1963.

It took some effort to drag myself away from Nha Trang – and its soft sands and succulent seafood – but the Super Express was calling once again. I booked into Soft Seat class for the final leg to the former Saigon, maximising the chances to grab snacks from the roving food trolley, and to solicit other passengers for recommendations.

Over the next eight hours, egret-stalked inlets, paddy-ringed villages and motorcycle-filled townships buzzed by, frozen into cinematic frames by the train windows.

Finally, shuttered houses closed in around the railway tracks and we clattered into the 1980s communist-utilitarian block that is Saigon Station.

Later, sipping iced *caphe* (coffee) surrounded by Saigon's French-era shophouses, I mulled over my 1072-mile (1726km) journey on Vietnam's mainline. From 1954 to 1976, this vital conduit was severed by conflict, but today it brings north and south Vietnamese together like a shared blood supply. The trip from Hanoi to Saigon would never be as symbolic – or as enjoyable – by road or by air. **JB**

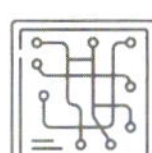

Start/Finish // Hanoi/Ho Chi Minh City (Saigon)
Distance // 1072 miles (1726km)
Duration // From 32hr
Ticket types // Hard Seat (wooden benches); Soft Seat (airline-style seating, air-con); Hard Sleeper (six-berth compartments); Soft Sleeper (four-berth air-con compartments); Livitrans, Violette, Lotus (all luxury private berths).
How to book // Booking through third-party sites like 12GoAsia (12go.asia/en) and Baolau (baolau.com) is easier than using the Vietnamese Railways site (dsvn.vn).
When to go // February to May, for lower humidity, drier skies and better views.
Things to know // Some trains have dining cars serving simple meals; others have roaming trolleys.
More info // Visit Vietnam (vietnam.travel).

Opposite top: Rice paddies outside the mountain town of Sapa. Opposite bottom: hectic Ho Chi Minh City, starting point for many an adventure

MORE LIKE THIS
VIETNAM'S BEST TRAIN RIDES

DALAT TO TRAI MAT

Short but as sweet as a cup of Vietnamese *caphe*, the train ride from Dalat to the village of Trai Mat oozes French-Indochina vibes. A locomotive resembling a model train tows a few tiny belle époque–style carriages for the 4.3-mile (7km) trip through a landscape of chalet-like villas, flower nurseries and polytunnel-covered fruit and vegetable gardens. Before the return journey, you'll have time to wander around Trai Mat village, dropping into Linh Phuoc pagoda, a mosaic-covered marvel dripping with porcelain dragons and tiered spires. As you rattle back to Dalat, consider the engineering nous required to construct this mountain railway; in the 1930s, the landscape was tangled with dense jungle.

Start // Dalat
Finish // Trai Mat
Distance // 4.3 miles (7km)
Duration // 30min

HANOI TO LAO CAI & SAPA TO FANSIPAN

We're cheating a little, as the journey from Hanoi to Vietnam's highest mountain involves one stage by road, but the trip takes in some of the country's most spectacular scenery. Step one is to board the express train from Hanoi to Lao Cai – most people go overnight but we recommend the morning train for uplifting views of country villages, waterlogged rice paddies and cocoa-brown rivers before the mountains pop up on the skyline. From Lao Cai, it's a one-hour minivan ride to Sapa, the hub of the highlands, where you can board the diminutive cog railway to reach Hoang Lien, connecting with the cable car to the 10,325ft (3147m) summit of Fansipan. En route, you'll be lifted high above the landscape on steel rails and cables, soaring past dizzying views of villages dwarfed by misty, forest-girdled mountains.

Start // Hanoi
Finish // Fansipan
Distance // 213 miles (343km)
Duration // 1 day

HO CHI MINH CITY TO PHAN THIET

Not everyone has time to go epic on the Reunification Express; for a quick taste of Vietnam's railways, consider the 116-mile (187km) trip from HCMC to the port city of Phan Thiet. As the line enters Binh Thuan Province, it slips into a fantasy landscape of dragon-fruit plantations, where endless lines of drooping cacti are tipped by the red, almost reptilian fruit from April to October. At Phan Thiet, you can drop in on a temple dedicated to the spirits of whales, visit Vietnam's largest Buddha atop Ta Cu Mountain or take a boat to the French-built lighthouse at Ke Ga, before hanging a 360 back to HCMC. To extend the ride, change trains at Binh Thuan on the return leg and roll north on the Reunification line to Nha Trang.

Start // HCMC
Finish // Phan Thiet
Distance // 116 miles (187km)
Duration // 4-5hr

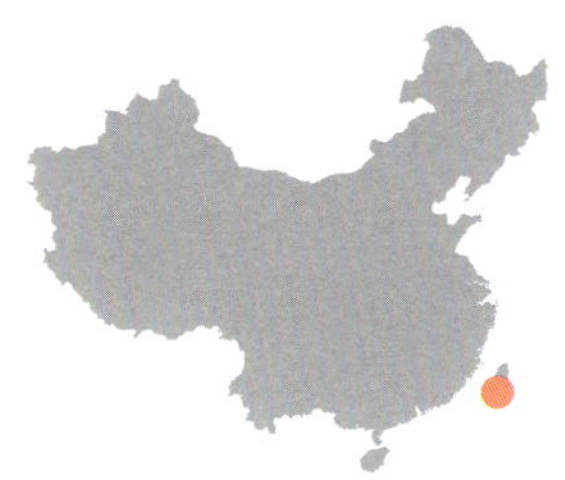

OUT OF THE WOODS ON THE ALISHAN FOREST RAILWAY

This century-old railway – Asia's longest narrow-gauge track – links the island's coast to its central mountains, offering engineering ingenuity, diverse ecology and history galore.

My aunt grew up on a tea estate on the way up Alishan mountain, and for years I used to visit her and her family there. Sometimes, it was difficult to get there because typhoons and earthquakes damaged sections of the railway, but I always made it, even if it meant swapping the train for a local bus. The visits ended up meaning more to me than I realised at the time.

On this June day, I'm taking my family up Alishan. After a 14-year closure, the railway's last section has reopened, so we can enjoy the entire line. I want to recreate my favourite memory here – boarding a packed train at Taiwan's largest wooden rail station in the Alishan National Forest Recreation Area to watch the sunrise. We'd start at 98ft (30m) above sea level in Chiayi and take the train for three hours to Alishan Station at 7270ft (2216m). At Alishan, we need to stop, get a hotel and rise early for another train at 4.20am for a half-hour journey to Zhushan, the highest rail station in Taiwan. Here we would witness the first rays of dawn.

On the train up, there's a running commentary, detailing the line's sixteen stations. Most of the passengers – retirees, families with children, groups of tourists and hikers – board at Chiayi and

alight at Fenqihu, best known for its bento boxes. We're assigned seats, but my partner moves between both sides of the train to get the best view. My daughter points at the tea fields out the window.

We get off and eat lunch at Shizilu where Wei-yang Huang, a fourth generation-wasabi farmer, makes us bentos filled with braised pork-knuckle, local bamboo shoots and mountain ferns. I watch the conductor carry his bento back on board, while my four-year-old plays with Mrs Huang's daughter.

While we wait for the next train, another local, Yu-Tao Pan, invites us to her home, where her family operates a timber transport company. The house is made of wood and is set next to the station.

'They used to carry the cypress logs over their shoulders. We'd help load them onto the trains,' she tells me. She's been here since 1948, and I can only imagine the hardship she and the loggers had to endure back then.

Since the entire railway reopened in 2024, the train's red engine has been pushing its five air-conditioned cars and 124 passengers uphill through a mosaic of ecosystems – tropical, subtropical and temperate climate zones. Near the peak, where it reaches its steepest gradient, the train moves in a Z-shape. The Taiwanese refer to this section as 'Alishan hits the wall.' My daughter thinks the whole thing is an amusement park ride.

Built in 1912 when the island was under Japanese rule, the railway transported timber to build Tokyo's Yasukuni Shrine. When the line returned to the Taiwanese after WWII, the route was gradually transformed into a tourist service to prevent any further deforestation of the now-endangered Taiwanese cypress. With angel's tear flowers brushing up against the carriages, cypress trees lining the tracks and the sharp S-curve turns unfurling, we find ourselves thankful for the foresight that protected this area. At the top, we take the cheapest hotel we can find – the historic Alishan Hotel being beyond our budget.

After a short night's rest, it's back on a train from Alishan Station to Zhushan for sunrise. In the darkness, there's a sense of hope and determination from the other passengers, most of whom plan to hike back. We alight in a blanket of mist and walk briskly to the viewing platform.

On arrival, we enter a scene from a Chinese scroll painting. The wait to see the sun seems like an eternity for my daughter, so I distract her with soy milk and *shao bing*, a traditional Taiwanese flatbread. The waves of clouds finally open up and their white brushstrokes across the various blues in the sky justify the early wake-up call. The sunrise reminds me of my last visit to the park with my aunt and father when he was still alive.

Later that day, we descend to Chiayi. The sound of ferns brushing against the train windows against a rhythmic click-clack

SUNRISE AT ZHUSHAN

Zhushan Station is Taiwan's highest at 8041ft (2451m), forms part of the highest track ever built by the Taiwanese and is the only part of the line that was built for tourism. Newly re-opened at the end of 2023, its crescent-shaped platform is based on the station's original design and is perfect for viewing the sunrise. Hiking and biking trails lead from the station to the rest of the park.

From left: Alishan Station; crowds gather to watch the sunrise; vistas of the Alishan National Forest; a tea plantation near Chiayi. Previous page: A diesel locomotive on the narrow-gauge line.

lulls my daughter to sleep. The engine is now towing us downhill. On the right, more cypress trees rise above us, while valleys of tea and betel nut trees – planted to prevent landslides – appear below.

The train suddenly slows, and we hear the conductor instructing the driver to look out for people close to the tracks. This group rushes on board at Doulin and fills our carriage until the next stop. We pass through tunnels, spiral around Dulishan mountain and then the train screeches to a stop for a second time – rocks have fallen onto the track and the driver must clear them.

We're now close to sea level and the altitude change makes itself known when my water bottle explodes. Typical farm life appears near Beimen Station – white-tiled buildings with Mediterranean-style roofs, a family's laundry next to the track and a moped parked in winter melon, garlic and lychee fields. Folk songs play over the loudspeaker.

We reach Chiayi and pull up alongside modern locomotives that travel the Taiwanese coast. Waving goodbye to the conductor, we've ended our trip. I feel lucky to have shared this journey with my family, one that I did many times in my youth. Though I trained as a scientist, I was always drawn back to my aunt's tea farm on Alishan mountain – so much so that I started a tea company and now own my very own farm. **CJL**

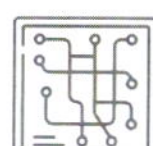

Start/Finish // TRA Chiayi Station (not to be confused with the THSR Chiayi Station)/Alishan Station
Distance // 44.5 miles (72km)
Duration // 3hr
Ticket types // One class of service. Children five and under travel for free but do not get a seat.
How to book // Book on the Alishan Forest Railway and Cultural Heritage Office website (afrch.forest.gov.tw/En). Tickets are available 14 days in advance. They can be purchased online but must be exchanged at the Alishan Forest Railway ticket window in the TRA Chiayi station.
When to go // Late spring or early autumn to avoid peak tourism and typhoons. March to May for cherry blossom.
Things to know // One train departs daily at 9am. Additional trains also run at 8.30am and 9.30am to cater to crowds on the weekend.

Opposite top: Playing on the track of the Pingxi Line. Opposite below: Colourful interiors on the Jiji Line.

MORE LIKE THIS
OTHER TAIWAN TRAIN TRIPS

PINGXI LINE

A former coal-mining route during the Japanese colonial era, the seven-station Pingxi Line runs through Taiwan's northern mountains along the Keelung River into deep valleys of conifers, ferns and waterfalls. With a maximum of four carriages, this diesel-powered, air-conditioned narrow-gauge tourist train with bench-style seating stops at Shifen, where passengers can release a fire-lit lantern – once used as safety signal – and view Taiwan's 'Niagara Falls', a mini curtain-style cascade. It terminates at Jingtong, a city decorated with written prayers on hanging bamboo sticks. No reservations are required.
Start // Ruifang
Finish // Jingtong
Distance // 8 miles (13km)
Duration // 55min

EAST COAST LANDSCAPES

Modern, spotless air-conditioned local services as well as express trains operate on this route, taking in mountainous terrain, rocky cliffs and gorgeous coastal views after leaving Taipei's high-rises. Part of the Taiwanese east coast railway, the train is usually filled with families, businesspeople, tourists and commuters. Heading south, the coast is on the left side, while steep slopes and possible landslides are on the right. Beyond the mountains, scallion farms fill vast open fields around Yilan, where you can surf on the volcanic-ash shores of Wai'ao Beach, or relax in a hot spring. At Hualien, continue your journey to Taroko National Park via bus, taxi or scooter. Within the city, remains of a narrow-gauge railway sit among former Japanese administrative offices at the Hualien Railway Culture Park. Advance reservations are recommended; Business and Standard seat classes are available; traditional Taiwanese bentos are sold at meal times, while at other times, there's a food trolley.
Start // Taipei
Finish // Hualien
Distance // 120 miles (194 km)
Duration // 2hr hours 22min (Puyuma Express or Taroko Express); 3hr 17min (local train)

JIJI LINE

Once used to build a hydroelectric dam in Sun Moon Lake, this single-track, narrow-gauge line was the first Taiwanese tourist railway. The diesel-powered, air-conditioned carriages run through central Taiwan into the island's largest tea-producing county, Nantou. Passing through pineapple, banana, dragon fruit and tea farms, the four-carriage Jiji Line is well-known among domestic tourists, while locals use it to get into town. The line's terminus is home to Taiwan's first hydroelectric plant and the Checheng Wood Museum. At Jiji Station, a restored Japanese-style station and the ruins of the original Jiji Wuchang Temple, which collapsed during a 1999 earthquake, are worth visiting. Engineering works are underway to repair the 83-year-old route, due to fully re-open in December 2025. The train runs every two hours, so planning is required. No advance ticket purchase is necessary.
Start // Ershui
Finish // Checheng
Distance // 18.5 miles (30km)
Duration // 1hr 5min

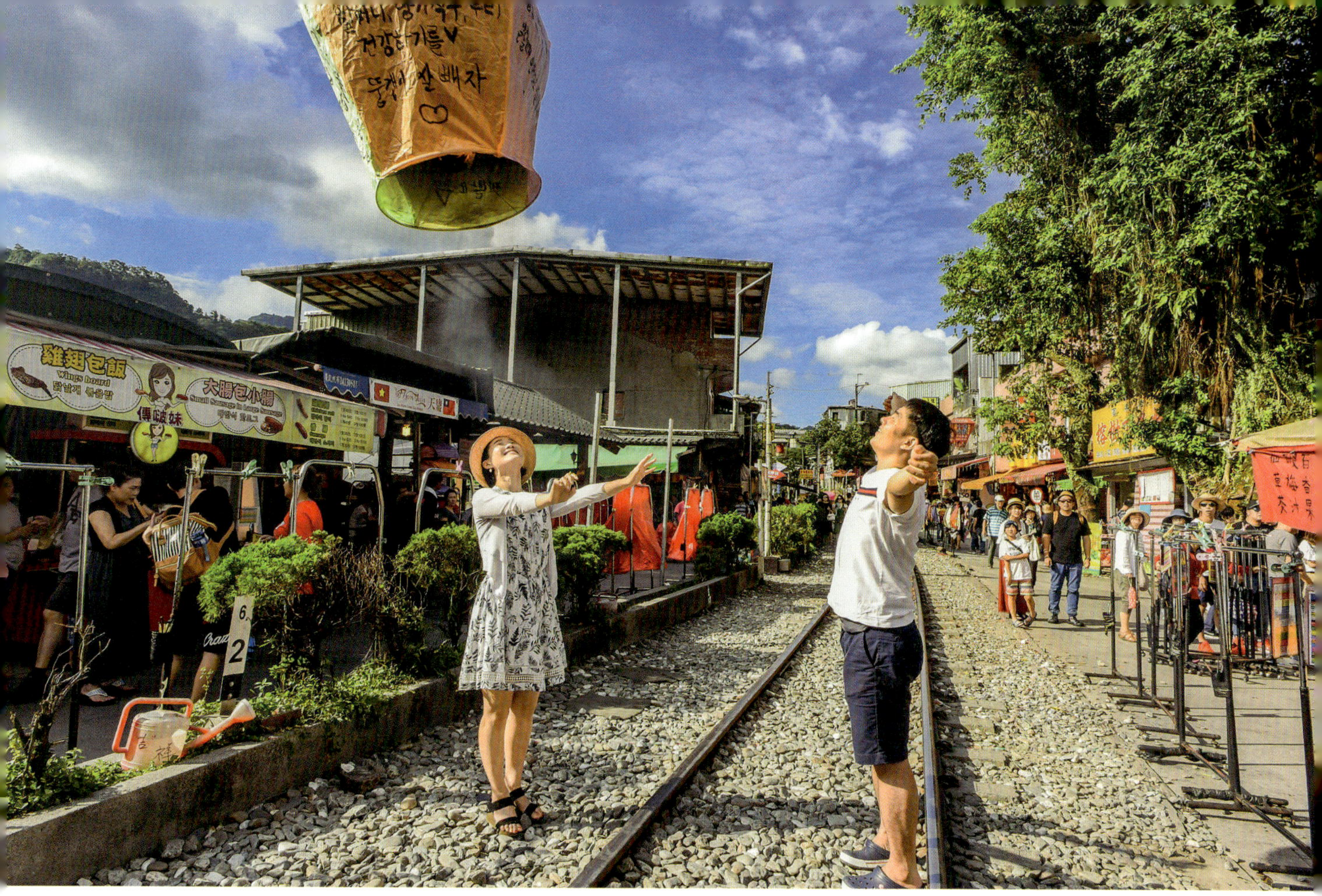

雞翅包飯
大腸包小腸

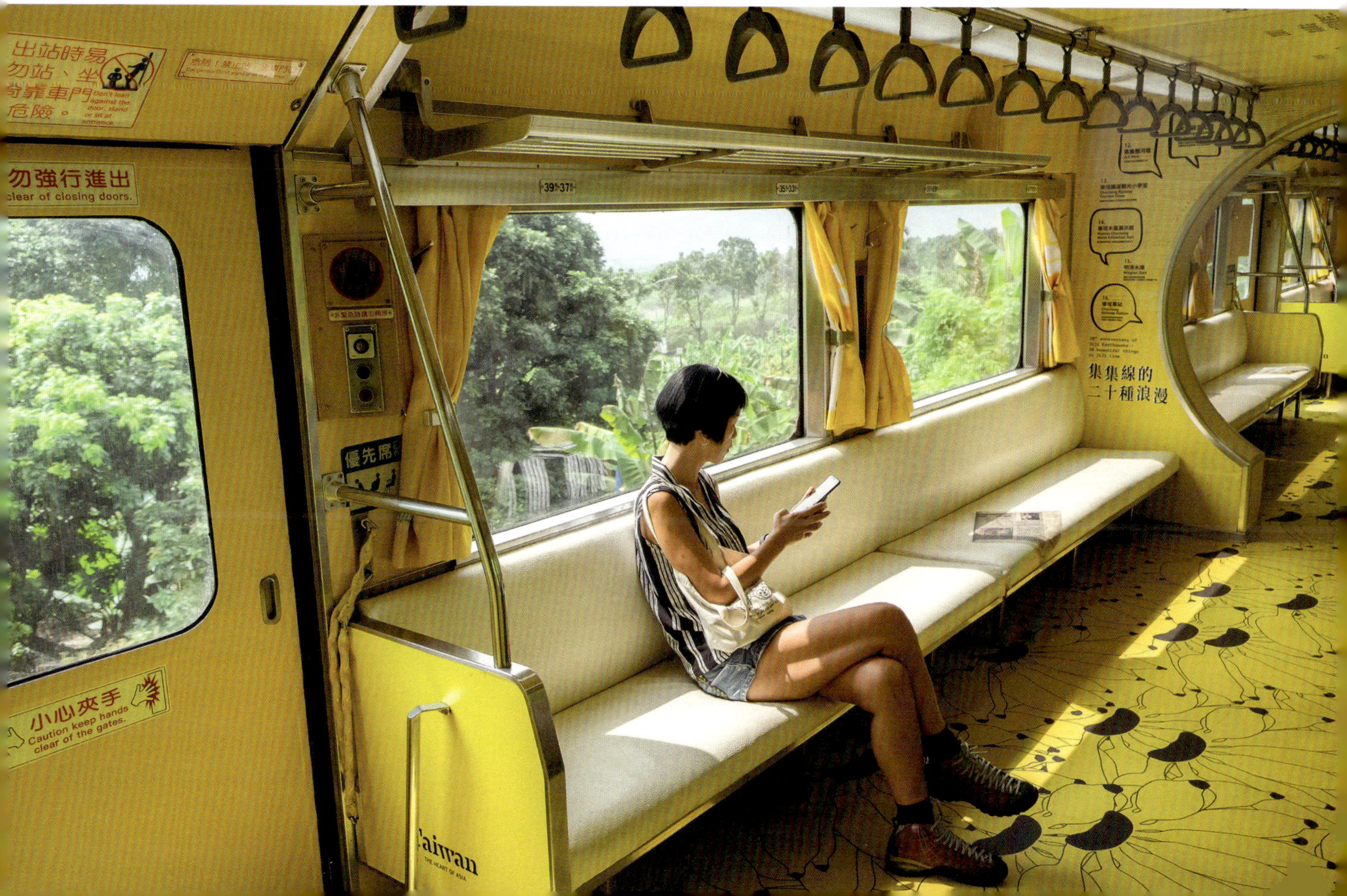

出站時易
勿站、坐
倚靠車門
危險。
勿強行進出
clear of closing doors.
優先席
集集線的
二十種浪漫
小心夾手
Caution keep hands
clear of the gates.

BITE THE BULLET ON THE TŌKAIDŌ SHINKANSEN

The iconic Tokaido Shinkansen, the world's first high-speed train, still impresses six decades on, providing a top-tier travel experience – and even a Mt Fuji cameo.

The Tōkaidō Shinkansen glides in and out of Tokyo Station with a precision that both fascinates and terrifies. It's been two decades since I took my first ride – the first of many – and it still leaves me in awe. Here, trains famously stop for just 12 regimented minutes – passengers have two minutes to disembark, after which a swift-footed cleaning crew has seven to sweep the whole train of 16 cars, readying it for the return journey. That leaves just three minutes for everyone – hundreds of people – to board, filing on in neat columns that form and reform like clockwork on either side of the doors. It's a mesmerising sight, with hypnotic rhythms not unlike another one of Japan's accidental tourist attractions: the iconic Shibuya Crossing intersection.

There are now eight Shinkansen routes (not including a handful of branch lines), plus extensions in the works; the Tōkaidō Shinkansen, however, remains the most popular. It's the one most people ride for the first time, as it travels to four out of five of Japan's largest cities: Tokyo, Yokohama, Nagoya and Osaka. Former imperial capital and popular tourist destination Kyoto is also a stop en route. There are three different services: the fastest, called Nozomi, does the trip in just under two-and-a-half hours. Before the Shinkansen, it took six hours to travel by train between Tokyo and Osaka, a distance roughly the same as London to Amsterdam, or Philadelphia to Boston. The other services, Hikari and Kodama, reach the same peak speed – 177mph (285km/h) – but take longer because they make additional stops.

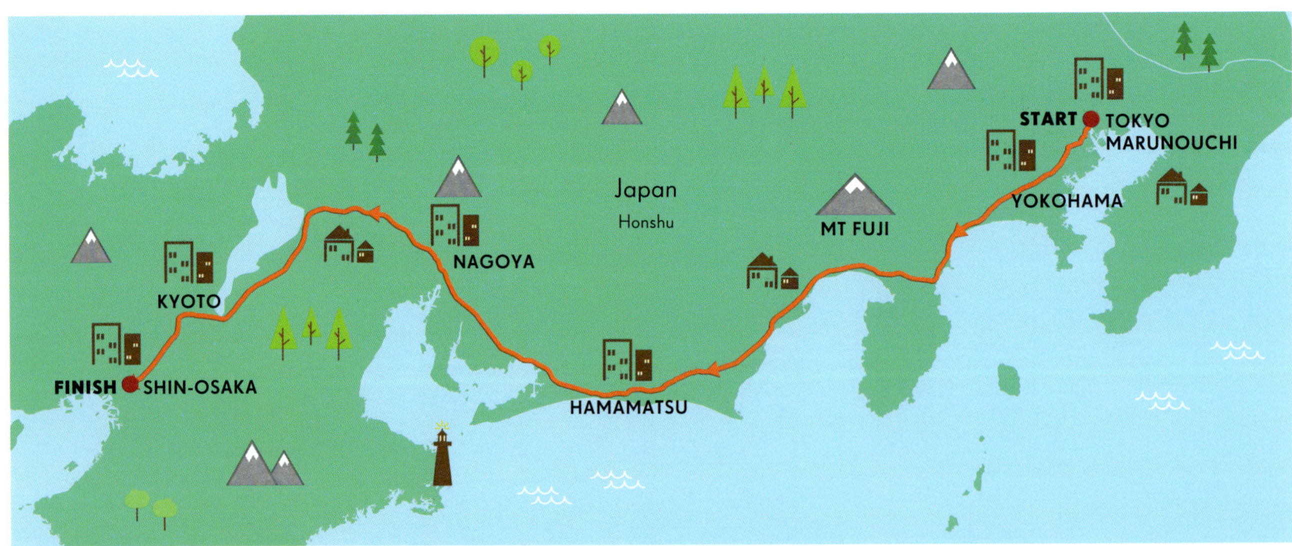

"This Shinkansen traverses one of the most densely populated urban corridors in the world, a near-contiguous metro area on Japan's Pacific coast that is home to roughly 65 million people..."

Regular riders – business travellers, for example, who use the Tōkaidō Shinkansen for day trips between branch offices – tap in and out of the automatic ticket gates like they're riding the subway. First-timers, however, should give themselves plenty of time to navigate Tokyo Station, which is one of the city's biggest and busiest, because the train will leave on time, whether you're on board or not (never mind that seat reservation). The ideal time to head to the platform is 10–15 minutes before departure, which gives you enough breathing room to comfortably find the correct spot on the platform to queue, but not so early that you're in the way, disrupting the natural flow of people.

As soon as the door closes – and maybe even before you've found your seat – the Shinkansen starts to accelerate swiftly. Not that you notice, really; that's how smooth the ride is. Tokyo Station, built in 1914, is smack in the middle of the capital, in the Marunouchi business district, and the Tōkaidō cruises on elevated tracks between skyscrapers, past housing complexes and alongside the metropolitan expressway. I love seeing the city from this vantage point. With a keen eye, I can pick out the details that define urban life in Japan: futons airing from residential balconies, pocket-sized parks, bus depots and high-school baseball fields enclosed in netting.

After Tokyo Station, the next stop is Shinagawa, also in Tokyo, followed by Shin-Yokohama, the station for Yokohama. It takes just 18 minutes to travel between the capital, Japan's largest city, and Yokohama, its second largest – were it not for the stations, however, you'd hardly know you'd left one city and entered another. The Tōkaidō Shinkansen traverses one of the most densely populated urban corridors in the world, a near-contiguous metro area on Japan's Pacific coast that is home to roughly 65 million people – or more than half the country's population. Trains depart approximately every five minutes (or every three minutes during peak hours), moving hundreds of thousands of people every day. If you think of this stretch as one giant megalopolis, then the Shinkansen is like its sophisticated, well-run metro.

This is not a scenic journey in the conventional sense. While the train runs near the coast, there are only a few glimpses of the water. Nor are there the kind of rural vistas that you get on the Tōhoku Shinkansen. What you do get, however, is a sense of Japan's built space. Past Yokohama, the landscape gradually shifts to the suburban: two-storey

EATING ETIQUETTE

While eating on public transportation in Japan is generally a no-no, dining on board the Shinkansen is a time-honoured custom. All Shinkansen stations have shops selling *ekiben* – a bento (boxed meal) from the train station ('eki') – packed neatly with chopsticks and a wet napkin. Look out for ones with local specialties; or get one in a souvenir container shaped like the iconic train.

Clockwise from top: Shinkansen services passing through Ginza, Tokyo; an N700 series train; a Shinkansen bento box. Previous page: Passing under Mt Fuji.

homes with slate-coloured roofs, modest allotments, planned 'new towns', hilltop mansions, shopping centres and shipping warehouses. There's some exurban – small factories and farms – too, and a lot of tunnels: about 15% of the route is tunnels, particularly notable in the stretch between Odawara and Mishima (stops on the slower Kodama service), where the Tōkaidō Shinkansen runs through mountains just outside of Fuji–Izu–Hakone National Park.

Just as it all starts to feel a bit same-y, the train rounds a bend and I glimpse the journey's majestic highlight – Mt Fuji, appearing on the right-hand side about 45 minutes into the trip, around Shin-Fuji Station. It's a spectacular view – if it's not cloudy – of not just the snowy crown but of the whole majestic cone rising abruptly from an alluvial plain. It's a thrilling, classic moment, two beloved symbols of Japan, the Shinkansen and Mt Fuji, together.

On the Nozomi service, the train won't stop again until Nagoya (Japan's third-largest city) – where it pauses for just one minute to let passengers off and on – followed by Kyoto and Shin-Osaka. The Shinkansen stations in Kyoto and Nagoya are centrally located, which means you get a (brief) look at these cities before the final stop, to the north of Osaka proper. I always know when I'm nearing the end of the line because the remaining passengers start gathering their belongings, knowing they and I have mere minutes to disembark before the magic starts again. **RM**

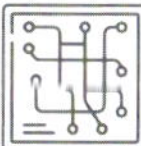

Start/Finish // Tokyo Station/Shin-Osaka Station
Distance // 320 miles (515km)
Duration // 2hr 22min (fastest service)
Maximum speed // 177mph (285km/h)
Ticket types // There are two classes, Standard and Green, which is akin to Business Class with bigger seats and onboard refreshment service.
How to book // Use the dedicated Smart Ex app or reserve in person at counters or via vending machines at major Japan Rail train stations in Tokyo and elsewhere.
Things to know // For Mt Fuji views, book window seat E (on the right-hand side) when travelling from Tokyo to Shin-Osaka.
Tip // Pay a little extra to reserve a seat; you also need to reserve space for large luggage.

Opposite top: Open-air carriages are a hallmark of the Sagano Scenic Railway. Opposite below: Autumn colours on the Kurobe Gorge Railway.

MORE LIKE THIS
JAPAN ON THE RAILS

THE HIDA

If you want to shift down a gear from the Shinkansen services and really take in the scenery, there's an equally stellar array of local trains. One example is the Hida – a limited express, meaning it's no slow coach, but neither is it going at super-fast speeds either. This classic route departs the megacity of Nagoya and makes its way north through the Japanese Alps, bisecting the island of Honshu and connecting the Pacific at Ise Bay with the Sea of Japan at Toyama Bay. Departing Nagoya's huge station (the tallest in the world), you begin by gliding north to Gifu. The landscape turns more rural, with forested hills rising as you trace the Hida River upstream past onsen (hot springs). On the last leg, the hills lapse into coastal plains and rice fields. As well as the views, the slick new trains themselves are part of the appeal.
Start // Nagoya
Finish // Toyama
Distance // 159 miles (256km)
Duration // 4hr

KUROBE GORGE RAILWAY

If the Hida whets your appetite for journeys through Japan's mountainous heart, Toyama Prefecture offers another glorious line in the form of the Kurobe Gorge Railway. Ride mainline trains to Unazuki Onsen to change for this tiny narrow-gauge line that scrambles its way through a correspondingly narrow gorge – soon you'll be climbing uphill in little open carriages that have a whiff of a fairground ride, switching back and forth over the course of the Kurobe River on bright red bridges. You'll also spot dams – the line was in fact built in the 1920s by the Kansai Electric Power Company to supply the Kurobe Dam, but has had a deluge of admiring passengers since being reinvented for tourists in the 1950s. The trip ends at Keyakidaira, where you can stew in nearby onsen.
Start // Unazuki
Finish // Keyakidaira
Distance // 12 miles (20km)
Duration // 1hr 20min

SAGANO SCENIC RAILWAY

Those craving respite from the bustle of Kyoto can find an escape in the form of the Sagano Scenic Railway – its rolling stock seductively known as the Sagano Romantic Train. It is indeed a railway that sets hearts fluttering when first glimpsed at Torokko Saga Station – where you might also fall for the vintage steam engines and a vast model railway. The diesel engine hauls old freight cars adapted for people, one of which is open-air, meaning passengers feel closer to nature as they trundle out of the former capital, tracking the Hozu River's twists and turns, terminating where the valleys open out in Kameoka. It's a line with different moods depending on the season, though it's most synonymous with autumn, when a thousand maple trees blaze red along the route.
Start // Torokko Saga
Finish // Torokko Kameoka
Distance // 5 miles (7km)
Duration // 25min

BANGKOK TO SINGAPORE: AN INTERNATIONAL ODYSSEY

Linking three of Asia's most captivating capitals, the train ride from Bangkok to Singapore offers a sampling platter of cultures and cuisines.

To qualify as truly epic, a train trip needs to start in one country and finish in another, taking in plural cultures along the way. It should last for days, connecting some of the world's most fabulous cities, creating a transect through a continent. With the 1200-mile (1900km) trip from Bangkok to Singapore, I definitely had a winner.

My first ride on this overland epic was during a stopover from London to Australia. Pausing in Bangkok and continuing from Singapore added nothing to the airfare, providing a chance to visit three bustling Asian capitals for the negligible investment of an extra week tacked onto my itinerary.

A few decades and several life milestones later, I decided to revisit the Bangkok to Singapore run to see what had changed, loosely following the route – though not the lifestyle – of passengers on the original Eastern & Oriental Express. My train snack shopping was a case in point: in the absence of silver service dining, I grabbed packs of larb-flavoured pretzels, cans of grass-jelly drink and a kilo of rambutans.

The favoured train for the Thailand-Malaysia leg is the overnight Special Express 45, which covers the 495 miles (797km) between Bangkok and Padang Besar in 16 hours, but there are ample opportunities to break the journey along the isthmus.

I was lucky enough to take the train from the mock-Renaissance terminus at Hua Lamphong, with its glazed archway and cheerful Dairy Queen franchise. Soon after, long-distance trains moved to the anodyne, airport terminal-style Krung Thep Aphiwat Central Terminal, shaving away a little of the charm.

Exiting Bangkok through a hazy cityscape punctuated by Buddhist temple rooftops, I was pleased to discover that little had

HKN

changed on the Special Express. Carriages still retained their chrome-edged Formica interiors – like the cabin of a 1960s airliner or a vintage barber's chair.

I wanted to cover some distance, so I skipped stops at Nakhon Pathom, with its 417ft (127m) high stupa, and the beach town of Hua Hin. This allowed time for a potently spicy Thai green curry supper, but not a full night's sleep. Creaking into Phun Phin in the wee hours, I checked into a Surat Thani hotel to make up the missing Zs.

A 48-hour stop was time enough for a fleeting trip by bus and boat to Ko Samui, whose castaway charms had been eroded – though not irrevocably – by a surge of resort development. But I was there as much for the seafood (swimmer crabs, giant prawns as fat as your wrist) as for the sand and surf.

I reboarded the Special Express early in the morning for the run to the Malaysian border. As the morning sun displaced the pre-dawn grey, we rolled into Hat Yai, once a busy hub for backpackers making the visa run to Malaysia, but now quieter because of rebel violence in Thailand's restive south.

We loitered lazily in the station while the train was divided, with half the carriages continuing to Padang Besar, and half turning east towards the less used border crossing at Sungai Kolok.

Easing back into motion with a jolt, the train rattled on past waterlogged rice fields and small villages with minarets poking up above the rooftops. There was a tangible cultural shift on board too, as the ethnic balance tipped towards Peranakan Chinese businessmen, Malay women in coloured headscarves and devout Kedah Muslim families immaculately dressed in white and black.

At Padang Besar – a mere blip of a town straddling the Thai-Malay border – immigration and customs procedures were handled efficiently on the platform, and I boarded a smartly modern Malaysian KTM Komuter train for the hour-long ride to Alor Setar.

Why stop at this sleepy backwater? Well, there's a grand mosque, a royal palace and some great food, fusing Thai and Malay flavours with Indian undertones. It's also a handy place to change to the KTM ETS train to Ipoh, one of Malaysia's most charming colonial-era outposts.

Disembarking at Ipoh's vintage train station, opened to great fanfare in 1917, I could immediately sense the British influence, but I was more focused on food – firstly the curries served on banana leaves in Ipoh's historic Indian quarter then the lip-smacking Chinese-style *tauge ayam* (chicken with beansprouts) doled out along Jalan Yau Tet Shin.

THE RAILWAY BUILT BY TIN

If you stop in Ipoh or Kuala Lumpur on the way south from Bangkok to Singapore, you'll be treading in the footsteps of the 19th-century tin miners. Both cities were jungle outposts before the British Empire constructed railway lines along the peninsula to transport this precious metal to the coast. Ipoh's Ipoh World museum has some interesting displays on Malaysia's tin-mining history.

From left: A street scene in Bangkok; Singapore's Gardens by the Bay; street food at Jalan Alor in Kuala Lumpur. Previous page: The old terminal of Hua Lamphong in Bangkok.

The journey on to Kuala Lumpur passed in a blur of conversations with Malay students, delving into culture, politics (British, not Malaysian) and religion (largely me explaining my lack of personal faith). Outside, the odd modernist mosque or dragon-topped Chinese temple caught my attention amid the trackside greenery.

Malaysia's multicultural capital has its own vintage train station – an Indo-Saracenic gem from 1910 – but I disembarked at the blandly functional KL Sentral Station for a day and night of mall shopping, architecture admiring and street food grazing (reassuringly, my favourite clay pot chicken stand was still in business).

The final run on to Singapore was much more complicated than it used to be. Singapore's elegant art deco railway station closed in 2011 and the modern journey from KL involves a train change in Gemas, then a shuttle train, bus or taxi from Johor Bahru across the causeway to Singapore.

Despite the slightly unsatisfying mode of arrival, it was a thrill to end the trip in the world's last fully functioning city-state. It's said the world gets smaller as you age, but travelling long-distance by train pops the globe back out to its proper dimensions. The trip from Bangkok to Singapore felt every inch of its 1200 miles, infused with the spirit of three nations, half a dozen cultures and one satisfied travel writer! **JB**

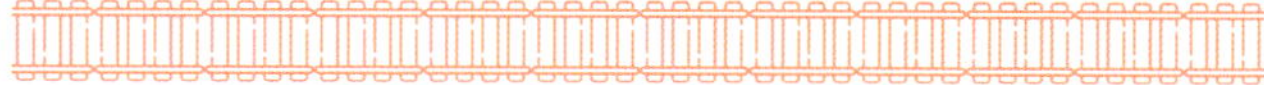

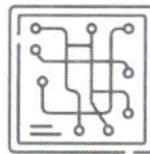

Start/Finish // Bangkok / Singapore
Distance // 1200 miles (1900km)
Duration // From 48 hours
Ticket types // Second Class sleeper Bangkok to Padang Besar; Standard or Second Class seats on KTM Komuter, ETS and EKS trains.
How to book // Each section of the route needs to be booked separately. Book through third-party sites such as 12GoAsia (12go.asia/en).
When to go // November to April
Things to know // Special Express 45 and Special Express 37 are linked as far as Hat Yai – make sure you're in the right half of the train when they separate!
More info // Man in Seat 61 (seat61.com/malaysia.htm)

Opposite top: The Korean coast at Gangneung. Opposite below: The great temple of Borobudur, not far from Yogyakarta on Java.

MORE LIKE THIS
UNSUNG ASIAN TRAIN RIDES

KHYBER MAIL

Despite once being part of Asia's most celebrated rail network, Pakistan lies off the radar for many rail enthusiasts. After Partition, India's railways expanded, while Pakistan's slowly declined, but there are still some thrilling Pakistani train rides and the Khyber Mail is one of the best. Punching from the capital to rugged Khyber Pakhtunkhwa province, this desert line hopscotches between Pakistan's greatest cities, offering a fascinating overview of the nation's richly layered history. Leaving Karachi at 10pm, you'll get a full day of views over increasingly arid landscapes as the train rattles north to Lahore, then it's on through the night to Peshawar, arriving just as dawn breaks over the Hindu Kush. Recommended stops include Multan, with its magnificent mausoleums, Lahore, with its mighty Mughal monuments, and energetic Rawalpindi, with its tangled, timeless bazaars.

Start // Karachi
Finish // Peshawar
Distance // 1096 miles (1764km)
Duration // 32 hr

SEOUL TO GANGNEUNG

High-speed trains crisscross South Korea, linking futuristic megacity to futuristic megacity, but smaller branch lines serve up some of the best scenery. Cutting east across the peninsula, the journey from Seoul to Gangneung will whisk you away from the urban sprawl to peaceful countryside, with the promise of a day on the beach before you zoom back to the capital. Starting off among Seoul's high-rises and *Blade Runner*-esque neon billboards, you'll whoosh east at 300kmph in a bullet train styled after Japan's legendary Shinkansen. It's a memorable way to appreciate the scenery, with sweeping views over farmland and rugged mountains in Gangwon-do Province. When you arrive in Gangneung, you can dip your toes in the East Sea or surf on beaches that bring a touch of Honolulu to the Korean coast.

Start // Seoul
Finish // Gangneung
Distance // 142 miles (229km)
Duration // 2 hr

JAVA MAIN LINE

Dutch engineers built Java's main line railway to feed the colonial machine with cane sugar and palm oil, but it outlasted both the Dutch Empire and the Japanese occupation. Today, the train trip from Jakarta to Yogyakarta offers a perfect vantage point for admiring the green, serene scenery in between Java's frenetic urban hubs. Just remember to pack warm clothes to combat the icy air-conditioning! En route from the capital to cultured Yogyakarta, you'll pass through an emerald wonderland of palm and banana-edged rice fields, broken up by scattered villages and towns and hazy hills. A few hours in, Bandung is a worthy stop for a day hike up the Tangkuban Perahu volcano, before you continue to Yogyakarta's museums and sultanate-era monuments.

Start // Jakarta
Finish // Surabaya
Distance // 116 miles (187km)
Duration // 4–5 hr

EUROPE

A HIGHLAND FLING ON THE CALEDONIAN SLEEPER

Britain's most celebrated train journey straddles two countries and two different landscapes, ushering passengers from the traffic-thronged English capital to the glorious Scottish Highlands.

In a city of spectacular stations, London Euston is by far the most disappointing.

St Pancras is a neogothic fantasia; Paddington has its famous bear and its undulating roof; Kings Cross has its Harry Potter fame. Meanwhile Euston looks like a multi-storey car park: a huge, shapeless dollop of concrete, packed chiefly with humdrum commuter trains. Look hard within their midst, however, and you'll find a train like no other in Britain. A little longer and more dapper than its companions, it's emblazoned with the motif of a proud stag, indicating that it is the monarch of the platforms. This is the Caledonian Sleeper, leaving Euston each evening to connect the capital with various points across Scotland. In a single snooze, passengers can be transported from the centre of one of Europe's biggest cities to some of the continent's most sparsely inhabited regions – straight from the rush hour rat race to the realm of rutting stags, from London grit and grime to pure Highland air. I have boarded the Caledonian Sleeper at Euston many times, and every time it is with an accompanying frisson of anticipation and excitement, knowing that when I next disembark I will be in another country, and in some senses another world entirely.

Look at the route map of the Caledonian Sleeper. It's vaguely like a flower in form – the stem rises from London, then forks into branches where carriages detach to serve different Scottish destinations. The shortest branches reach the cities of Edinburgh and Glasgow in the country's densely populated Central Belt; two more branches stretch northeast, serving both the Highland capital of Inverness and the oil capital of Aberdeen. The most celebrated variant of the

023

"I drop my bags and dash to the club car to grab a precious seat and to savour the uncommon thrill of a dining car on a British train."

Caledonian Sleeper, however, is the so-called 'Deerstalker' – that service which glides out of Euston, through Glasgow, and on into the West Highlands, navigating a succession of glens to Fort William, where the sea laps at heathery mountains. The promise of all this stirring scenery is at the forefront of my mind as the Deerstalker nudges out of London and into the gathering night.

On midsummer departures there is sometimes enough residual light to get a sense of the world outside the train – the Camden Roundhouse perhaps, or the twilit rise of the Chiltern Hills. But on my journey it is pitch black outside, and so the focus of attention is the train itself. Staff with tartan ties tactfully steer passengers to comfortable compartments with simple bunk beds, where Scottish confectionery is neatly placed on the pillows. But experienced sleeper passengers, me included, know there is no time to linger in your accommodation – I drop my bags and dash to the club car to grab a precious seat and to savour the uncommon thrill of a dining car on a British train.

It is here I am happiest – many passengers get an appetiser of Scotland in the form of starters of Scottish trout pâté or mains of haggis, neeps (turnip) and tatties (potato) in a whisky sauce. But my favourite thing to plunder is the whisky menu – the Caledonian Sleeper stocks no less than seven distinguished single malts – a peaty prelude for the whisky-fuelled nights that await north of the border. They provide perfect sipping as the nightscapes of England flash past – the industrial estates of Milton Keynes, the moonlit canals of the West Midlands. When I stumble back to my compartment, the rocking motion of the train on the tracks is hard to tell apart from the aftereffects of my nightcaps.

As sleep comes, I'm only dimly aware of the goings on of the railway around me: briefly woken as the train idles for a moment in a midnight siding; gently disturbed by other small-hours wanderers of the rails. And then the real magic comes the following morning, when the sunlight begins to peek through the thin curtains to coax my hungover head from its slumber. A new day breaks over the sublime geography of the Scottish Highlands.

I rise very early to see the train skirt the forested slopes that rise over the saltwater inlet of Loch Long. I'm still in my pyjamas as the train flirts capriciously with the wide open expanse of Loch Lomond – offering glimpses of its archipelago of islands and the southernmost of the munros

LOOKING TO THE FUTURE

The Caledonian Sleeper has a pedigree dating back to 1873, but the current rolling stock counts as some of the newest running on the rails in Britain, introduced in 2019 to a generally favourable response. New innovations include wider, longer beds and the option of booking compartments with double beds and en suites (though some sleeper old timers bemoan the loss of the lounge car with its very squidgy sofas).

Clockwise from above: The Club Car; the Steall waterfall near Fort William; a Royal stag. Previous Page: The sleeper with new livery.

(Scottish peaks over 3000ft/914m), Ben Lomond.

But it's after the junction at Crianlarich that the landscape reaches its swaggering best – just in time for passengers to stumble to the club car for a breakfast of porridge or Lorne sausage. Many let their food get cold, unable to take their eyes off the majestic scenes revealed beyond the thin pane of glass. The sleeper trundles over the Allt Kinglass Viaduct and then rolls on into the lunar, pancake-flat expanse of Rannoch Moor. There's a brief stop at Corrour Station – the highest on the UK mainline and immortalised in the famous 'It's shite being Scottish' scene in *Trainspotting*. I reach the opposite conclusion by the time the train begins its final approach into the Highland hub of Fort William, and the craggy mass of Britain's highest peak, Ben Nevis, slides into view. Well rested, passengers disembark the sleeper to make tracks in the surrounding landscapes under their own steam – mountain bikes are unloaded, backpacks heaved onto the platforms, boots laced, binoculars unsheathed.

Just like London Euston, Fort William is a workaday station with no airs and graces. Nonetheless, the empty sleeper train that stands briefly on its platforms is the stuff of which railway dreams are made. **OS**

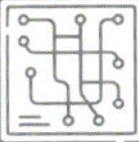

Start/Finish // Euston Station, London/Fort William
Distance // 418 miles (673km)
Duration // 12hr 42min
Ticket types // Caledonian Sleeper tickets are divided into Classic compartments (without en suite), Club compartments (en suite) and Double rooms. If travelling on a budget, opt for reclining seats.
How to book // Book direct at sleeper.scot.
When to go // The Caledonian Sleeper is worth a journey year-round – winter adds snow-appeal to the landscapes, while autumn arguably has the richest colour palette. Be aware that summer sees the Highland air busy with midges (tiny biting insects).
Things to know // The sleeper terminates at Fort William but the rails don't: continue to Mallaig via the Glenfinnan Viaduct, immortalised in the Harry Potter movies.

Opposite: The beachside railway line into Penzance, Cornwall.

MORE LIKE THIS
BRITISH SLEEPER ROUTES

LONDON TO INVERNESS

The second most beautiful variant of the Caledonian Sleeper is the one that continues north from Edinburgh to the city of Inverness. While not quite as spectacular as the Deerstalker, it has its quota of drama for travellers – from Perth, the train traces the River Tay upstream, before reaching Scotland's highest whisky distillery at Dalwhinnie. Look out the right-hand window and you soon spy the crags of Cairngorm National Park – a range of mountains often regarded as Britain's last wilderness and containing five of the country's six highest peaks. Many sleeper passengers alight in the outdoor capital of Aviemore, with its historic Swiss-style station, for adventures in these hills. Finally, the train swerves northwest to draw into the slate-grey station at Inverness – perfectly placed for days scouring the surface of Loch Ness or touring the fabled distilleries of nearby Speyside.
Start // Euston Station, London
Finish // Inverness
Distance // 443 miles (712km)
Duration // 11hr 30min

LONDON TO ABERDEEN

The most unsung of Caledonian Sleeper routes runs from London to Aberdeen – it's popular with business travellers working in the oil and energy sector, though a trickle of tourists also make the journey to Scotland's third city. Departing Edinburgh, the train crosses the Firth of Forth and bucolic Fife farmland before hauling into the city of Dundee (rise early and you might just spot the city's impressive V&A museum as you roll over the Tay Bridge). As the journey continues, a mosaic of golf courses, sandy beaches and shallow wooded valleys flash by – though this route has little in the way of Highland drama, North Sea sunrises go some way to compensate. Once you've arrived, Aberdeen's excellent Maritime Museum is conveniently located just across the road from the station.
Start // Euston Station, London
Finish // Aberdeen
Distance // 396 miles (637km)
Duration // 10hr 35min

LONDON TO PENZANCE

The only overnight train operating in Britain aside from the many variants of the Caledonian Sleeper is the Night Riviera, departing London's Paddington Station bound for Southwest England's coastal counties of Devon and Cornwall. It's unlike the Caledonian Sleeper in that the train departs London very late (almost midnight), the journey is shorter and the food and drink offering is more rudimentary. Nonetheless, it works as an effective way to beat the traffic jams that blight the roads to the Southwest – get up early on a westbound journey to enjoy crossing Brunel's bridge over the Tamar Estuary, the border between Devon and Cornwall. You'll get little in the way of sea views until the train hauls into Britain's southernmost station at Penzance – the platform is right beside bobbing boats in the town's harbour.
Start // Paddington Station, London
Finish // Penzance
Distance // 253 miles (407km)
Duration // 8hr 14min

THE PYRENEES' MELLOW YELLOW WONDER

Call it the Little Yellow Train, the Canary or the Ligne de Cerdagne – this beloved train offers a portal into the French Pyrenees.

In my experience, morning commutes don't often involve chatting to a shepherd on his way to work. But today on the Petit Train Jaune – the high-altitude 'Little Yellow Train' that winds across the French Pyrenees – I spend a half-hour discussing the art of sheep wrangling with Claude, a silver-haired, sexagenarian *berger* returning after the Transhumance, the twice-yearly movement of his flocks between mountain and lowland pastures.

'Traditions still matter in the Pyrenees,' he says, looking out over green pastures speckled with lupins, gentian, orchids and saxifrage. 'Many things here are still as they were in my grandfather's day. *Il fait bon vivre dans les montagnes*. Life is good in the mountains.'

I know what he means. Over 25 years of exploring France, it's the Pyrenees I've returned to most. This is France's wild side: a geographer's textbook of valleys, cirques and arêtes, plateaus and saw-toothed peaks. Many villages have changed little in a hundred years. Famously, this is one of the only corners of France where wolves and brown bears still roam wild (to the consternation of shepherds like my new friend Claude).

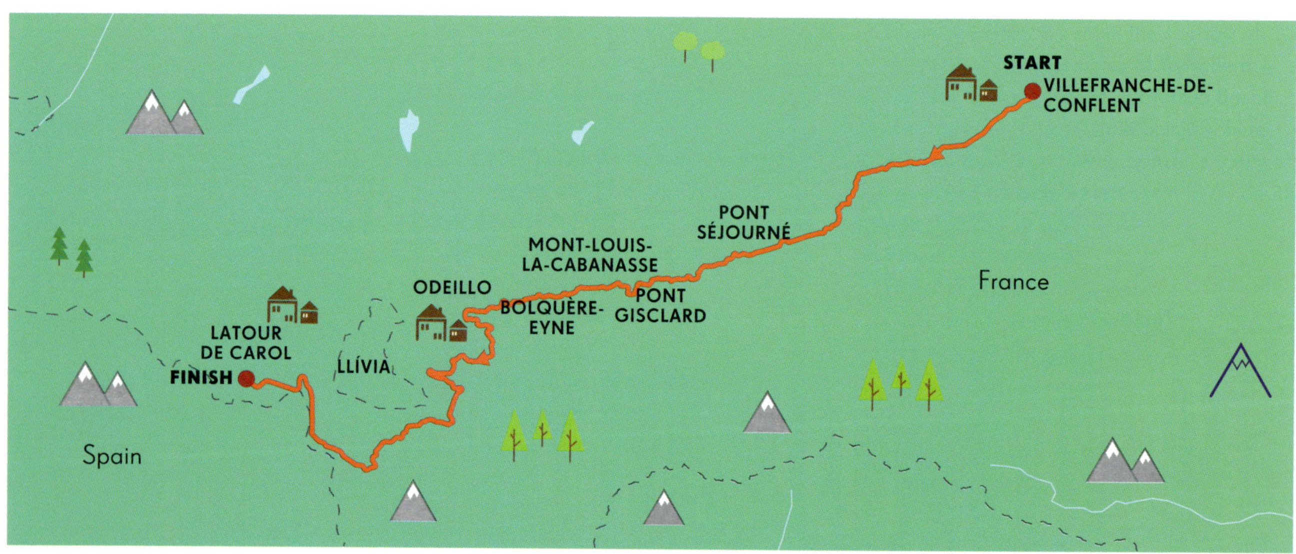

Until the late 19th century, much of the Pyrenees was only accessible on foot or by donkey, following old drovers' paths largely known only to locals. But in 1903, the decision was made to build a railway between the mountain towns of Villefranche-de-Conflent and Latour de Carol. It was to be one of the great engineering projects of the early 20th century. Unfortunately, it also turned out to be one of the most difficult.

To complete the 38-mile (62km) route, the railway was required to traverse precipitous gorges, circumvent sheer-sided mountains and punch through miles of granite, siltstone and limestone. Nineteen tunnels were blasted, and two landmark bridges built: the 213ft-high (65m) Pont Séjourné and the 262ft-high (80m) Pont Gisclard, France's only railway suspension bridge. It took a quarter of a century to complete the line, which finally opened in 1927.

Nowadays, the Ligne de Cerdagne – or Train Jaune, as it's affectionately known – is one of France's most beloved railways. Its jaunty red-and-yellow livery is inspired by the Sang et Or (blood and gold) colours of the Catalan flag, accounting for its other nickname, Le Canari (the Canary). But while its dinky carriages look like they've tumbled out of a child's toy box, they are surprisingly robust, running in all weathers and all seasons. A snowplough remains on standby in winter, and every morning, the train team sets out to clear the route of icicles, snowdrifts and avalanches.

My journey begins on a summer morning in Villefranche-de-Conflent, a walled mountain town about 31 miles (50km) west of Perpignan. As I wait for my train to depart, I walk around the town's hulking battlements, devised by Vauban, the mastermind of French martial engineering; in the distance looms Mont Canigou, the sacred mountain of the Catalan people, still capped by its crown of winter snow. A toot-toot of the horn signifies departure, and I clamber aboard, finding a spot alongside Claude the shepherd in one of the Train Jaune's beloved open-top carriages. The Canary is on its way.

"Soon, we're rattling through a Pyrenean panorama: forests, valleys, gorges, waterfalls, hilltop villages."

Soon, we're rattling through a Pyrenean panorama: forests, valleys, gorges, waterfalls, hilltop villages. Streams gush down the mountainsides. Cows mooch on the slopes. Occasionally, the train slows down and chugs to a stop to pick up passengers; most of the 22 stations along the line are *arrêts facultatifs* (request stops), and to hail the train, you simply stick out a thumb, catch the driver's eye and clamber aboard. Locals use the Train Jaune like a bus service, and for hikers, bikers and climbers, it offers a way to reach the Pyrenees' most remote trailheads.

The Train Jaune is one of only a few narrow-gauge railways still running in France. It averages only 19mph (30km/h), but when you're in a roofless carriage, it feels considerably faster – a wind-in-the-hair ride, as much rollercoaster as railway. The line is electrified, with power supplied by a hydroelectric dam higher up the Têt Valley, so there's no rumbling diesel engine to disturb the

STOPPING POWER

The Train Jaune goes big on brakes. Each train has not just one, but three separate braking systems: standard mechanical brakes, Westinghouse air brakes, and electrically powered rheostat brakes. This triumvirate system is a wise precaution, ensuring that it's practically impossible for the train to experience brake failure – reassuring given the formidable gradients.

From left: The iconic rail suspension bridge at Pont Gisclard; the fortified town of Villefranche-de-Conflent at the line's eastern end. Previous page: Crossing the Pont Séjourné.

silence – and I soon find myself tuning into the meditative tick of the train wheels on the track.

About halfway, the train crawls up through Mont-Louis–La Cabanasse before reaching its highest point at Bolquère-Eyne – which, at 5223ft (1592m), is the highest station on the French rail network. Here, passengers clamber out to snap the obligatory selfie next to the station sign, then climb back on board for the final stage of the journey.

From Bolquère-Eyne, the Train Jaune passes France's first solar power station at Odeillo before terminating at Latour de Carol, 15 miles (25km) or so further west. From here, it's possible to link up with mainline services to Toulouse and Barcelona – Latour de Carol is famous among train nerds as the junction of three different railway gauges.

But if you catch an early Train Jaune, Latour de Carol makes the perfect place to stop for lunch before the return journey back to Villefranche. Having bid farewell to my companion Claude, I head off to one of the little bistros near the station for a bowl of hearty *garbure* (stew) and a *pichet* or two of local red wine. In an hour or two, there'll be another Train Jaune to catch – but in the meantime, I'm content just to soak up the mountain scenery and indulge in a dose of *la vie douce* (the sweet life), Pyrenean-style. Life, as my shepherd friend Claude says, really is rather good in the mountains. **OB**

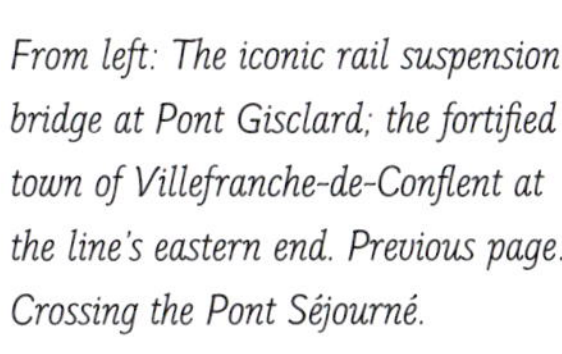

Start/Finish // Villefranche-de-Conflent/Latour de Carol
Distance // 38 miles (62km)
Duration // 3hr
Ticket types // The Ligne de Cerdagne runs both old-fashioned vintage cars and modern air-con trains (look for *ancien* or *moderne* on timetables). Vintage trains have a maximum of six carriages; usually a couple are open-top, and the rest are covered.
How to book // The Train Jaune site (letrainjaune.fr) has timetables and info. Book online (ter.sncf.com/occitanie).
When to go // Spring for wildflowers and snowy views, autumn for forest colours and fewer crowds.
Things to know // Let the driver know well in advance if alighting at an *arrêt facultatif* – don't leave it to the last minute or you may miss your stop.
More info // Pyrénées Cerdagne Tourism (pyrenees-cerdagne.com).

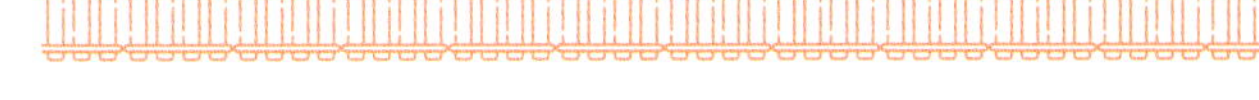

Opposite: The Swallows' Line is at its most spectacular around the town of Morez, once a centre of clock production.

MORE LIKE THIS
FRANCE'S SLOW RAILWAYS

LIGNE DES HIRONDELLES

Alongside the Alps and Pyrenees, France's third great mountain range is the Jura – and the Swallows' Line here offers another fantastic way of appreciating the scenery. Running for 76 miles (123km) between Dole and Saint-Claude, the three-hour trip takes in many of the Jura's key sights including the Bienne Valley, the plateau of Grandvaux and the Forêt de Chaux, the second-biggest hardwood forest in France. Along the way, the train passes through 36 tunnels and 18 viaducts, which are best seen on the stretch between Morbier and Morez. The Swallows' Line is also an ideal way to enjoy one of the other great pleasures of the Jura: its wines. You'll pass plenty of vineyards along the way, and riding the train means you can indulge in a spot of *dégustation* without having to worry about nominating a designated driver.

Start // Dole
Finish // Saint-Claude
Distance // 76 miles (123km)
Duration // 3hr

TRAIN DES PIGNES

Provence's 'Pine Cone Train' offers something special: the chance to travel all the way from the Mediterranean into the Alps in a single day. You could spend the morning rollerblading along the Promenade des Anglais in Nice, and end the day skiing down the slopes or soothing yourself in a hot tub in Digne-les-Bains. Covering 94 miles (151km) of formidable alpine terrain, the train is said to have got its name because when it was first built, the locomotives often had to slow down so much due to the gradient, passengers could hop off to collect pine cones and still have time to climb back on board. These days, the whole trip lasts about three and a half hours. If you'd prefer a more old-fashioned experience, vintage steam locomotives (traindespignes.fr) in their original hand-painted livery puff between Puget-Théniers and Annot between April and November.

Start // Nice
Finish // Digne-les-Bains
Distance // 94 miles (151km)
Duration // 3hr 30min

CANNES TO MENTON

The hairpin corniches of the Côte d'Azur offer one of France's top road trips, but a more sedate way to enjoy the Riviera scenery is to board the local TER train in Cannes and ride the rails along the coast all the way to the pretty seaside town of Menton, near the Italian border, famous for its annual lemon festival. Along the way, you could hop off in Nice for a visit to one of its fantastic art museums or a wander around the shady Old Town, or stop in the self-governing principality of Monaco to visit its world-class aquarium, ogle the superyachts or place a bet like James Bond at Monte Carlo Casino. The Riviera views along the route are dazzling: don't forget your *lunettes*.

Start // Cannes
Finish // Menton
Distance // 40 miles (63km)
Duration // 1hr 15min

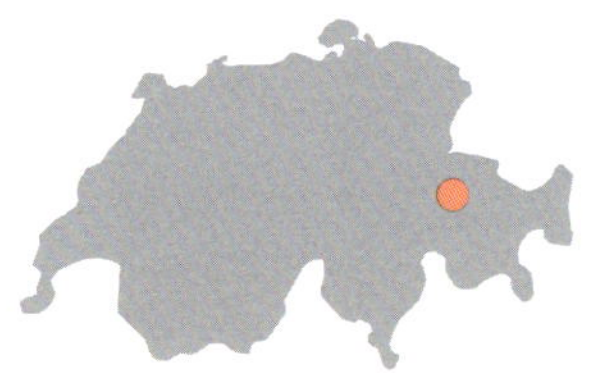

THE HIGH LIFE ON THE BERNINA EXPRESS

The Alps' superstar train ride is the Bernina Railway, whose little red trains climb to ear-popping elevations as they traverse a windswept pass between Switzerland and Italy.

A great many railways cross the Alps. Express trains burrow through the long, gloomy tunnels of the Simplon and the Gotthard. Freight trains whoosh across the fabled Brenner Pass where forested slopes brood above. And yet none traverse these ranges as stylishly as the Bernina Express, which runs for a modest 54 miles (87km) but still manages to number among the world's most hallowed railways. This metre-gauge line connects two countries, Switzerland and Italy, and in doing so traverses a watershed between Northern and Southern Europe. It also unites two different worlds: the barren, snowbound uplands of the Alps and the lush green meadows of the valleys. For railway aficionados across the world, this Swiss highland railway sits at the highest spot on their wishlist. I was no exception.

I took the Bernina Railway as part of a transcontinental odyssey, riding the rails all the way from London to Venice. The journey involved intricate connections – changing from Eurostar services to lightning-fast TGV Lyrias bound for the Swiss frontier. I navigated rush hour on Paris' metro. On Zürich's underground I grimaced at the armpits of commuters thrust in my face. But the capstone in the whole journey – its crowning central link – was the Bernina. Its iron rails are UNESCO-listed – like St Mark's Basilica and the Rialto Bridge – but in truth, those bright red trains were a greater part of the appeal than the water-bound city that lay at my journey's end.

I boarded a branded Bernina Express train at Chur. The panoramic carriages were decked out with glass ceilings perfect for enhanced views. We hauled out of Chur Station and onto the Albula Railway which, while served by the Bernina

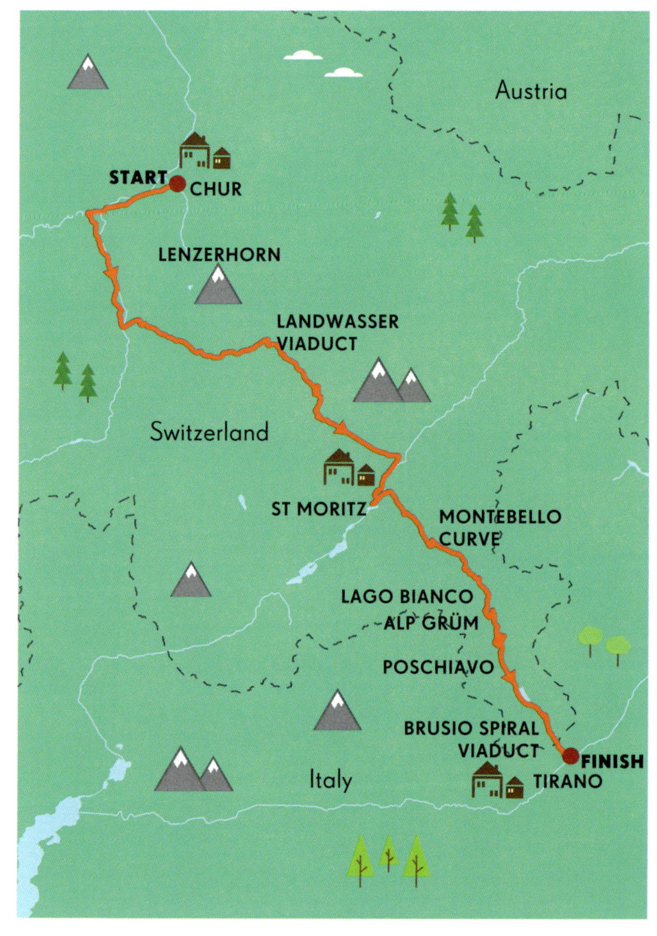

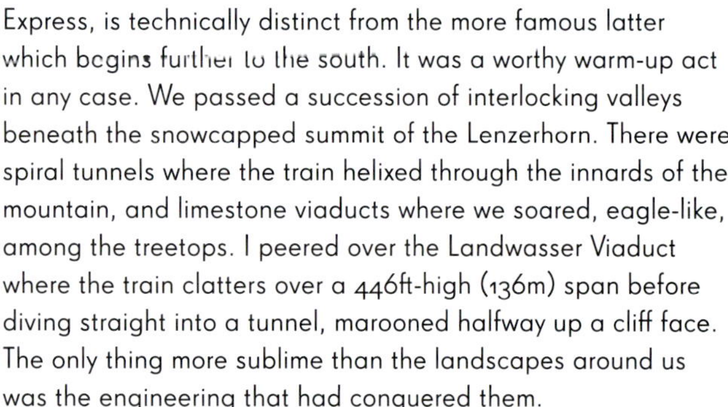

Express, is technically distinct from the more famous latter which begins further to the south. It was a worthy warm-up act in any case. We passed a succession of interlocking valleys beneath the snowcapped summit of the Lenzerhorn. There were spiral tunnels where the train helixed through the innards of the mountain, and limestone viaducts where we soared, eagle-like, among the treetops. I peered over the Landwasser Viaduct where the train clatters over a 446ft-high (136m) span before diving straight into a tunnel, marooned halfway up a cliff face. The only thing more sublime than the landscapes around us was the engineering that had conquered them.

Eventually we arrived in the ear-popping heights of St Moritz, the luxurious ski resort beloved of the great and the good, but mostly of the wealthy. I walked a lap of its little lake, and paid a visit to the legendary Cresta Run skeleton course, devoid of winter ice. But it was the Bernina Line proper I was here for – its own route diving and swerving with the capriciousness of a toboggan.

The next day I arrived at the station early, watching the distinctive gliding hands of the Swiss railway clock run down the minutes to departure. Soon we were trundling over mountain streams gorged with glacial meltwater, and the Bernina Express began its skyward ascent. There came the Montebello curve – the train navigating a horseshoe as the mass of the Morteratsch Glacier swung regally into view. Phones in camera mode were raised in unison. Noses were pressed on the windows, leaving smudges. The azure waters of Lago Bianco reservoir marked the highest point of the railway at a thin-aired elevation of 7392ft (2253m). They also mark the watershed between the Danube and the Po rivers: rain that falls to the north of the lonely Ospizio Bernina Station will pass through Vienna and Budapest before emptying into the Black Sea; showers to the south will ebb across the great Italian plain and spill into the balmier Adriatic.

"Soon we were trundling over mountain streams gorged with glacial meltwater, and the Bernina Express began its skyward ascent."

The lake also marks a linguistic watershed. We entered the Italian-speaking Poschiavo Valley where the line reaches its operatic finale, passing Alp Grüm – a place accessible only by railway in the depths of winter, with the residents having groceries and furniture imported by train. Then we rummaged about a series of switchbacks, pulling turns worthy of a driver at Monza.

A CLASSIC CLOCK

The Swiss railway clock has been a design icon since it was created in the 1940s. What marks it out is its unusual movement – the red second hand doesn't tick, but rather glides continuously around the face, hovering for a second and a half at the 12 o'clock mark, and then resuming its journey. Seen on platforms across Switzerland, the clocks are a symbol of punctuality and efficiency.

From left: Leaning out of the window on the Bernina Line; the spectacular Landwasser Viaduct seen from below; descending into the Poschiavo Valley; a train navigating the Montebello curve. Previous page: glacier-spotting from the Bernina.

The line is truly a miracle of engineering. A passenger departing from Chur will pass through some 55 tunnels and almost 200 bridges by the time they arrive in Italy. They were built at the dawn of the 20th century, partly to access the hydroelectric stations high on the pass, but mainly to bring visitors to the burgeoning resorts of the Alps. There were bumps along the way – rockfalls routinely blocked the line; trains have been buried under avalanches – and the original operation once went bankrupt. But today, as at its inception, tourists are at the heart of the Bernina Line.

Slowly pine and fir lapsed into palms and cypresses: olive groves too, lay not far from the tracks. Passing through little towns, I noticed the realm of the Alpine *stube* (traditional inn) had changed into the domain of the pizzeria and trattoria. You could sense the border drawing nearer, but there was one last encore – the Brusio spiral, where the train loops the loop to lose elevation, and travel its last mile on Italian soil. When I disembarked in Tirano, my journey wasn't over. I took a local service along the shores of Lake Como to Milan's temple-like station. I boarded a Frecciabianca train to Venice, gliding across the silver waters of the lagoon. It took a whole family of trains to shuttle me across the continent from London to Venice. But one in particular marked a geographical and personal high. **OS**

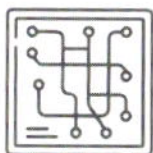

Start/Finish // Chur, Switzerland/Tirano, Italy
Distance // 54 miles (87km)
Duration // 4hr
Ticket types // Bernina Express services are divided between First and Second Class – First is more spacious. There's no dining car, though there is a trolley service. Ordinary Rhaetian Railway services also travel the Bernina and Albula lines – they don't have the panoramic windows but some travellers consider them more authentic.
How to book // Buy online at rhb.ch.
When to go // The Bernina Express runs year-round – a snowplough often clears the route during winter, when the frosty scenery is even more spectacular than in summer.
Things to know // You'll need your passport to travel the entire Bernina Line – border officers await you on the Italian frontier at Tirano.

Opposite top: Drinks service on the Treno Gottardo. Opposite below: A modern train travelling on the historic Semmering Railway.

MORE LIKE THIS
RAILWAYS ACROSS THE ALPS

SEMMERING RAILWAY, AUSTRIA

Swiss railways hog the limelight, but Europe's first mountain railway was actually Austria's Semmeringbahn – another UNESCO-listed marvel of engineering, traversing the relatively modest peaks of the Northern Limestone Alps. It was a pioneering feat when construction began in 1848, and a century and a half after completion, it's still going strong – not as a tourist railway but as part of a fully functioning mainline. Board a service from Vienna to Austria's second city Graz and you'll likely travel it. The line proper begins in the town of Gloggnitz, Lower Austria. Soon after, trains waltz through wooded hills. Then comes the double-arched Kalte-Rinne-Viadukt and the Adlitzgraben Viadukt – both spans provide views over hills dotted with summer villas. The town of Mürzzuschlag, in the state of Styria, marks the end of the Semmering Railway (though Graz-bound trains continue to follow the Murz River westwards). Ride this route now – a new tunnel is set to usurp the Semmering in the coming years.

Start // Gloggnitz
Finish // Mürzzuschlag
Distance // 25 miles (41km)
Duration // 50min

TRENO GOTTARDO, SWITZERLAND

The Treno Gottardo is another service linking Switzerland's German-speaking heartlands with the Italian-speaking south. In any other country this would be the most scenic railway line, but among the pantheon of Swiss trains it gets overlooked. Departing Zürich Hauptbahnhof, the train strikes south – after Lake Zürich, more freshwater panoramas unfurl in the form of lakes Zug and Lucerne. All the spellbinding mountain scenery disappears as trains plunge into the Gotthard Base Tunnel – the world's longest and deepest rail tunnel, measuring 35 miles (56km) long. Recent times have seen the tunnel close for maintenance, meaning trains instead cross the original 9-mile (15km) Gotthard Tunnel. Whichever one you end up passing through, you'll eventually emerge into the Swiss Canton of Ticino, rumbling under the great castles of Bellinzona and ending in Locarno on the sun-dappled shores of Lake Maggiore.

Start // Zürich
Finish // Locarno
Distance // 84 miles (136 km)
Duration // 3hr 10min

BRENNER RAILWAY

The Brenner Pass has been a highway across the Alps since prehistory – stomped by Iron Age tribes, Roman centurions and Holy Roman Emperors. It was Austro-Hungarian engineers, however, who laid out the Brenner Railway – a strategic 171-mile (275km) link between the Austrian mountain town of Innsbruck and fair Verona in Italy. It remains a magnificent route – travelling southbound, trains roll through the Wipp Valley and squeeze into the gap between the Stubai and Zillertal Alps. Entering Italy, you pass under the shadow of the Dolomites and through shady vineyards en route to the city of the star-crossed lovers. Austrian railways have added new swanky rolling stock to the Brenner route in recent times.

Start // Innsbruck
Finish // Verona
Distance // 171 miles (275km)
Duration // 4hr 30min

STEAM DREAMS IN NORTH WALES

Two of Britain's most revered heritage railways can be combined in a long journey through magnificent scenery, with castles, quarries and mountains as an unsurpassed backdrop.

With the possible exception of the Himalaya, there's nowhere in the world more renowned for narrow-gauge steam than North Wales. This Celtic heartland is home to a profusion of preserved locomotives, from the rather diminutive to the positively tiny, a little fleet which whistles and wheezes about the landscapes charming children and trainspotters alike. Some skirt lakes, others race seaside promenades, one or two scale mountains or rattle under castle battlements. The Welsh Highland and Ffestiniog Railways do all the above. Combine the two, and over a day you can travel some 38 (and a half) miles to the soundtrack of chuffing locomotives and rattling rails.

My journey starts in Caernarfon, in the shadow of one of Europe's best preserved medieval castles. Its 13th-century octagonal towers stand in sharp contrast to the clean, modern lines of the station. Then again, this terminus of the Welsh Highland Railway (WHR) is a relatively recent addition to the town

– the 25 miles (40km) of track stretching south were only fully laid in 2011. The Welsh Highland line is a modern reimagining of an older railway of the same name that existed in the 1920s, which closed when the local slate industry collapsed (and travellers opted to take quicker buses instead). Speed is not a priority for passengers these days, I note, as my service toots to announce its snail-pace departure from Caernarfon.

Soon the towers of the castle retreat behind us and we are rolling into the Arcadian Gwyrfai Valley, the massif of Yr Wyddfa (also known as Snowdon) rising to the left, and the treacherous spine of Nantlle Ridge just visible to the right through plumes of steam. Narrow-gauge railways are common in North Wales owing to the topography – smaller engines can more deftly navigate inclines, descents and tight curves. This is soon very evident. After a halt at Rhyd Ddu (a trailhead for hikers ascending Yr Wyddfa), the train slaloms through conifer forests and zigzags down the contours into the heart of Beddgelert, arguably the prettiest village in the area.

Here, among stone pubs and dapper tearooms, the train meets its companion, the River Glaslyn, whose course it will race downstream all the way to Porthmadog. It's the stretch from Beddgelert that is perhaps the most glorious, the train barging through a series of tunnels, reemerging in a narrow canyon flanked by invasive rhododendrons, with the ghostly wreckage of old copper mines littering the summits above. I'm here in summer and spot swimmers bathing in the shallow pools of the river, while others hop over the stepping stones. The sudden cool of the tunnels provides welcome respite from the heat.

The port of Porthmadog is soon announced by the cry of seagulls. The rails of the Welsh Highland Railway briefly and bizarrely trespass on a major road, before coming to a halt by the harbour. Here, many passengers disembark to take pictures of the mighty Garratt engines that have hauled them over the hills. What catches my eye, however, are the distinctive Fairlie locomotives – a Frankenstein's monster of a machine, with boilers at both ends. These locomotives are the signature of the Welsh Highland's compatriot, the Ffestiniog Railway – now part of the same company and using the same station at Porthmadog, albeit with a very different history.

The Ffestiniog Railway was originally a horse and gravity operation, built to connect the slate mines at Blaenau Ffestiniog to waiting ships at Porthmadog, from where the slate would be exported to rooftops around the world. Wagons would roll downhill under gravity, before noble steeds would clip-clop uphill, dragging the empty wagons behind them. It was in 1863 – some 30 years after its inception – that steam engines arrived on the Ffestiniog Railway: soon after passenger services followed. Unlike the Welsh Highland Railway, the Ffestiniog segued from a working line to a heritage operation with very little hiatus in the late 1950s – today, travelling aboard its restored rolling stock, you get an intimate sense of what it was like riding the line in

A NORTH WALES LOOP

With some planning, it's possible to complete a railway circuit from Caernarfon without retracing your tracks. First, board a Welsh Highland service to Porthmadog, before changing for a Ffestiniog train to Blaenau Ffestiniog. Here, you join the British national network – ordinary trains run north up the beautiful Conwy Valley to Llandudno Junction where you can change for a westbound train to Bangor. From Bangor it's an easy 30-minute bus ride back to Caernarfon.

Clockwise from top: The town of Blaenau Ffestiniog surrounded by slag heaps; relics of slate mining in the mountains of Eryri; a mighty Garratt engine on the WHR. Previous page: the WHR passing under Yr Wyddfa.

its Victorian heyday. Simple, no-frills quarrymen's coaches are the authentic choice, but ride the luxury Pullman-style carriages – with plush armchairs and cups of tea clinking on linen-clad tables – and you might imagine yourself a top-hatted director of the line.

Departing Porthmadog, my Ffestiniog Railway service huffs across the Cob – a man-made embankment shored against the shifting sands of the Mawddach Estuary, with the pyramidal peak of Cnicht bearing down from the east. It's after passing the railway works at Boston Lodge that the hills close in, the line passing through thick woodlands before creaking to a stop at the midway station of Tan-Y-Bwlch. Fans of railway engineering delight as the train ascends the Dduallt spiral – the only railway spiral in the United Kingdom. Very soon forests turn to wind-whipped moorlands, the mood turns more sombre and the immense wreckage of slate workings loom, Mordor-like, beyond the Tanygrisiau Reservoir. Their leviathan forms provide a poignant reminder of the genesis of this line – and, to a degree, of the Welsh Highland Railway too.

Today, both lines are busy with happy day-trippers, but the iron rails were once laid to steal the heart out of these mountains. Workers hacked away at strata with sinew and pick and dynamite, many losing their lives to extract slate that found its way to buildings around the world. Gazing up at the spoil heaps from a train arriving into Blaenau Ffestiniog is, I find, a moving experience. The railways help keep the memory of this industry and those labourers alive. **OS**

Start/Finish // Caernarfon/Blaenau Ffestiniog
Distance // 38½ miles
Duration // 5hr 30min (dependent on a change at Porthmadog)
Ticket types // Seat options on the Welsh Highland and Ffestiniog Railways vary according to the particular train, but broadly include Standard Class and First Class, the latter subdivided into Pullman and Observation coaches. Food and drink are available on some departures, including cream teas with Welsh cakes.
How to book // Book direct for both railways at festrail.co.uk.
Things to know // Be aware that not all routes cover the length of the line: on the Ffestiniog Railway the 'Woodland Wanderer' makes a return trip from Porthmadog only as far as Tan-y-Bwlch, while on the Welsh Highland, the 'Gelert Explorer' runs from Caernarfon to Beddgelert.

Clockwise from top: A view of Dolbadarn Castle and Llyn Padarn, home to the Llanberis Lake Railway; carriages on the Brecon Mountain Railway; a cutting on the Talyllyn Railway.

MORE LIKE THIS
WELSH NARROW-GAUGE ADVENTURES

LLANBERIS LAKE RAILWAY

Running parallel to the Welsh Highland Railway but on the opposite side of Yr Wyddfa/Snowdon, the Llanberis Lake Railway is the same gauge as its counterpart (specifically 1ft 11½in/60cm) and has the same pedigree of transporting slate. That said, it's a far more sedate and shorter ride – trains travel for just 2 miles (3km) northwest from the National Slate Museum, with wooded slopes and spoil heaps rising up on the right hand side while the mirror-like expanse of Llyn Padarn draws the attention on the left. Motive power comes in the form of a trio of characterful and colourful little Hunslet steam locomotives, with a few diesels in support. Enjoy views, too, of Dolbadarn Castle, a poetically ruined fortification built by Llywelyn the Great in the 13th century – it still guards the Llanberis Pass, centuries since the last English invasion.

Start/Finish // Llanberis
Distance // 5 miles (8km) round trip
Duration // 1hr

TALYLLYN RAILWAY

Mid-Wales' Talyllyn line is yet another railway connecting slate quarries with the sea – and, though a little less famous than some of its North Wales siblings, it can justifiably claim to be a pioneer. In the 19th century this was Britain's first narrow-gauge line granted permission to use steam engines. Then, in the 20th century, it was the first 'heritage' railway to be saved by volunteers – a model that has since been emulated the world over. These days many families come because of its connections with the Reverend Awdry – author of *Thomas the Tank Engine* – who was a volunteer at Talyllyn and drew inspiration from its characterful cast of locomotives. All comers enjoy the gentle ride along a lush green valley, shuttling between the shadow of the old quarries at Nant Gwernol to Tywyn Wharf, where the historic line intersects with the modern Cambrian Coast track for onward travel.

Start/Finish // Tywyn Wharf
Distance // 14 miles (22.5km)
Duration // 2hr 30min

BRECON MOUNTAIN RAILWAY

South Wales doesn't have the same proliferation of narrow gauge found in the north – with the honourable exception of the Brecon Mountain Railway. Setting out from the outskirts of the former coal mining town of Merthyr Tydfil, the route runs northward beside the banks of the Pontsticill Reservoir, and across the threshold into the Bannau Brycheiniog National Park (formerly known as the Brecon Beacons). A curious feature of the line are the Philadelphia-built Baldwin engines – not typical of Welsh narrow-gauge railways, but rather redolent of the Old West.

Start/Finish // Pant
Distance // 10 miles (16km)
Duration // 1hr 30min

No 3

MADRID TO BARCELONA BY HIGH-SPEED RAIL

Madrid to Barcelona is a breeze on the flagship route of Spain's high-speed network, buzzing from the centre of the Iberian Peninsula to the sea.

Spain is high-speed rail heaven, with rapid routes out of Madrid radiating to the country's other great cities. Along key lines, there's a fast-expanding choice of trains which, while all thundering along at roughly the same speed, offer varying levels of price, choice of seating class and onboard service. Arguably the flagship of the network is the service from the Spanish capital to Barcelona – the first and most obvious starting point in the country's efforts to get travellers off planes and onto the rails. In what was once Europe's busiest air corridor, today this service handles three-quarters of all journeys between the two cities.

Starting my own journey one morning in Madrid, I wasn't sure if it was early or still late as I checked out of my hotel. Madrid is a city that stays out till the wee hours, and plenty of revellers were strolling down the streets as dawn broke. Disconcertingly for this middle-aged Northern European, many were older than me: Spanish pensioners heading home from all-nighters mingled with groups of younger Madrileños, both parties still going strong. As I got closer to Atocha Station, I enjoyed swapping pleasantries with some of these stragglers as the ambience slowly changed from one-more-beer naughtiness to coffee and, for me, the start of a wonderful journey.

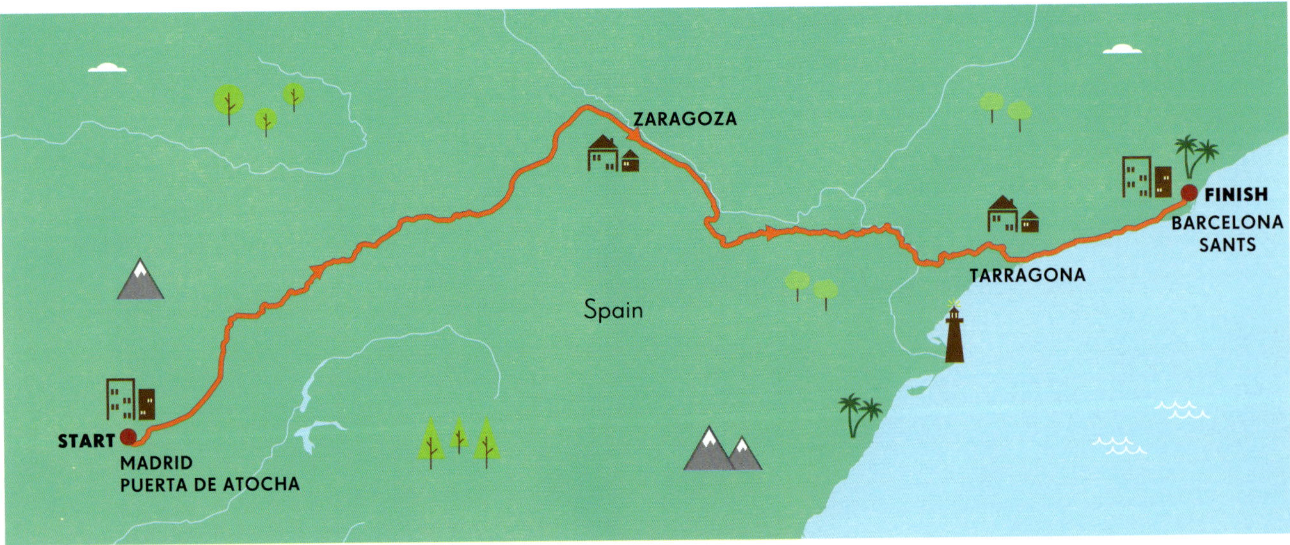

BURGER KING

Arriving on foot, my first view of what is more formally known as Estación de Madrid Atocha was the curvaceous girders of its original 1892 trainshed, now somewhat sunk below a mesh of modern highways. Upon entering the station by what felt like a side door, I descended onto the old platform level. For Atocha's centenary, this vast indoor area was reimagined as a tropical garden, with palm trees and looming greenery interspersed with good-looking eating and drinking options to continue last night's fun. Beams of sunlight shot here and there, casting spotlights on commuters arriving for a day's work.

Departure formalities before boarding Spanish high-speed trains require a little extra time than you might be used to. These involve passing through slimmed-down airport-style security, then hanging out in a departure hall above the station's modern platforms before joining – what was for me – a lengthy line for a ticket check. Sense of wonder about this journey returned quickly when I got to platform level and saw my unquestionably handsome Renfe AVE (Alta Velocidad Española) fast train. In fact, I saw several at the same time. The lineup of locos waiting to depart was as impressive as the tropical atrium on the other side: a sleek-looking assortment of trains, united in their capacity to travel at speeds of up to 186mph (300km/h).

Express trains make the Madrid–Barcelona trip in about two and a half hours, but taking a stopping service can pay

"By the time we had passed briefly through Camp de Tarragona, the deep blue of the Mediterranean Sea appeared between hills, heralding our arrival at the seaside and Barcelona."

dividends, despite the slower journey time (an extra 20-45 minutes). Direct trains generally cost more, being the fastest, and while breaking up a high-speed journey might seem anathema if your priority is racing the plane, there is some logic to stop-offs in places like Zaragoza, especially if there's time for an overnight stay. What was once the Roman city of Caesaraugusta is now one of Spain's gastronomic capitals, with an Old Town bursting with bars and cafes. You can also detour up the single-track line to Canfranc in the Pyrenees, home to a station that was a white elephant for decades, now reborn as a high-end hotel on a railway to nowhere.

My journey, however, was all about speed, so a Zaragoza stopover was for another time. I'd booked onto Renfe's AVE direct service in Standard Class, which meant I didn't qualify for the in-seat food and drink service, but I still got a large window seat and, as no one turned up to sit next to me, plenty of room to spread out. Departing Atocha, the first sight was a vast train yard where many of the workhorses of this route come to rest at night. Leaving the city behind, the scrubby hinterland gave way to a mix of undulating terrain and broad plains dotted with towns and villages basking in the sunshine.

By the time we had passed briefly through Camp de Tarragona, the deep blue of the Mediterranean Sea appeared between hills, heralding our arrival at the seaside and Barcelona. Though I was thrilled to be rolling in on time to one of the world's most beautiful cities, Barcelona's Sants terminus made for an unromantic arrival point, with platforms buried deep beneath street level. I followed the crowds up the escalators and out of the modern concourse into the sunshine of the Catalan morning. Visitors need to continue on by metro or suburban train to find the Barcelona of their dreams, whether that's taking in the city views from Montjuïc hill, strolling the Barri Gòtic or heading to the port for an onward ferry to the Balearic Islands.

If Madrid to Barcelona is too short to be an epic train ride in itself, this need not be journey's end. The tracks rumble beneath the city from here, pretty much right under the Sagrada Familia, and then the high-speed line thunders to Figueres and the French border at Perpignan. AVEs travel deep into France to Marseille and Lyon, and if Trenitalia's expansive plans to link Madrid with Paris come to fruition, direct services may soon link the Spanish and French capitals for the first time since the demise of the night train in 2013. Whatever the future may hold, Madrid to Barcelona is an essential cog in the great European rail machine. **TH**

TRAIN OPTIONS AND OPERATORS

As well as Renfe's AVE and low-cost AVLO services, Spain has high-speed services run by Ouigo (owned by France's SNCF) and Iryo (part-owned by Italy's Trenitalia). All have different seats, classes and catering options. You need to take a low-cost (but still high-speed) AVLO train between Madrid and Barcelona to ride the distinctive Renfe S102 and 112 models, nicknamed *pato* (duck) for their bill-shaped cars.

Clockwise from top left: Cycling the seafront in Barcelona; Las Ramblas in Barcelona; Pato services at Atocha; dining out in Barcelona. Previous page: The gardens at Atocha Station.

Start/Finish // Madrid Atocha/Barcelona Sants
Distance // 314 miles (506km)
Duration // 2hr 39min (direct)
Ticket types // AVE trains have three types of fare: Básico, Elige and Prémium. Básico is the cheapest and least flexible Standard Class option. Elige tickets, offering greater flexibility, can be bought for Standard or Comfort Class, the latter being a premium seat. Prémium fares give you a Comfort seat and the widest range of options when rebooking.
How to book // Check Trainline (trainline.com) to explore all available options per route.
Things to know // Because of the pre-boarding procedures for Spanish high-speed trains, allow 30 minutes (or longer) to comfortably get through security and ticket checks, and find your carriage.

Opposite top: The seafront at Donostia/San Sebastian. Opposite below: Valencia's magnificent City of Arts and Sciences.

MORE LIKE THIS
SPANISH HIGH-SPEED ROUTES

BASQUE Y

Named after the y-shape outline of the planned network, this under-construction line will connect Donostia/San Sebastián and Irun, close to the French border, with the other key Basque cities of Bilbao on one fork and Vitoria-Gasteiz on the other. Services are expected to begin in 2027, when these 106 miles (172km) of new high-speed lines will link up with the rest of the Spanish network, slashing journey times to Madrid. The projected travel time between Bilbao and Donostia/San Sebastián could be as swift as 38 minutes, with travel between Bilbao and Madrid cut to two hours 15 minutes. With extensions planned to high-speed lines on the French side of the border too, there may be future possibilities for international connections on this route.

MADRID TO MÁLAGA

Given the smoothness and speed of the journey, it might be tempting to do little more than board a seaside-bound AVE from Madrid and nod off for a few hours until you reach the Med. Sleeping to Málaga would, however, mean missing out on a stopover two hours from the capital in Córdoba, home to the Mezquita, one of Spain's most significant Islamic buildings. An hour further along the line, Málaga delivers on cultural attractions with its Alcazaba palace-fortress, as well as a museum devoted to hometown boy Pablo Picasso, plus the Spanish offshoot of the Centre Pompidou.
Start // Madrid Atocha
Finish // Málaga María Zambrano
Distance // 258 miles (416km)
Duration // 3hr 6min

MADRID TO VALENCIA

The scenic highlight of what is otherwise a breathtaking blur of Spanish countryside comes around two-thirds into this route, when trains pass by the bright-blue waters of the Embalse de Contreras reservoir in the Hoces del Cabriel Nature Reserve. Journey's end is the modern Valencia-Joaquín Sorolla Station, but don't miss checking out the art nouveau Estación del Norte, one of Europe's most beautiful stations, while exploring Valencia. Note that, slightly confusingly, most trains to Valencia depart Madrid's northerly Chamartín Station (where services to the north and west of the country more commonly start); some trains, however, depart from Atocha. Check before travel, and allow additional time to get to Chamartín if this is your departure point. As well as Renfe services, Iryo and French-owned Ouigo trains compete on this route.
Start // Madrid Chamartín or Atocha
Finish // Valencia-Joaquín Sorolla
Distance // 188 miles (303km)
Duration // 1hr 40min

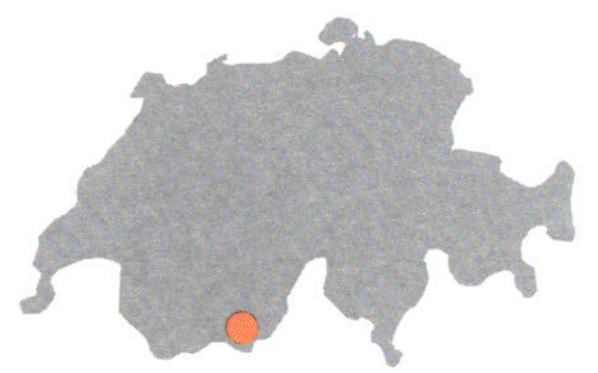

THE GLACIER EXPRESS: SWITZERLAND'S ICE QUEEN

Enjoy a slap-up lunch, vintage wines and amazing views of some of Switzerland's highest peaks on the ultimate high-altitude Alpine train.

Few trains take so long to travel so short a distance as the Glacier Express: just 180 miles (290km) in seven and a half hours, at an average speed of 24mph (39km/h). The bullet train it is not; it's sometimes been called the world's slowest express train. On the other hand, there are even fewer trains where you find yourself so unbothered by its frankly lethargic speed. In fact, by the end, you'll probably wish it had taken twice as long. This is because the Glacier Express offers its passengers a front-row seat for the kind of scenery ordinarily only accessible to elite mountaineers – only this seat is padded, comes with a gourmet lunch set down in front of it, a glass or two of Riesling to wash it down with and a Swiss chocolate or two to finish things off. It's Alpinism for the indolent.

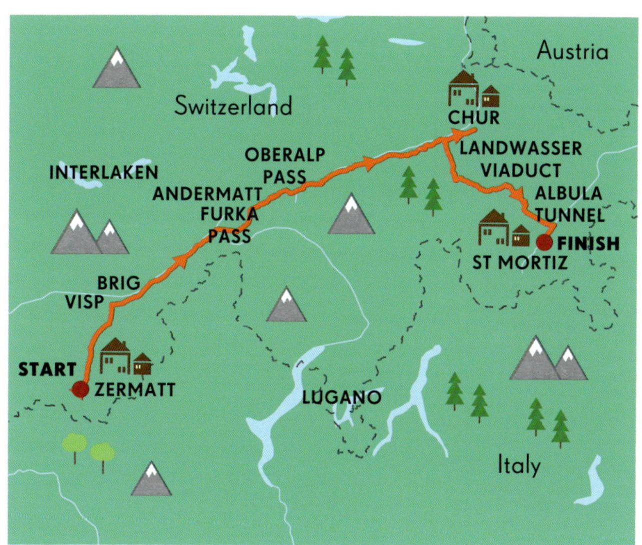

Running between Zermatt and St Moritz, the first Glacier Express departed on 25 June 1930. For the first 50 years or so, it was strictly a summer-only service, as the two high-mountain passes over which it crosses – the Furka and the Oberalp –

"I settle back, sipping my drink as we pull out of St Moritz Station, feeling a tingle of anticipation shooting through my veins that's not entirely down to the booze."

were impassable in winter. However, the construction of the 9.5-mile-long (15.4km) Furka Tunnel has meant the trains can now run year-round (though services do pause between mid-October and early December). For me, the prospect of making the journey in the middle of winter, when even the hardiest mountain climbers don't dare pull on their crampons, is simply too good to pass up – and so it is that I find myself in St Moritz on a bitter January day, wrapped up in mittens, balaclava and scarf, barely able to feel my fingers.

As I trudge towards the *bahnhof* (station), it's bone-bitingly, lip-crackingly cold. Snowdrifts stand knee-high on the streets. A steely grey sky promises more blizzards to come. But as I step aboard the Glacier Express, into a toasty carriage with windows as big as a greenhouse, I feel the cold melt away. A cheery concierge shows me to my seat and asks whether I'd like something to warm me up: a hot chocolate, perhaps, a glass of schnapps, or a mug of *glühwein*? I settle back, sipping my drink as we pull out of St Moritz Station, feeling a tingle of anticipation shooting through my veins that's not entirely down to the booze.

Soon, we're lost in a world of white. Fresh snow cloaks the mountainsides, pristine as cake icing. I spy the summits of Piz Bernina and Piz Languard as we trundle over the Engadin Plateau, then turn up the Val Bever, climbing to an altitude of 5955ft (1815m) where we enter the 3.6-mile-long (5.9km) Albula Tunnel, one of 91 through which the Glacier Express passes. There are even more bridges than there are tunnels: 291 in all, to be precise. Soon we cross the best-known of them, the Landwasser Viaduct, whose six stone arches tower 213ft (65m) above the valley floor. Looking over the frozen gorge as we follow a graceful curve over the viaduct, it seems hard to believe anyone could possibly have contemplated building it – but here it stands, 122 years later, a monument to the great age of European railway building.

After stopping in Chur, the Glacier Express cuts west along the wooded Rhine Valley, then ascends to the high point of the route at Oberalp Pass, 6670ft (2033m) above sea level. Here, we are remarkably close to the source of the River Rhine, and at the top of the pass stands a lighthouse, modelled on one which, for more than 70 years, stood at the opposite end of the river 764 miles (1230km) further north at Hook of Holland in the Netherlands. It's a very curious thing to see poking up in the middle of the mountains, but most of

A WORLD HERITAGE RAILWAY

The Glacier Express is one of only a few railways in the world that travels through a UNESCO World Heritage Site. Inscribed in 2008 as the Rhaetian Railway in the Albula and Bernina Landscapes, the site recognises the architectural importance of the railway, as well as the cultural value it holds for the area's mountain communities which, prior to its arrival, were effectively cut off from the rest of Switzerland for much of the year.

Clockwise from top: The Matterhorn; inside the trains; approaching Andermatt; the train snaking through Andermatt itself. Previous page: Winter majesty.

my fellow passengers barely give it a second glance.

From the apex of the Oberalp Pass, we rattle on down to Andermatt, and I sit down for lunch, watching snowy vistas whistle by as I tuck in. There's barley soup and fresh bread, *Bündner capuns* (stuffed chard leaves, a Graubünden specialty), a generous *Käseplatte* (cheese plate) and a slice of *Engadiner nusstorte* (nut cake) to finish off. 'The food is good, *ja*?' says Kurt Haglof, a sprightly, white-haired septuagenarian gent with whom I've shared my table for lunch. 'A lot better than normal train food!' he laughs, sipping enthusiastically from a frothy stein of lager.

The finest scenery of the day is saved for last. We pass through the Furka Tunnel, make stops in Brig and Visp, and then begin the final climb, a snaking ascent along the Matter Vispa River and up towards Zermatt. Serrated peaks loom on all sides, white as bone, sharp as shark's teeth. As the train pulls into Zermatt, I get a glimpse of the mightiest of them all: the Matterhorn, 14,692ft (4478m) high, rising like a pyramid at the head of the valley. Icy cliffs encase its flanks; spindrifts twirl from its summit. It almost looks too theatrical, too painterly, to be real – a mountain as imagined by a Romantic poet, rather than something that really exists. And yet there it is.

'*Ja, das Matterhorn*,' Kurt says, as we shake hands vigorously on the platform and say our farewells. 'I have seen it many times. Even climbed it once, when I was a much younger man. But every time I return, it is like seeing it for the first time again.'

As I watch the summit blush pink in the afternoon light, I know precisely what he means. **OB**

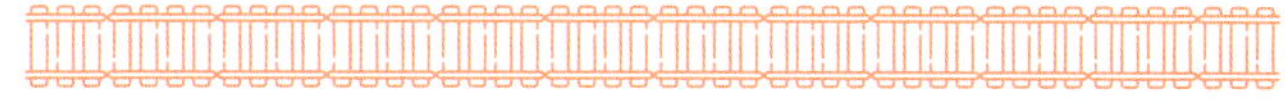

Start/Finish // Zermatt/St Moritz
Distance // 180 miles (290km)
Duration // 7hr 30min
Ticket types // There are three classes: Second, First and Excellence. In addition to your ticket, you must also pay a mandatory seat-reservation fee.
How to book // Full-fare tickets can be booked directly (glacierexpress.ch). It may be cheaper to buy a Saver Day Pass from SBB (sbb.ch).
When to go // There's no Glacier Express service from mid-October to December.
Things to know // The difference between classes is mainly comfort. In Second Class, meals are served at your seat; First Class passengers have their own dining car and three-course menu; Excellence Class has an exclusive cocktail bar and five-course menu.
More info // Switzerland Tourism (myswitzerland.com).

Opposite top: The Jungfraubahn waiting on the platform. Opposite below: The GoldenPass Belle Epoque near Rossinière, Lake Geneva.

MORE LIKE THIS SUPER SWISS RAILWAY JOURNEYS

JUNGFRAU RAILWAY

This gravity-defying Swiss railway travels at altitudes that would turn even the most experienced climbers pale and clammy. After catching the Eiger Express cable car from Grindelwald, the train leaves from Kleine Scheidegg Station at 6762ft (2061m). It then ratchets 0.9 miles (1.5km) up the mountainside to Jungfraujoch, the highest station in Europe, at 11,332ft (3454m) – more than 10 times the height of the Eiffel Tower. At points, the railway navigates an incline of 1 in 4 (25%). From Jungfraujoch, you can set off on an array of stunning treks, or just enjoy views over iconic Swiss mountains including the Eiger and Monch. Operating at these elevations, especially in winter, requires constant vigilance – snowploughs and snow-blowers are on constant standby to keep the rails free of ice and snow.

Start // Kleine Scheidegg
Finish // Jungfraujoch
Distance // 5.8 miles (9.3km)
Duration // 40min

GORNERGRAT RAILWAY

The Gornergrat Railway was, for 14 heady years, Europe's highest railway until it was pipped to top spot by the opening of the Jungfrau in 1912. While it may no longer hold the title, it's still well worth experiencing – not least because it arguably offers better views, as the Gornergrat relies on fewer tunnels than its loftier neighbour to reach its apogee. From the top, at 10,134ft (3089m), you get a panoramic view of several glaciers and 29 Swiss peaks over 13,123ft (4000m). This is one trip that's definitely worth saving for a clear day, especially if you want to snap some quality photos of the Matterhorn.

Start // Zermatt
Finish // Gornergrat
Distance // 5.8 miles (9.3km)
Duration // 33min

GOLDENPASS EXPRESS

This is the train trip to take for chocolate-box Switzerland: green meadows, clear mountain lakes, cows grazing the pastures and timber-framed inns perched on the hilltops. Travelling from Freddie Mercury's adopted home in Montreux to the resort town of Interlaken, it covers pretty much every Swiss scene you could ask for in just over three hours. Like the Glacier Express, this is a luxury-first service, with three classes to choose from: for the ultimate experience, go Prestige for widescreen windows and super-comfy, heated rotatable seats, and order some caviar and champagne to be delivered to your seat. Unlike many of Switzerland's other trains, the GoldenPass Express is actually pretty new: it's been running since 2022, built at the eye-watering cost of CHF89 million (US$100m).

Start // Montreux
Finish // Interlaken
Distance // 72 miles (116km)
Duration // 3hr 15min

JUNGFRAUBAHN
221
NGFRAUBAHN
BDhe 4/8
215

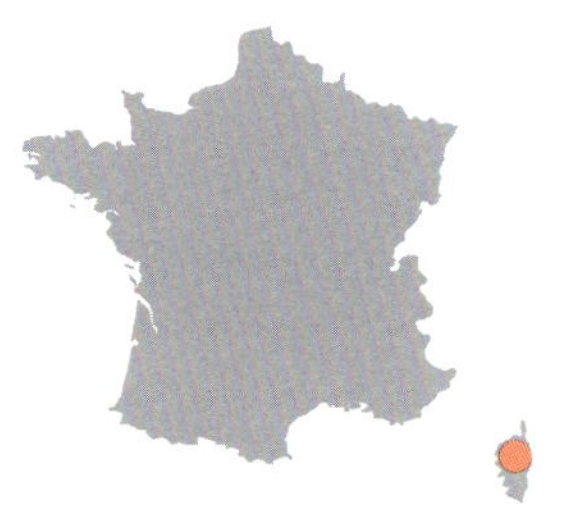

U TRINICHELLU: A LITTLE CORSICAN WONDER

Climb aboard Corsica's vintage railway line for a boneshaking ride into the rugged, maquis-cloaked heart of the 'Island of Beauty'.

Kalliste, the Greeks called it – the most beautiful. Anyone who's ever visited Corsica will find it hard to disagree. Only a shade smaller than Cyprus, this ravishing Mediterranean island packs in every form of terrain you can think of: pine forests and crimson cliffs, limestone gorges and secret caves, high mountains and beaches ranging in colour from pearl white to dusky orange to coal black. Outside the towns, the island remains fabulously wild, cloaked in the hardy, scented scrub known as maquis. And while its hairpin roads are a thrill to drive, there's another way to explore – and that's U Trinichellu (the Little Train).

Looking at Corsica's topography, it seems like an act of lunacy to even contemplate building a railway here. But in 1878, the island's Ministry of Public Works commissioned engineers to construct one between its two main towns: the west-coast capital of Ajaccio, and Bastia on the northeast shore. Unfortunately, there was a rather large – and very spiky – obstacle in between: the spine of mountains that runs down Corsica's centre like the back of a stegosaurus.

It took more than 20 years and the effort of 20,000 labourers to complete it, although the railway – including the spur to the coastal town of L'Île Rousse – wasn't officially declared finished until 1934 (another stretch along the east coast was destroyed by bombing during WWII, and never rebuilt). The Little Train has been threatened with closure many times since, but local outcry has (at least so far) ensured its survival.

Today, I'm riding the line from northeast to southwest, leaving from Bastia late morning, with a plan to watch the sunset over supper in Ajaccio. In summer, the train gets packed, thronged with backpack-toting hikers heading into the mountains; but today, in early spring, Bastia's station is curiously quiet, and I'm one of only a handful of people on this cross-island adventure.

For the first section, the train rolls along the coast, offering flashes of the Mediterranean before veering west at Casamozza, where it begins its long, slow climb up into the mountains. Maquis carpets the hillsides. When I lean my head out of the window, I catch hints of its herby perfume – rosemary, thyme, bay, eucalyptus. The track steepens, and the train slows, mostly trundling along at a steady 19mph (30km/h) as it crawls along steep-sided valleys and beetles over rickety river bridges.

Historically, the Little Train had another nickname: the Trembler, a reference to the bone-shaking, teeth-rattling ride afforded by the line's tracks, which were almost entirely laid by hand and, as such, tended not to be level or parallel. Until the early 2000s, vintage carriages known as Michelines were still running on much of the network, with wooden seats and dinky windows that made them look like something from a Disney cartoon. Sadly, most of the Michelines have been phased out in favour of modern carriages sporting air-con, widescreen windows and padded seats – but a few were kept on, and are now generally wheeled out only for special occasions. These trips offer a nostalgic glimpse of the Trinichellu of old, and are always packed to capacity.

"Maquis carpets the hillsides. When I lean my head out of the window, I catch hints of its herby perfume – rosemary, thyme, bay, eucalyptus..."

We reach the halfway point, Corte, around noon. Located high in the island's mountainous heart, this fortress town was the focus of Corsican resistance under local hero Pascal Paoli in the mid-18th century, when it briefly served as Corsica's capital. These days, it's a rough-around-the-edges, tumbledown kind of town that feels a world away from the glitzy harbours and ports of the Corsican coast: independence slogans are graffitied on the walls, and many road signs are peppered by shotgun pellets. I hop off the train to explore, pay a visit to the history museum and stop for a spot of lunch: a plate of delicious *cannelloni au brocciu*, flavoured with the island's tangy sheep's cheese, followed by chestnut cake, another Corsican staple. Contentedly stuffed, I rejoin the train for the run down to the coast.

From Corte, the Trinichellu meanders on over the mountainsides, offering views of the island's dagger-like peaks before crossing one of its most famous landmarks: the Viaduc sur

Philip Lee Harvey/Lonely Planet

CORSICA'S LOST BRIDGE

Originally, U Trinichellu was designed as part of a plan to build a line across Corsica and its neighbour, Sardinia. Napoleon III thought it would cut transport times between France and its African colonies, and plans were drawn up for a bridge to cross to Sardinia. Needless to say, the cost would have probably bankrupted France, and the plans were quietly shelved.

From left: U Trinichellu passes from coast to coast; the fortress town of Corte marks the midway point; a stone bridge in the interior. Previous page: the Pont du Vecchio, designed by Gustave Eiffel.

le Vecchio, the 558ft-long (170m), 308ft-high (94m) iron viaduct over the Vecchio River, designed by none other than Gustave Eiffel. Soon afterwards, it reaches its highest point, the 2972ft-long (906m) Tunnel de Vizzavona, before beginning the plunge down towards the west coast. Occasionally, we stop off at little stations to let off hikers, and I watch rather enviously as they trudge into the sunbaked hills, picking their way through the maquis. I wonder if any of them are planning on tackling the GR20, Corsica's legendary high-altitude trail, said by many to be the toughest walk in all of France.

I sit back and watch the Corsican countryside roll by. Olive groves and drystone walls zigzag over the hillsides. Goats watch us trundle past, bells tinkling through the pastures. Little country towns flash by, their terracotta roofs standing out against the green hillsides. We clatter over rivers and through pine woods, and whizz through stations – Bocagnano, Tavera, Ucciani – with names that sound more Italian than French, a reminder of the island's proximity to Italy and its historic links to Genoa. And then, before I know it, the Mediterranean is filling the windows once again, and we're pulling into Ajaccio, where Corsica's most famous son, Napoleon Bonaparte, was born, and U Trinichellu reaches its journey's end.

As I walk down to the harbour, reflecting on my day's journey, I can't imagine a better way to see the Île de Beauté. **OB**

Start/Finish // Bastia/Ajaccio
Distance // 98 miles (158km)
Duration // 3hr 30min to 4hr
Ticket types // €50 buys the Pass Liberta, a seven-day ticket giving free travel across Corsica's train network.
How to book // Buy the Pass Liberta online (cf-corse.corsica); individual tickets are sold at stations or on the train.
When to go // Corsica gets very busy in July and August. April, May and September are much calmer months, and you'll find it easier to find a seat on the train.
Things to know // As with many of France's rural trains, many stations on the Trinichellu line are request stops (*arrêts facultatifs*), so you need to remember to signal to the driver if you want to disembark.
More info // Corsica Tourism (visit-corsica.com)

Opposite: The vintage tram at Sóller, passing right under the beautiful facade of the Església de Sant Bartomeu.

MORE LIKE THIS
LITTLE ISLAND RAILWAYS

ISLAND LINE, ISLE OF WIGHT

At the turn of the 20th century, more than 55 miles (89km) of track ran across the Isle of Wight, a product of the insatiable Victorian passion for railway building – but cuts in the 1950s and '60s closed all save for this stretch along the island's east coast. Despite the reduced service, it's possible to travel by train (almost) all the way from London Waterloo: hop off at Portsmouth Harbour, catch the ferry, and then hop back on the Island Line at Ryde Pier Head to Shanklin, with Channel views along the way. Train buffs might notice something peculiar about the trains: most are ex-London Underground rolling stock that have been shipped over and put back into service. On the return journey, disembark at Smallbrook Junction and catch the Isle of Wight Steam Railway for 5.5 miles (9km) to Wootton.
Start // Ryde Pier Head
Finish // Shanklin
Distance // 8.5 miles (14km)
Duration // 30min

TRÉN DE SÓLLER, MALLORCA

Lisbon and San Francisco might be famous for their vintage trams, but the ones in Sóller are just as handsome. These charming wooden-sided trams have been trundling around the town since 1913, and put to all kinds of uses – transporting fish, fruit and vegetables, carrying coal, even carting munitions. Equally photogenic are the vintage carriages of their cousin, the Trén de Sóller, which shuttle a far longer distance – between Sóller and the island capital, Palma. With their hand-painted livery and wooden construction, they offer a glimpse of train travel as it was a century ago – and you'll be treated to views of the island's olive groves, pine forests and the Serra de Tramuntana, Mallorca's main mountain range. Look out for the Cinc-Ponts Viaduct, named after its five arches.
Start // Sóller
Finish // Palma
Distance // 17 miles (27km)
Duration // 1hr

INSELBAHN LANGEOOG, GERMANY

There's a very good reason to use public transport on Langeoog, one of the seven inhabited East Frisian Islands: cars aren't allowed, which means everyone on this sandy atoll gets around by bike, horse, cart or, quaintest of all, aboard the Inselbahn. This train was originally built to serve the island's port, and with its brightly coloured carriages and locomotives, it looks bizarrely like a child's impression of a train that's chugged straight off the sketch pad. It was horse-drawn until 1937, after which diesel engines were introduced. Its main claim to fame, however, is its status as Germany's shortest train trip: seven minutes from start to finish. You'll barely have time to sit down and get the snacks out, so you might want to ride it a few times.
Start // Langeoog Bahnhof
Finish // Langeoog Anleger
Distance // 1.6 miles (2.6km)
Duration // 7min

9

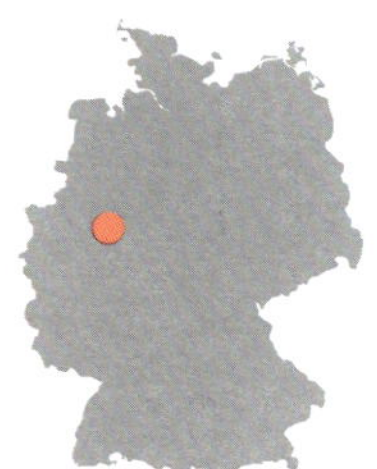

A RAILWAY RIDE BESIDE THE MIGHTY RHINE

Ride a beautiful, best-done-slow rail route along one of Europe's great transport arteries, taking in awe-inspiring vineyard views, mysterious castles and cobblestone-clad townscapes.

The Rhine is a world of its own. Carving a course from deep in the Alps, the river defines the natural and political borders of much of Western Europe. At 760 miles (1233km) in extent, it's second only to the Danube in the list of the region's longest rivers. The continent's history is, unsurprisingly, indelibly linked to the Rhine, which formed the northwestern boundary of the Roman Empire and today serves as a border between several of the countries it passes through. Happily for train travellers, tracks line much of the river's course, and one section in particular, the West Rhine Railway, offers what might just be Europe's best historical rail journey.

Plan carefully before starting out. The fastest journeys between Cologne and Mainz often take the high-speed line, bypassing the river. Make sure of a route that goes along the West Rhine tracks via Bonn and Koblenz, taking around two hours without stops. Better still, don't book at all and travel the route on a series of local trains, which allows for breaks in your journey and ferry connections along the way.

However you traverse the Rhine, Cologne is a fantastic station to leave from. Its gleaming glass-and-steel facade is startlingly close to the city's cathedral, just steps across Bahnhofsvorplatz, offering the chance for a quick look round one of Europe's greatest churches before getting on your way. Cologne Hauptbahnhof is also a sensible place to stock up on supplies for the journey.

I grabbed breakfast here, and everything I needed for a train picnic later in the day, before boarding a train heading upstream towards Bonn.

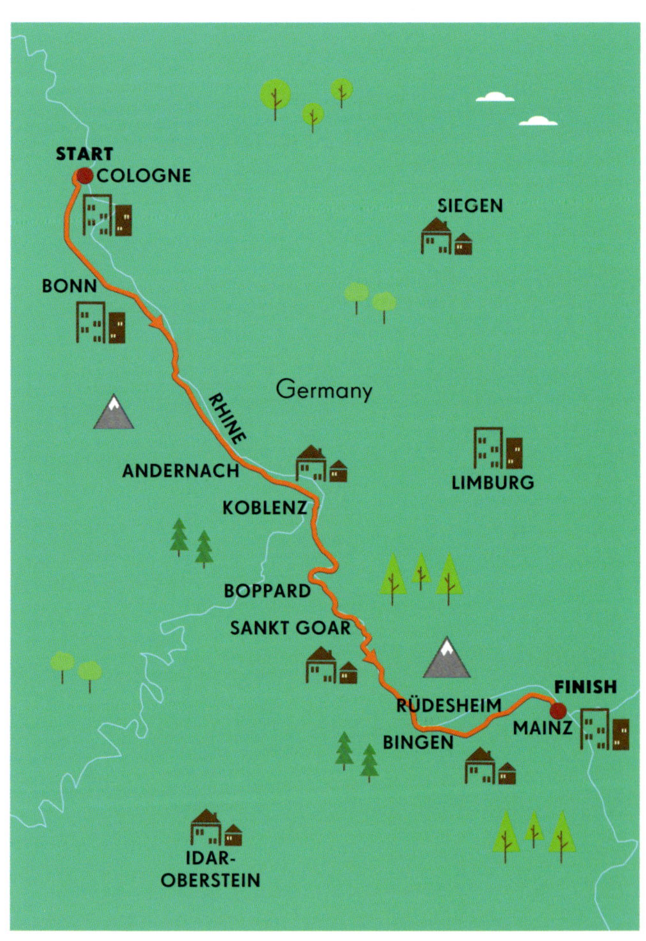

The former capital of West Germany, Bonn has a modern centre with medieval remnants, including a gatehouse with a severe-looking portcullis – visitors were not always as warmly welcomed as they are today. Most beeline to the house of Ludwig van Beethoven, a Bonn-born boy who died a few decades before the railways arrived in these parts. He missed a treat. From here, my train performed strange magic, seeming to go back in time. At Andernach there was another taste of the medieval: an ancient town wall with turret-studded towers. The Rhine narrowed. More towers began to appear on its banks. Changing trains in Koblenz – where the spontaneously inclined can veer upstream along the Moselle River to the ancient city of Trier – the broader waters of the Rhine held my attention. I took a quick break and walked down to Deutsches Eck, where a vast riverside monument to German unification is crowned by a statue of Kaiser Wilhelm I. A cable car stretching from Deutsches Eck to the Ehrenbreitstein Fortress across the river forms the most unusual Rhine crossing. What's visible of this long-standing fortress, however, are primarily 19th-century defences.

My next train travelled from Koblenz to Boppard in a flash, taking just a little longer than the cable car over the river. Arriving in Boppard felt like the first immersion into the deep Rhine, the stretch which is often celebrated, synonymous with the word 'romantic'. If love was in the air here, it was of the dreamy sort: quiet cobbled streets echoing to the sound of church bells; the steep-banked Rhine Valley bathed in sunshine; heavily laden touring cyclists tinkling bells and weaving round selfie-snapping visitors. Less obviously romantic but impossible to ignore was the procession of commercial shipping – mostly long, thin boats carrying industrial cargo, with the quirky sight of a car of two belonging to the crew hoisted up onto the deck.

The other extraordinary aspect of this section of the Middle Rhine is the vast number of castles – intact and ruined – that come into view from the train window. While many flash past in an instant, it's worth making a few stops to explore some further, not least because the views from their ramparts are generally spectacular. Possibly best explored after a lunch pause, Schloss Rheinfels is a 20-minute uphill amble from the station at the tiny riverside town of Sankt Goar, also an excellent place to detour to the east (right) bank of the Rhine by ferry, headed for its sister settlement Sankt Goarshausen. Once on this side, a lovely walk goes to and around Loreley, a rocky peninsula at the heart of many river myths.

BIG WINDOW VIEWS OF THE RHINE

For a nonstop zip down the Rhine and beyond, consider the daily Hamburg–Zürich EuroCity service, leaving Cologne mid-morning and following the West Rhine line. Its Swiss Railways First Class carriage has large windows that open up views of the river, and the dining car promises lunch with a fine backdrop – a taste of Swiss scenic services down the line, but at no extra cost to a regular First-Class fare.

Clockwise from left: A regional train passing under Katz Castle beside the Rhine; historic buildings in Mainz; the riverfront in Koblenz. Previous page: the Hohenzollern Bridge next to Cologne Cathedral.

Though mainly used for freight services, roughly hourly local trains roll along the East Rhine Railway from Sankt Goarshausen to Rüdesheim in 30 minutes, offering a chance to explore more tumbledown ruins and steep-sided vineyards. These key elements of a Rhine journey collide at Rüdesheim, where the remains of Schloss Ehrenfels are enclosed by grapevines. The Upper Middle Rhine was designated a UNESCO World Heritage Site in part because of its large number of castles, and nearby Brömserburg is one of the oldest within the UNESCO boundaries. Eibingen Abbey, the principal shrine to 11th-century mystic, composer and polymath St Hildegard of Bingen, is also close by. Hildegard was one of medieval Europe's most important women. Her music and spiritual legacy echoes along the river, and there is an exhibition on her at Bingen's Museum am Strom, reached by a ferry.

Back on the West Rhine Railway, the landscape flattened after Bingen, and it was from here that my final train left the UNESCO World Heritage area. Though far smaller than Cologne, Mainz provided a modern, big-city bookend to the tiny riverside stops I'd made in the Middle Rhine – and the best place from which to delve deeper into Europe. Though after a day on the West Rhine, you may feel you've seen many of the continent's highlights flowing past already. **TH**

Start/Finish // Cologne/Mainz
Distance // 121 miles (195km)
Duration // From 2hr 20min
Ticket types // Buying station-to-station tickets is the best option for following this route, though a rail pass covering Germany or all of Europe will also be valid. The good value Deutschlandticket, good for one month, is accepted on regional trains, but is primarily aimed at the German domestic market.
When to go // Visit late May or early October to get the balance between good weather and smaller crowds. Winter is quiet with more limited opening times for attractions and reduced ferry services, and many eating options close entirely.
How to book // You can buy regional and local tickets at stations shortly before travel.

Opposite: A vintage steam engine chuffing through wintry forests on the Harz Railway.

MORE LIKE THIS
GERMAN MOUNTAIN MAJESTY

HARZ RAILWAY

The narrow-gauge Harz Railway runs 37 miles (60km) from Nordhausen in the south of Germany to Wernigerode in the country's north, with an 11-mile (18km) branch line to Brocken. If that sounds prosaic, what makes it (and the neighbouring Selke Valley Railway, running from Nordhausen to Quedlinburg) so special is the widespread use of steam locomotives on all the lines. Not every service is steam-hauled, especially in winter, though many are. With careful attention to the timetables, this makes for the perfect slow-travel adventure, with gently determined steam services going about their daily business as they have for decades, unlocking a quiet corner of Germany.

Start // Nordhausen
Finish // Wernigerode
Distance // 48 miles (77km)
Duration // 3hr 30min

BLACK FOREST RAILWAY

Part scenic train, part regular Deutsche Bahn regional service, the Schwarzwaldbahn (Black Forest Railway) crosses over, around and through the mountainous Black Forest in Germany's south. Branching southwest from the Rhine Valley Line, the railway follows several river valleys and navigates tunnels and loops – managing some 2133ft (650m) in elevation changes. The trains stop at numerous attractive villages, including Triberg, home to Germany's highest waterfalls, and Donaueschingen, the source of the Danube River.

Start // Offenburg
Finish // Singen
Distance // 93 miles (149km)
Duration // 2hr 10min

ZUGSPITZE RAILWAY

Literally heading into Germany's highest mountain, the Zugspitzbahn packs a lot into a short route. It passes the Kreuzeckbahn and Alpspitzbahn cable cars and pauses at Eibsee, a beautiful little Alpine lake that's blue-green in summer and often frozen in winter. Driven steeply uphill by cogwheels – one of only four such railways in Germany – the Zugspitzbahn climbs the northern flank of Zugspitze, then zigzags through a 3-mile-long (5km) tunnel inside it, before emerging at the Glacier Station at 8530ft (2600m). From here, a cable car continues to the summit itself, where a Bond-villain-style complex of buildings and a viewing platform offer panoramic views. Bring warm clothes for the top, where temperatures will be significantly cooler than the lower stations.

Start // Garmisch-Partenkirchen
Finish // Zugspitze
Distance // 11.8miles (19km)
Duration // 1hr 15min

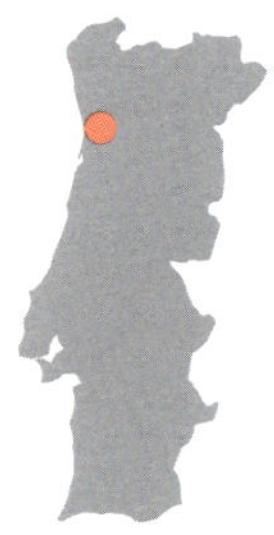

A VINTAGE JOURNEY ALONG PORTUGAL'S LINHA DO DOURO

The Linha do Douro train line through the Douro Valley, northern Portugal's legendary wine growing area, is considered one of Europe's most beautiful rail journeys.

I'm in Porto's São Bento Station, a UNESCO World Heritage Site and an officially recognised national monument within Portugal. But it's not yet 7am, and I'm not quite ready to take in the majesty of the station's floor-to-ceiling, early 20th-century tile murals that depict both the country's history and scenes from rural, northern Portuguese life. What I really need is coffee. I exit, grab some caffeine at one of the city's seemingly infinite *pastelarias* (pastry shops), then return to the station to board a sleek, modern commuter train – a jarring contrast with the scenes depicted in those murals. I'm awake at this hour so I can catch the first train to Pocinho, a dusty village at the eastern extent of the Douro River Valley, the country's famous wine region.

Sign up for a tasting at one of the ancient port cellars that spill down to the river's edge in Porto, or pop open an elegant red, and you're tapping into the Douro River Valley's claim to fame. The oldest demarcated wine-making area in the world (and another UNESCO World Heritage Site) is the source of the grapes that end up in Portugal's most lauded and expensive bottles. For millennia, these wines

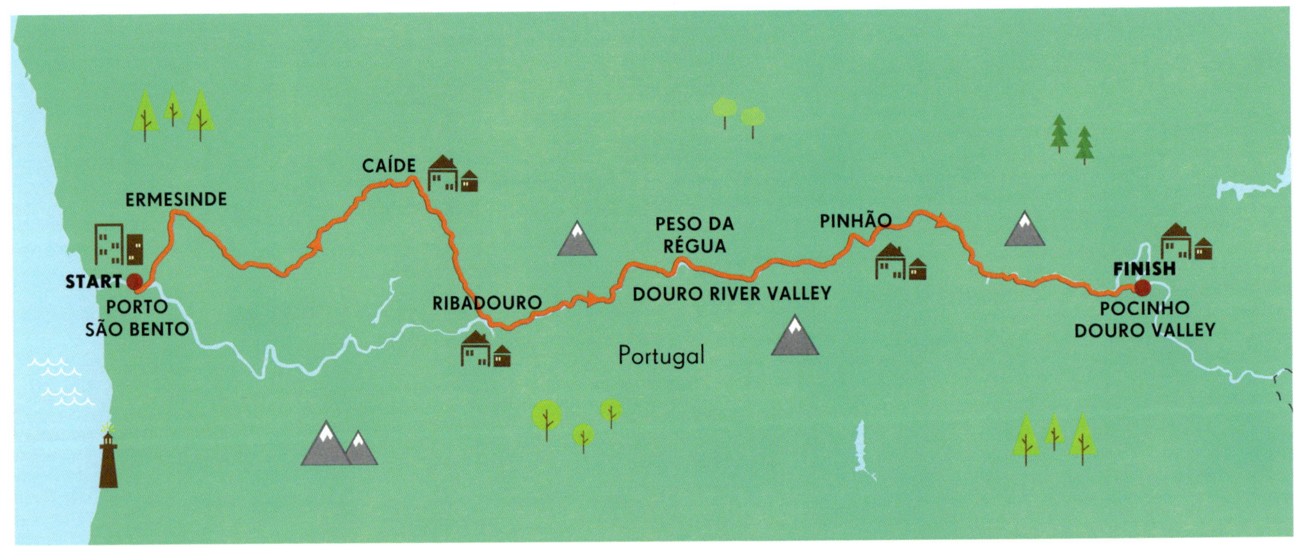

were transported via *barco rabelo*, traditional wooden cargo boats, but in the late 19th century, engineers completed a train line, linking Porto with the estates upriver. These days, grapes and wine bottles alike travel by truck, but the train continues to run its route, and I wanted to see the Douro Valley from this vantage point.

Just outside Porto, in the town of Ermesinde, I change trains, boarding a rattling, 1970s-era carriage decked out in shades of orange and purple that could easily feature in a Wes Anderson film; this is my ride into the Douro Valley proper. We pull out of Ermesinde and the next hour is distinctly uneventful: it's January, and the seemingly endless industrial-feeling suburbs – a thousand shades of grey – and perpetual mist and rain make me wonder if I've somehow boarded a train in northern England.

Then, suddenly, it all changes. In Caíde, we enter our first tunnel (one of 23 along this route), and when we emerge, the landscape has shifted to that of steep hills and greenery. A bit later, above the tiny village of Ribadouro, we round a corner and catch our first glimpse of the Douro. It could be said that the trip really begins here.

From this point on, the train hugs the north bank of the river, sometimes appearing to run only metres from the current. This proximity is due to the fact that the Douro Valley is incredibly steep, with little space for trains. It's observing this that I gain a new appreciation for wines from here, one that has little to do with aromas, body or tasting notes. Simply planting, maintaining and harvesting vineyards on these impossibly sheer slopes is itself an accomplishment of engineering.

> *"Clusters of houses and tiny villages cling to hills, and I spot the occasional winery, a manor house surrounded by neat lines of vineyards."*

As we chug east, parts of the valley are obscured by mist while the sun threatens to emerge, illuminating only the hilltops, and giving me the impression that we're skimming a coastline beside a chain of islands. Clusters of houses and tiny villages cling to hills, and I spot the occasional winery, a manor house surrounded by neat lines of vineyards. But because it's January, the vines have neither leaves nor grapes.

We approach Peso da Régua, one of the larger towns along the line and an opportunity to stretch the legs or have a meal, but I stay on board. My interlude instead comes in Pinhão. This riverside village is the terminus for boat trips from Porto, and is a confounding blend of crusty old winemakers and wide-eyed tourists. I disembark at the town's station, which is decked out with tile murals that depict the grape harvest, and walk along the riverfront. The hills that encircle Pinhão are home to a handful of wineries, and if you time your trip right, a stop can involve a meal, a

END OF THE LINE

The Linha do Douro used to have five branch lines: the last closed in 2009. Additionally, the line didn't terminate in Pocinho but rather in Barca d'Alva, on the border with Spain, where it was possible to connect with local trains. When Spain discontinued its counterpart in 1984, Portugal made Pocinho the terminus, though in recent years, there's been talk of once again linking the two lines.

From left: Azulejos at a station; vineyards high above the Douro; a traditional Portuguese pastel de nata *in Porto; waterside dining in Porto. Previous page: For much of the journey the line skirts the Douro.*

wine tasting or both. I cross the town's bridge on foot. The mist has been burned away by now, so I get an excellent view of the vineyards and estate houses that ring the city.

At 3.43pm, I catch the next train east to continue my journey. This is by far the most dramatic part of the trip, where the Douro Valley becomes even narrower and rockier. At Ferradosa, the train crosses a bridge (one of 35 along the way) to the south bank of the Douro. I swap to the left side of the nearly empty carriage to see tiny train stations – shelters, really – that link to trailheads, abandoned wineries and vineyards.

Approaching Pocinho, the topography abruptly flattens and steep hillsides studded with grapevines transform into wide valleys spiked with fruit trees. I spy the terminus and a smattering of railroad infrastructure; until 1984, it was possible to continue riding this train to Spain, less than 20 miles (32km) away, and onward towards the university town of Salamanca. After the extremes of the Douro Valley, pulling into tiny, flat Pocinho doesn't exactly feel triumphant.

I snap a picture of the old wooden station, use the bathroom, then board the same train again; at 5.14pm we leave Pocinho, bound for Porto. After a half hour or so, back in that steep valley, the sun and mist combine to give me a rainbow, something I take as my reward for putting the journey over the destination. **AB**

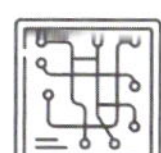

Start/Finish // São Bento Station, Porto/Pocinho
Distance // 106 miles (171km)
Duration // 3hr 30min
Ticket types // Standard Class
How to book // Visit the Comboios de Portugal website cp.pt.
When to go // Late summer and early autumn are best if you want to witness the grape harvest; the winter months can be rainy and misty, obscuring views.
Things to know // From July to October, the Douro Historical Train, a circa 1925 steam engine complete with vintage cars, runs part of this route. The five carriage train links Régua and Tua, a distance of 22 miles (35km), never exceeding a speed of 30mph hour (48km/h) – all the better for the views. Details can be found at cp.pt.

Opposite top: The Alhambra of Granada makes for a wonderful finish for a train journey from Almeria. Opposite below: Viana do Castelo Cathedral is a stop on the journey from Porto to Vigo.

MORE LIKE THIS
IBERIAN ESCAPADES

ALMERÍA TO GRANADA, SPAIN

Known as Línea 68, this 'medium distance' train links Almería, on Spain's Mediterranean coast, with the fabled city of Granada, in Andalucía. Departing from Almería, the first part of the journey passes through a landscape so studded with fruit- and veg-growing greenhouses it's known colloquially as the *mar de plástico* (sea of plastic). Heading inland, the plastic shifts to dry flatlands – thought to be Europe's only proper desert, and the film location for many spaghetti westerns. From here, make sure you've chosen a seat on the train's left side for views of the dramatic, perpetually snow-capped Sierra Nevada range. In the town of Guadix, don't miss the cave-like houses some residents live in. At the time of writing, the trip takes around three hours, but there are plans to replace this line with a high-speed rail.

Start // Almería
Finish // Granada
Distance // 113 miles (182km)
Duration // 3hr

BARCELONA TO VALENCIA, SPAIN

Inaugurated in 1997, the Euromed is a high-speed train that runs along Spain's Mediterranean coast. The full route links Figueres, in the country's northeast, with Alicante, south of Valencia, connecting intermediate stops Barcelona and Valencia in just over two and a half hours. Exiting Barcelona, the first part of the route is largely inland. It's not until after Tarragona that the train skirts the water, passing through the green wetlands of the Ebro Delta on the left-hand side and the Serra del Montsià on the right. Handsome seaside villages form much of the remaining landscape. Sit on the left-hand side and turn your moveable seat in the direction you prefer for best views.

Start //Barcelona-Sants
Finish // Valencia-Joaquín Sorolla
Distance // 218 miles (351km)
Duration // 2hr 30min

PORTO, PORTUGAL TO VIGO, SPAIN

Known in Portuguese as the Linha Celta (Celtic Line), this trip runs from Porto in Portugal to Vigo, the largest city in Spain's Galicia region. An hour north of Porto, the countryside is more Ireland than Iberia: emerald green and misty, with granite villas rather than tile-fronted houses. Along this stretch, it's common to see pilgrims en route to Santiago de Compostela walking beside the train tracks. The train, a slow, rattling Comboios de Portugal Série 592, makes a stop in Viana do Castelo. Just north of here, it follows the coast and is sprayed by foam from the rough Atlantic. At Caminha, the journey turns inland and follows the Minho River, eventually crossing it – the border between the two countries – in Valença (Portugal)/Tui (Spain). At the time of writing, this is the only international service between Portugal and Spain, though a high-speed rail route is being planned.

Start // Porto-Campanhã
Finish // Vigo-Guijar
Distance // 109 miles (175km)
Duration // 2hr 30min

RACING RIVERS ON THE BOHINJ RAILWAY

This short, sweet relic of a railway runs from the Italian border into Slovenia's Julian Alps, rumbling slowly enough to take in views of beautiful river valleys and mountains.

The first time I rode this line, it was so mind-blowing that I knew I had to return and do it again. Back then, the train was a rusty, graffiti-covered, single-carriage diesel idling on the platform at sleepy Jesenice Station near Slovenia's border with Austria. With almost unbelievably inexpensive tickets in our hands, my family and I waited on a deserted platform and doubted whether this train was going anywhere that day. But it did, running through increasingly dramatic high-altitude scenery to Bled Jezero, a hermitage-style station overlooking Lake Bled (the body of water after which it is named). It wasn't hard to fall for this humble train and the small-but-perfect country that it trundled through. I watched it pull away towards Lake Bohinj and the Italian border and vowed to make another visit – this time I would explore the entire line.

When the day of my return came, I found myself standing at the other end of the route, my feet astride two countries. On one side of the border was Gorizia, a quiet Italian city midway between Venice and Trieste, dominated by its castle; on the other, its Slovenian twin of Nova Gorica. Information boards explained how this was once a very different frontier – with tight controls, high fences and tension where Western Europe met the former Yugoslavia. Today, both countries are EU members and part of the Schengen Area. I crossed decisively into Slovenia and aimed for the enormous cream-and-white edifice of Nova Gorica's station, a few steps ahead. Looking robustly Austro-Hungarian, the station felt like an entry point into a new country. It was very different to the country where I'd just been standing – on the platform,

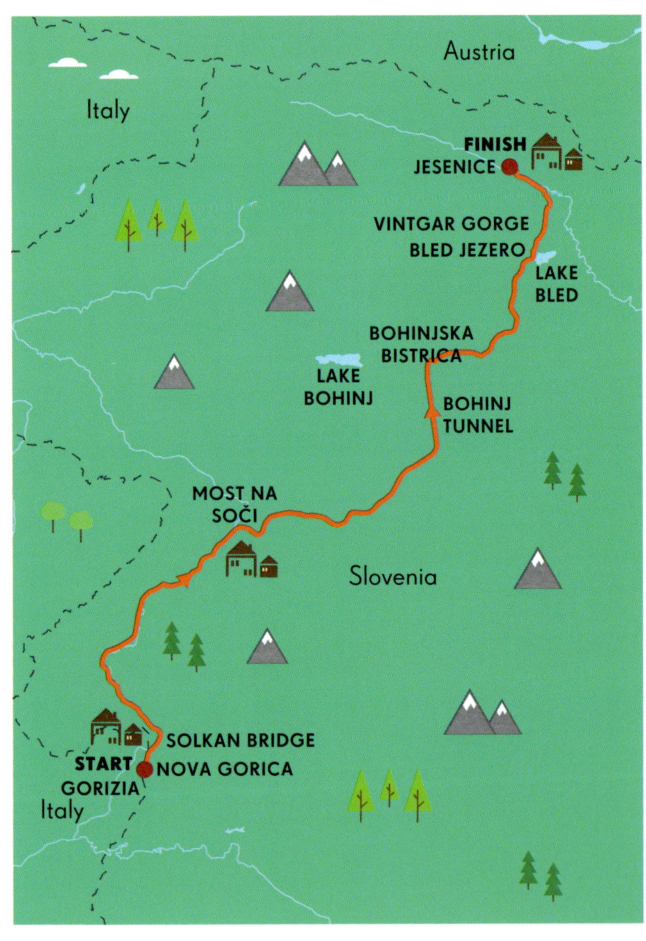

I found the same sense of peace I'd found at the other end of the line in Jesenice a few years before.

A bright red train emerged through the tunnel to my right – my ride for the morning. More modern than the last time I'd been here – though still on a small scale – this train was the kind of regional service that shuttles up and down lines across Europe. There were a handful of carriages, a spray of graffiti and a distinct sense of the everyday. A small group of passengers, some carrying bags of shopping, strolled out of a cafe that doubled as a waiting room. The driver grabbed a quick coffee, exchanged a laugh with the waiter and, with a reassuring blow on the conductor's whistle, we were on our way.

The track immediately took up residency alongside the Soča River, whose bright green waters we'd follow as they became narrower and led higher into the Julian Alps. First we crossed the river via the Solkan Bridge: at 279ft (85m), it's the world's longest stone arch railway bridge. As with many remarkable sights on the line, I seemed to be the only passenger gaping in awe at what we passed. The local-bus atmosphere continued as we travelled slowly up the valley, one or two people getting on or off at small halts.

At Most na Soči things started to take on a holiday vibe, with hikers and paddleboarders in evidence, obviously aiming for the lovely lake of the same name. This was also the starting point for that great rarity of the rails: a car-carrying service. Here, a separate 35-minute journey sees cars transported through the Bohinj Tunnel, with 4 miles (6.4km) of track offering a shortcut to almost two hours of mountain driving. Continuing uphill along the side of an ever-steepening valley, our little train seemed to be careering straight into towering green mountains, only to suddenly plunge into the tunnel, its darkness contrasting with the bright sunshine outside.

"Our little train seemed to be careering straight into towering green mountains, only to suddenly plunge into the tunnel..."

At the other end of the tunnel, the train emerged into scenery that was, if anything, even more glorious. We passed the town of Bohinjska Bistrica and ran alongside the waters of the Sava Bohinjka – a river flowing out of Lake Bohinj and eventually meeting the Danube in distant Belgrade. Pitch-roofed houses and barns with piles of neat-stacked logs formed a rustic

A RIDE THROUGH HISTORY

A century ago, modern-day Slovenia was part of the Austro-Hungarian Empire, and the Bohinj Railway formed part of new rail link to the empire's port at Trieste. Ownership of the territory straddling the line was split between Italy and the Yugoslavian state after WWI, then then subsumed almost wholly into Yugoslavia after 1945.

From left: Bled Island in the lake of the same name; the Solkan Bridge seen from above; the border between Italy and Slovenia at Gorizia/Nova Gorica. Previous page: a local train crossing the Solkan Bridge.

backdrop. One station appeared to have its own small farm, using one end of the platform for growing produce. It came as a bit of a surprise to be suddenly back in the modern world at Bled Jezero, the nearest stop on the line to Slovenia's most famous postcard scene, Lake Bled. Anyone choosing to hop off here could stroll down to the lake, have a swim in its perfect green waters with Bled's famous island church in sight, take a leisurely lunch at the campsite next to the beach and then wander back uphill for the next train on to Jesenice. Alternatively, there's an even shorter walk from the next stop, Podhom, to the Vintgar Gorge, a mile-long (1.6km) chasm of raging water that's bridged by the Bohinj Railway. Stopping off guarantees a close-up view of the gorge rather than a moment's glance as you cross it on the train.

The journey was by now in its final stages, and the hills became dotted with factories and apartment blocks as Jesenice, the junction with the mainline, came into view. From here, Villach in Austria is a short journey to the northwest, while elegant Ljubljana is just an hour and a half to the southwest. Or there's the tempting option of staying on board one of Europe's best short train journeys, taking the return journey back over the mountains to the Italian frontier, and the grand Austro-Hungarian station. **TH**

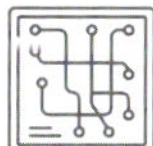

Start/Finish // Nova Gorica/Jesenice
Distance // 55 miles (89km)
Duration // 1hr 54min
Ticket types // There is only one (Standard) class of travel on the train, and no reservations are possible.
How to book // Tickets can be purchased at any station along the line.
When to go // Early or late summer is ideal, allowing you to combine exploring the line with making the most of summer in the Julian Alps. The area around Lake Bled, in particular, can be busy in July and August.
Things to know // Suspended at the time of research was the Summer Museum Train service, offering a steam locomotive experience from the Ljubljana Train Museum. Check zelezniskimuzej.si for future summer operations.
More info // Slovenia Tourist Board (slovenia.info).

Opposite: The great Ottoman bridge at Mostar – destroyed during the Bosnian war in 1993, and rebuilt in 2004.

MORE LIKE THIS
THE BEST OF BALKAN RAILWAYS

BELGRADE TO BAR, SERBIA & MONTENEGRO

Threading from the Serbian capital to the Montenegrin coast, this is one of Europe's most scenic journeys. On departure, the line heads into the hilly countryside south of Belgrade. Eager map readers will notice a brief meander into Bosnia & Herzegovina, though it's hard to take your eyes off the views, which get progressively more mountainous once in Montenegro. The highlight is Europe's tallest railway viaduct, Mala Rijeka, before the train returns to earth and the Montenegrin capital, Podgorica. Once across Lake Skadar, on the border with Albania, the final run skirts the Adriatic coast before the journey's end at Bar, a modern seaside destination with the atmospheric ruins of its Byzantine Old Town a few miles distant. If you're travelling in summer, there's a day train (Tara) and a night option (Lovcen) for this stunning route. Year-round, it's just the night train, with glorious morning views if riding to the sea.

Start // Belgrade Centar
Finish // Bar
Distance // 296 miles (476km)
Duration // 11hr

SEPTEMVRI TO DOBRINISHTE, BULGARIA

Departing from the Sofia–Plovdiv mainline at the convenient halfway point of Septemvri, Bulgaria's last narrow-gauge service reaches high into the Rhodope, Rila and Pirin ranges. This defiantly old-school diesel service tops out at Avramovo (at 4156ft/1267m) before continuing to the country's premier ski destination, Bansko. Unless you're a committed railway enthusiast planning on a very long day out from Sofia or Plovdiv, Bansko is the best place to pause for an overnight stay along the line. From the train window, you'll see wooded valleys and river gorges, and you'll chug around four spiral loops of track (encountered over the especially dramatic 28-mile/45km section from Velingrad to Yakoruda) while riding this determined feat of Balkan railway engineering.

Start // Septemvri
Finish // Dobrinishte
Distance // 77.7 miles (125km)
Duration // 4hr 30min

SARAJEVO TO MOSTAR, BOSNIA & HERZEGOVINA

Buses dominate intercity travel in many parts of the Balkans, but this line is an excellent opportunity to see an underappreciated region from the comfort of a modern train. The route can be travelled as part of the twice-daily service running from Sarajevo to the Croatian port of Ploče: on leaving the Bosnian capital, the track ascends tree-covered hills and, on arriving at lofty Bradina (2480ft/756m), crosses the watershed between the Black Sea and the Adriatic. The route then rolls downward past Lake Jablaničko, trundling in and out of tunnels before hugging the emerald Neretva River all the way to Mostar.

Start // Sarajevo
Finish // Mostar
Distance // 80 miles (129km)
Duration // 2hr

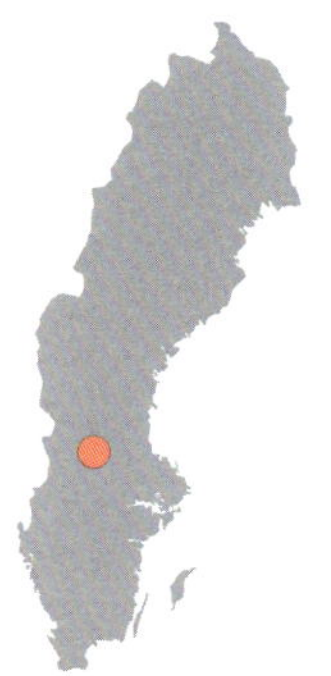

CATCH THE INLANDSBANAN INTO SWEDEN'S WILD HEART

The Inlandsbanan is one of the world's most wilfully eccentric railways, travelling at snail's pace from the lakeland of central Sweden high into the Arctic Circle.

The Inlandsbanan is a train you'd expect to find in a children's bedtime story. A bright-red, single-carriage service that putters up a single-track line, through wildflower-dotted meadows, occasionally creaking to a stop at remote and tiny stations, deep in forests that prompt visions of gingerbread cottages and malignant trolls. At certain spots, the driver has been known to hit the brakes so passengers can get out and forage for berries, swim in lakes or otherwise stretch their legs. This is a train that timetables stops for everyone to have lunch in lineside restaurants, and then resume their train journey as they digest. It sounds like it's made up, but the Inlandsbanan is very real. I know this because I've travelled its length up the backbone of Sweden, from the silvery lakes of the south to its northern terminus in the land of the midnight sun.

My story began, once upon a time, in the little waterfront town of Mora, itself a four-hour train journey from Stockholm. The salty air of the capital and its archipelago felt distant in this Swedish idyll – a land of slow-growing pine, birch and spruce forests, sprinkled with scarlet cabins and chequered by still lakes. It was this quiet, sparsely inhabited territory that the Inlandsbanan was built to exploit at the dawn of the 20th century. The 'Inland Railway' had two objectives: to provide the Swedish military a north-south supply line in the event of a Russian invasion from the east; and to exploit the timber and minerals in the relative terra incognita of the interior. By the 1990s traffic had dwindled to a trickle and the line was threatened with closure. Only more recently has it been reinvented as a route for tourists

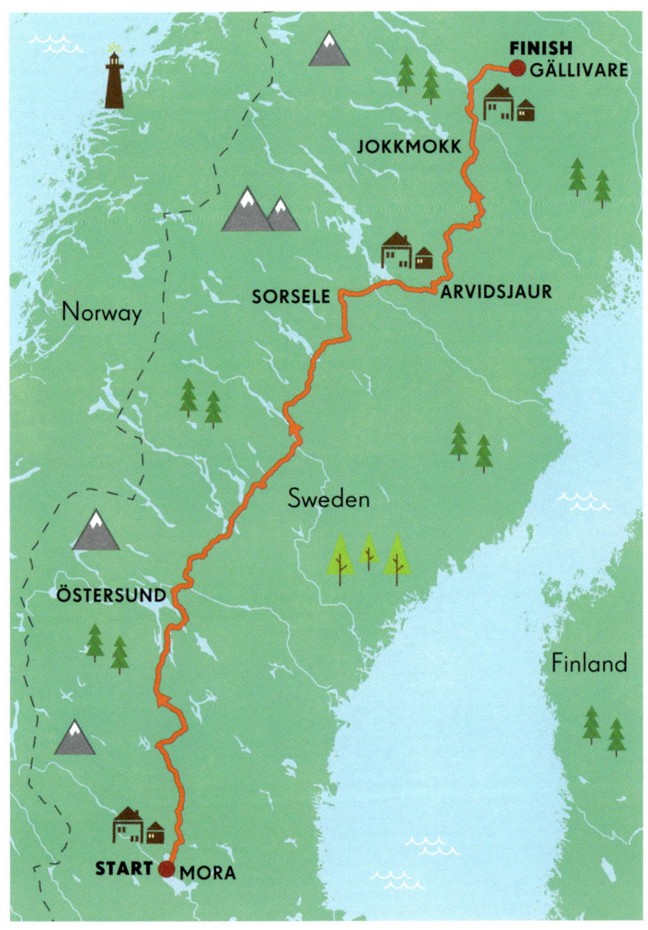

NGE

– sometimes foreigners, but mostly native Swedes who wish to see another, less familiar side to their country from a window seat. Speed is not a priority on these dawdling journeys through the woods – nor is this a showstopping display of soaring bridges and dizzying inclines, like Swiss mountain railways or routes just over the border in Norway. Rather an Inlandsbanan journey is about slowing your heartbeat to match the clank and clatter of woodland rails, spending idle hours chatting to fellow passengers, napping, reading books, inhaling the woodland air. It's also about scanning the line ahead for signs of reindeer, elk, wolf, wolverine, bear and other creatures whose tracks briefly intersect with those of the train.

I boarded a northbound service at Mora's lemon-yellow station – a 1981 Fiat railcar, far from its balmy Piedmontese homeland at these northerly latitudes, but whose lo-fi bus-on-rails profile has been part of the Inlandsbanan experience for decades. Upon departing, we skirted the shores of Lake Siljan, a body of water famous for Dala Horses, the little wooden models whittled into shape at lakeside workshops – and supposedly painted red so it won't show if you cut your hand making them. Soon our equally red train was cutting its course northward, away from settlements, roads and people, into the boreal forests. Once or twice we ground to a halt and hikers disembarked at request stops, heading off to spend a night alone in the

"Once or twice we ground to a halt and hikers disembarked at request stops, heading off to spend a night alone in the woods..."

woods. Here and there we slowed out of respect for fellow travellers of the rails – logging trains stacked with timber – occupying the sidings. But most of the time the train moved forth at a steady 31mph (50km/h) – only a shade faster than Usain Bolt at maximum speed.

Though the journey takes two days, the Inlandsbanan is no sleeper train, meaning all northbound and southbound through-passengers must break their journey mid-route. Like most people, I stayed two nights at the halfway point, the likable university town of Östersund, hugging the vast and island-studded Lake Storsjön – its depths are supposedly home to a creature much like the Loch Ness Monster. I grew tired of scanning the water for it and headed to Jamtli, Östersund's excellent museum of Swedish life, similar to the more famous Skansen in Stockholm. It has recreations of historic living in the interior – people dressed as bakers, milkmaids and farm hands busy in recreated farmsteads, evoking a world before the railway arrived in the early 20th century and modernity started to encroach. I spent an afternoon here before boarding a northbound service on the last leg of the Inlandsbanan.

The forests thinned out, and we entered more rugged, boulder-strewn terrain. The fells of the Norwegian border country began to rise up to our left, concealing the cold fjords beyond. At these latitudes, the summer sun loiters on the horizon at the day's end, scattering golden rays, before climbing once again in the small hours, having granted the world barely a blink of darkness. Eventually the train passes the Arctic Circle and enters Lapland, home to Europe's only recognised indigenous people, the Sámi. Stops along the Inlandsbanan offer a small window on Sámi life. Jokkmokk is home to a famous market, while in Arvidsjaur you can see a cluster of preserved wooden buildings. I disembarked just short of the northern terminus of Gällivare at Sorsele to visit a traditional Sámi homestay high in the hills, learning about their nomadic traditions and the seasonal movement of reindeer herds.

At the end of my trip I reflected on the Inlandsbanan, one of the most remote threads of the European rail network, reaching far north to the domain of the Sámi, of reindeer and endless summer days. Having narrowly escaped the axe in the 1990s, it deserves to have the sun shine on it for many years to come. **OS**

PAUSING FOR REFRESHMENT

In the early days of rail travel it was not uncommon for trains to stop and passengers to dine at establishments beside the line. It's a tradition that's all but vanished, though not on the Inlandsbanan. Hosts take orders on board the train to be eaten at restaurants during scheduled halts. Arctic char is a classic dish in the far north – but don't linger long or you'll miss your onward journey.

Clockwise from top left: A Fiat railcar travelling through the forests; a steam engine preserved at Arvidsjaur; crossing a girder bridge near Ostersund; traditional Sámi buildings in the hills near the Norwegian border. Previous page: A train in the Arctic.

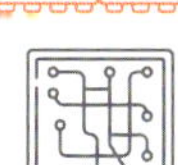

Start/Finish // Mora/Gällivare
Distance // 680 miles (1094km)
Duration // 2 days
Ticket types // There's one class on Inlandsbanan – seats are comfy but typical of a rural stopping service. You also get an onboard host offering a running commentary throughout the trip and serving drinks and snacks.
How to book // Book at inlandsbanan.se. Holiday packages are available, including accommodation along the line and, in some cases, excursions into Norway. Alternatively, get an Inlandsbanan card that entitles you to two weeks unlimited roving up and down the line.
When to go // The Inlandsbanan runs mid-June to mid-August. A winter service operates on the southern half between Östersund and Mora, from December to April.
Things to know // Pack plenty of insect repellent.

Opposite top: The Nordlandsbanen line connects Trondheim with Bodø to the north. Opposite below: Reindeer can be found in the landscapes beyond the town of Rovaniemi.

MORE LIKE THIS
ARCTIC RAILWAY LINES

STOCKHOLM TO NARVIK

Intrepid though the Inlandsbanan may be, it doesn't actually count as Europe's northernmost railway. That distinction belongs to the train that runs from Stockholm Central Station to the Arctic port of Narvik (actually just over the border in Norway). This sleeper hauls out of the Swedish capital early in the evening. Depending on the time of year, you might be able to glimpse the towers of Uppsala Cathedral, watching over Sweden's most famous university town. You'll likely be snoozing as the service skirts the Gulf of Bothnia before striking inland and briefly meeting up with Inlandsbanan services at Gällivare. Rubbing your eyes the next morning, you'll find trains trundling along a railway known as the 'iron ore line' – it's here that the scenery is most impressive. After crossing into Norway, the route hugs the southern flank of the Rombaken fjord, arriving in Narvik – Europe's northernmost station – in time for lunch.

Start // Stockholm
Finish // Narvik
Distance // 629 miles (1012km)
Duration // 18hr

NORDLANDSBANEN

Norway's Nordlandsbanen runs roughly parallel to the Inlandsbanan on the opposite side of the Scandinavian Mountains, journeying from Trondheim to the port of Bodø. It's another epic railway ride, stretching for over 450 miles (720km), and had been under construction for more than 80 years before it finally reached Bodø in the 1960s. After leaving Trondheim and tracing the banks of its eponymous fjord, the line veers inland, with the peaks of the Lomsdal–Visten National Park materialising out to the west. The most scenic stretch sees trains tracking a succession of fjords on approach to the industrial hub of Mo i Rana, but the final leg into Bodø is also scintillating – look out for the Saltstraumen, a narrow strait that's home to some of the fastest tidal currents in the world. Sleepers also run on this route.

Start // Trondheim
Finish // Bodø
Distance // 452 miles (727km)
Duration // 10hr

HELSINKI TO ROVANIEMI

Finland's railways offer a seasonal favourite in the form of the Santa Claus Express, adorned with a characterful livery of reindeers, owls and depictions of the white-bearded fellow himself. This double-decker sleeper train travels north from capital Helsinki bound for the Arctic Circle and, needless to say, is particularly popular with families wishing for Christmas-themed attractions. After passing through the country's second city, Tampere, the line continues north, flirting with the Bothnian shore around the towns of Kokkola and Oulu. Opening your curtains after a night in a bunk is akin to opening presents on Christmas morning – especially if you're gazing out over Narnia-like landscapes on approach to Rovaniemi, a town laid out like a reindeer's antlers.

Start // Helsinki
Finish // Rovaniemi
Distance // 438 miles (705km)
Duration // 12hr

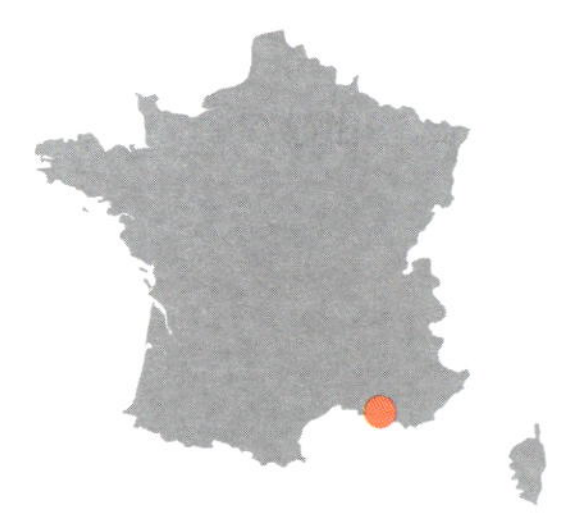

FRENCH CONNECTIONS FROM PARIS TO MARSEILLE

This gallop includes France's original high-speed line and melds the convenience of super-frequent services with a dash of Riviera glamour.

The old and the new mingle together on a Paris–Marseille TGV (Train à Grande Vitesse; France's fast trains). Curving down the spine of the country, in a graceful arc from the capital to the republic's oldest city, this route has origins reaching back to the dawn of French railways. The line also tells the story of the transformation of the national railway system – and how it inspired the high-speed revolution that continues across Europe today.

Technically, this route travels along three Lignes à Grande Vitesse (LGV; high-speed lines), adding up to one hugely popular three-and-a-half-hour link between France's two largest cities. The LGV Sud-Est from Paris to Lyon became the continent's first high-speed line when it opened in 1981. Eleven years later, the LGV Rhône-Alpes continued the southward march, the route completed by the opening of the LGV Méditerranée in 2001, slicing journey times between Valence and Marseille and along the Paris–Marseille route overall. Not only have faster trips seen rail travel endure as an alternative to driving, but the TGV model of quicker times and city-centre departure and arrival points has proved an appealing alternative to the stress, inconvenience and higher carbon cost of flying.

As tempting as it is to focus on how TGV trains have shaped the future of rail transport, this journey also serves as a reminder of France's railway heritage. The predecessor of this service – the classic route from Paris to Marseille via Dijon and Lyon – was promoted enthusiastically by Napoleon III to speed up French industrialisation. The line was a success, but railways never quite altered the character

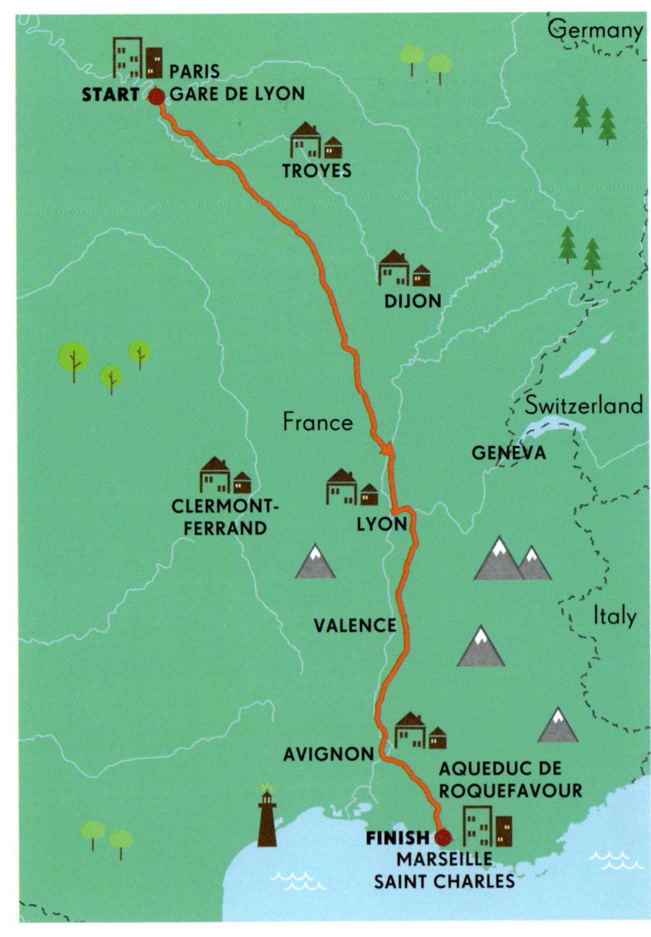

of France, which retains its huge swathes of resolutely rural country. This delight of a journey showcases that pastoral vision from the train window.

One of the pleasures is starting a journey from Paris' Gare de Lyon, a station that feels as though it's been transported straight to the banks of the Seine from the sunny shores of the Mediterranean. Built for the 1900 Paris Exposition, the clock tower, palm-tree-lined forecourt and sunlight-trapping glass roof make this one of the world's finest places to catch a train. That's assuming travellers don't lose track of time while they over-indulge at Le Train Bleu, the station's almost ridiculously ornate on-site brasserie, and miss their connection altogether. The Train Bleu name comes from a famously upmarket night service from Calais to Nice that ran in the interwar years. It paused here to pick up Riviera-bound passengers in the capital, in the process dripping glamour onto French rails.

Paris to Marseille today is an extremely popular route, with 23 daily services. While this may sound like a turn-up-and-go service, booking is recommended – partly to be sure you can get on and partly to get the best prices. In early summer, I had booked about a month in advance and, on boarding around lunchtime, found myself in the company of the expected seaside-bound crowds. My train was branded as an inOui service, distinct from fewer-frills Ouigo trains. Regardless of logo, TGVs don't so much as wait at a platform; they brood in anticipation of departure as the passengers

"With an elegant Gallic nose pointing towards the sea, we soon passed into classic French rural scenery dotted with silent villages and single-lane roads..."

jostle through the ticket barriers, eager to hop on. This enthusiasm may be due to the excitement of travelling on the double-deck carriages which operate on this route – the best views are from upstairs, while a calmer, quieter atmosphere generally prevails on the lower deck.

With everyone safely on board, the doors shut with a reassuring crescendo of beeps, and the power car released its pent-up energy with a smooth acceleration, leaving the grace of central Paris instantly behind for the suburban hinterland. With an elegant Gallic nose pointing towards the sea, we soon passed into classic French rural scenery dotted with silent villages and single-lane roads where only the occasional vehicle passed. It was pleasant enough, but the speedometer, nudging 186mph (300km/h) was the main focus of attention. In under two hours, we skirted Lyon and headed south, following the Rhône, a river we crossed once just past Valence. Leaving Avignon's ancient centre to our left – many services pause at out-of-town Avignon TGV station – we pushed on. Gone in a flash was the Aqueduc

THE SLOW TRAIN THROUGH PROVENCE

For a more leisurely roll through the Provençal section of this journey, board a Lyon-bound TGV from Paris, then pick up one of the slower trains that take around four hours to travel the 'classic' line. With services stopping along the way, you can take in Orange's Roman amphitheatre and Avignon's famously truncated Pont St-Bénézet, reaching Marseille at a gentler pace.

From left: Inside Gare de Lyon; Paris cafe culture; the waterfront in Marseille. Previous page: A TGV service slicing through vineyards on the Paris-Marseille route.

de Roquefavour, a 19th-century engineering feat that, despite being the world's largest stone aqueduct, is often mistaken for the Roman Pont du Gard to the northwest. Slowing down at last, passing by the port area of Marseille offered a first glimpse of the Mediterranean. Soon we were at Marseille Saint-Charles Station. I'd expected a bustling port city arrival and hadn't banked on such an elegant entrance to Marseille. A stroll past the ranks of statuary lining the Grand Staircase was a graceful connection from the somewhat out-of-the-way terminus with the Boulevard d'Athènes.

If this sounds like it happened rather quickly – and it did – there is a beautiful sequel. Slower services bound for Nice weave around the coast and inland via Toulon, Saint-Raphaël and Cannes. Along the way, the line passes pretty beaches, then the rocky coves and red hills of the Massif de l'Esterel, where the trains also run along the dramatic seafront viaduct at Anthéor. At times, the distant Alps appear behind the blue sea; this dramatic contrast is at its best in winter when the Alps shine white with snow. It takes almost as long to get from Marseille to Nice as it does to do the whole route from Paris to the coast. An even longer route is the Intercités de Nuit night service from Paris Austerlitz to Nice, where you can admire the coastal view of the scenic section without even getting out of bed. **TH**

Start/Finish // Paris Gare de Lyon/Marseille Saint-Charles
Distance // 409 miles (658km)
Duration // 3hr 22min
Ticket types // Different ticket types are available in First and Second Class, all working like airline-style dynamic pricing. Buy early for the best prices. You'll always be booked onto a specific journey, but you can change it before departure by paying the difference in fare and an administration fee.
How to book // sncf-connect.com or trainline.com
When to go // Avoid high summer, especially the peak French summer holiday weekends in July and August.
Things to know // The downside of double-decker trains is having to carry heavy luggage up and down narrow stairs. If you've got big bags, try to board early, and for the smoothest exit let those in a hurry get down the steps first before trying to navigate them yourself.

Opposite top: Mont St Michel is easily accessible from the Breton capital of Rennes. Opposite below: the Place de la Bourse in Bordeaux.

MORE LIKE THIS
FRENCH HIGH-SPEED FUN

PARIS TO STRASBOURG

The ultra-fast TGV Est takes some beating. The speed record for a conventional train – 357mph (575km/h) – was set on a section of this line in 2007. Without too many major obstacles on its path through the regions of Champagne, Lorraine and Alsace, this is a long and essentially straight-line of a journey – one to sit back and enjoy watching the peaceful fields of northeastern France slip by. The principal stops on the Strasbourg routes are out-of-town stations like the modern Champagne-Ardenne TGV, from which connections are available to Reims, deep in sparkling-wine territory. Strasbourg itself retains a medieval heart – the Petite France district of its Grande Île is filled with half-timbered buildings winding down to quiet, centuries-old canals. But it's also a modern city, a few miles from the Rhine River and the German border, at the heart of Europe's political, culinary and artistic scenes.

Start // Paris Est
Finish // Strasbourg
Distance // 246 miles (396km)
Duration // 1hr 50min

PARIS TO BORDEAUX

Hurtling out of Paris on the LGV Atlantique line through the Loire Valley, double-decker TGV Océane trains soon fork south, following the Sud Europe Atlantique route. Slightly slower services stop at Poitiers and Angoulême. Bordeaux's 19th-century Saint-Jean Station is a fittingly riverside starting point from which to explore this city steeped in wine and food. Many TGV services continue, at a slower speed, to connect Paris and Bordeaux with Toulouse, Biarritz and Hendaye on the Spanish border. Plans are afoot to construct a high-speed Bordeaux–Toulouse line, so services in this part of France will likely see faster journeys within the next 10 years.

Start // Paris Montparnasse
Finish // Bordeaux Saint-Jean
Distance // 310 miles (410km)
Duration // 2hr 25min

PARIS TO BREST

Travelling a route synonymous with the famously painful Paris–Brest–Paris cycling event, trains on the Bretagne-Pays de la Loire LGV line barely give a backward glance to another iconic sporting name – Le Mans, the home of the 24-hour motor race – en route to Brittany. An hour and a half from Paris, trains pause for breath at Rennes, the eastern gateway to the Celtic corner of France. From here onwards, services are more leisurely. Passing Guingamp, Plouaret-Trégor and Morlaix stations, branch lines serve seaside destinations like Paimpol, Lannion and the port of Roscoff. The TGV rolls onwards to the line's end at Brest, where the wild coves and Atlantic beaches of Finistère feel a very long way from the shadow of the Eiffel Tower.

Start // Paris Montparnasse
Finish // Brest
Distance // 313 miles (417km)
Duration // 3hr 45min

RIDE THE BERGENSBANEN OVER THE SPINE OF NORWAY

The Bergensbanen between Oslo and Bergen is an intercity odyssey – an adventure that spans deep fjords, snow-covered mountains and forests of rich and mesmerising greens.

Oslo and Bergen are Norway's capital and its second city respectively. Business travellers commute between these two historic ports, families shuttle back and forth on public holidays, goods are in constant flow in one direction or the other. Any rail link between two such economic hubs you'd expect to be a humdrum, workaday affair – a London-Birmingham or Paris-Lyon type artery perhaps.

But not in Norway. To travel from Oslo to Bergen is to scramble over the mountainous spine of the country on a rhapsodic rail adventure linking two salty sea fjords: one beside the Skagerrak Strait; the other trailing into the wild Atlantic. The Bergensbanen trains that traverse these highlands do not exactly dawdle, but then nor is this a high-speed line, meaning you are able to fully appreciate the glorious views that unravel outside the windows. It's unusual in being a line used daily by locals but also beloved of railway aficionados. As one of the latter, I had always wanted to ride it.

I boarded a westbound Bergensbanen train amid the sunken platforms of Oslo Central Station. After plunging into tunnels

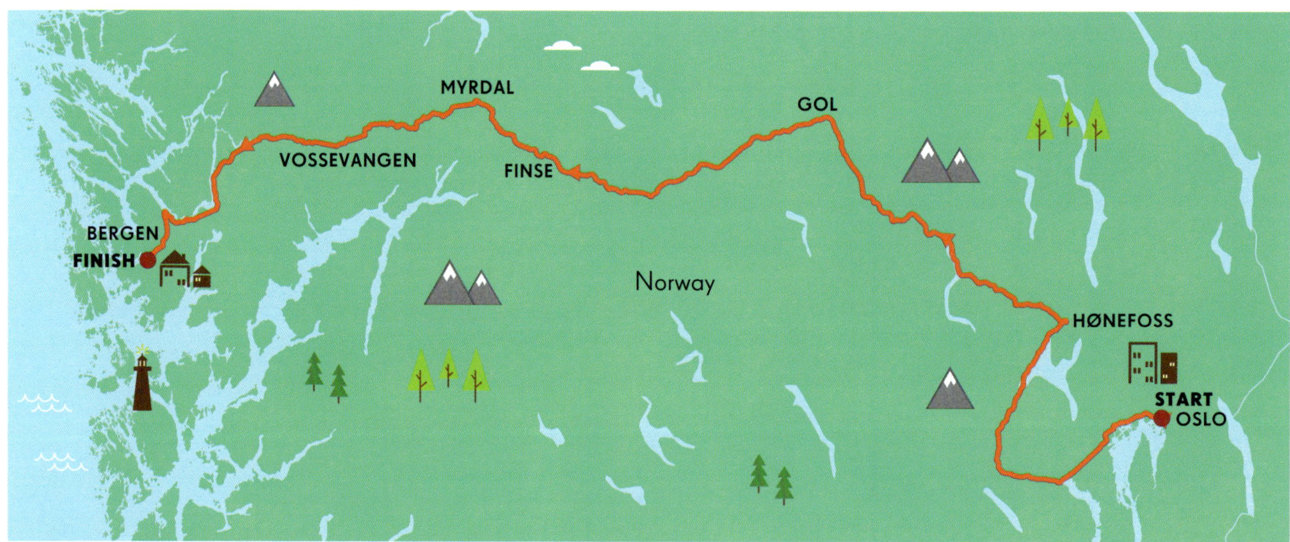

beneath the Norwegian Royal Palace, the train reemerged beside the shores of the sunny Oslofjord, with snatched glimpses of yachts out on its silver leagues. Eventually suburbs segued into countryside, and we skirted a series of wide crystalline lakes. So far, so ordinary for most fellow travellers it seemed – business folk barely looked up from their laptops to admire classic Norwegian scenes of woodlands interspersed with cabins painted blood red and mustard yellow. Soon the contours began to steepen, and the challenges facing the original Bergensbanen builders became fully apparent.

The Oslo-Bergen Railway was a revolutionary project at its inception in the 19th century. Until then, travel between the two cities had required a five-day steamship passage along the Norwegian coast – a serious undertaking, albeit not quite as serious as crossing the inhospitable terrain of the interior, where routes were blocked for much of the year by shoulder-high snowdrifts. Most of all, it was the uninhabited (and unwelcomingly named) Hardangervidda plateau whose uplands, roamed by reindeer and raked by glaciers, defied and daunted engineers. Among the first to vanquish this wilderness was the explorer Fridtjof Nansen. Nansen is best known for his attempts to reach the North Pole – less well known, however, were his exploits crossing the interior of his homeland. In 1884 he made the first ski-crossing over the Hardangervidda. A few years later it was decreed a railway could perform the same feat.

Set at a confluence of valleys, the town of Gol is a gateway into the mountains. From its station passengers can crane their necks to try to spot its spectacular Stave Church – a replica of a famous 12th-century structure which has long since been relocated to Oslo. In its design you can still catch an echo of the Viking Age. The valley narrowed by the time my train arrived in the outdoor hub of Geilo. Climbing higher still, tree cover thinned out, replaced by and revealing lakes, a lonely hydroelectric power station and horizons of bare gneiss, garlanded by lichens. There is something alien in these mountains – or so it must have seemed to George Lucas in the late 1970s.

The Bergensbanen has a chequered history. After being opened by the Norwegian king in 1909, it was used by the country's Nazi occupiers during WWII. But one of its most celebrated chapters was the role it played in the making of *Star Wars: The Empire Strikes Back*, in which the nearby Hardangerjøkulen glacier served as a double for the ice planet Hoth. Props, cameras, cast and crew travelled by rail to Finse – the station that marks the highest point of the Norwegian railway network. Unfortunately filming coincided with one of the most fearsome storms in modern history: temperatures sank to minus 40, and camera lenses froze over. Harrison Ford had to make his way up to the film set in Finse by bribing a railway worker with vodka to drive a special snowplough.

I rested midway along the line at the Hotel Finse 1222 – historically a springboard for expeditions in the mountains – before catching another train westward the next morning. At

A STATION FAR FAR AWAY...

One of the highlights of riding the Bergensbanen is encountering remote mountain stations that aren't serviced by public roads. Finse is one of them. More peculiar is little Hallingskeid, perched at 3642ft (1110m) and housed within a snow tunnel. It's unstaffed and serves no local population, existing as a jumping off point for hikers taking on the Hardangervidda plateau.

From left: The Oslo skyline; travelling the interior; the historic district of Bryggen; inside the cab of a Bergensbanen train. Previous page: a service deep in the mountains.

Myrdal the solitary single-track Bergensbanen suddenly acquired a sibling as we reached a junction with the Flåmsbana – a tourist-oriented branch line which makes a sharp 2789ft (850m) descent from the mountains to the tongue of the Aurlandsfjord.

The descent of the Bergensbanen, however, is a more stately and sedate affair – I watched as we trailed mountain streams downhill, and a landscape of boulder and bog returned to one of green meadows and country towns. West of Voss, the train slalomed through a succession of lakes and fjords, before entering a tunnel beneath the landmark mountain of Ulriken, and screeching to halt in Bergen's sombre-looking station. Disembarking, I soon found my way to Bryggen – Bergen's preserved port district, where merchants once uploaded goods from North Sea and Baltic ports. I toured the fine crop of museums dotted around Norway's second city.

And lastly I caught the cable car to the top of Ulriken itself – whose summit commands a view west to Bergen's warehouses and wharfs, and the distant Atlantic. Most visitors had their cameras pointed in this direction – to where the town and the great ocean met. But just as beguiling to my mind was the view eastward in the opposite direction – to the snow-capped peaks of the interior. A returning Bergensbanen train would soon be rumbling far beneath our feet, running out of Ulriken and into those frosty fells. **OS**

Start/Finish // Oslo/Bergen
Distance // 308 miles (496 km)
Duration // 6hr 30min
Ticket types // Trains divide into Standard and Premium classes – both are very comfortable, but in Premium you get complimentary tea and coffee.
How to book // Reserve online at vy.no.
When to go // The Bergensbanen runs year-round: winters sees the train soldiering through pretty, snowy landscapes, though at this time of year, at these latitudes, there are fewer hours of daylight for admiring the scenery. Spring sees the lineside waterfalls in full spate.
Things to know // Norwegian railways can be very expensive – as ever, booking in advance can keep costs lower. The classic 'Norway in a Nutshell' tour incorporates the Bergensbanen, the Flåmsbana and a fjord boat ride, offering an excellent-value introduction to the country.

Opposite: The Raumabanen passing through the spectacular Romsdalen Valley, en route to the sea.

MORE LIKE THIS
NORWEGIAN RAIL RIDES

FLÅMSBANA

The Flåmsbana is Bergensbanen's chief rival for the title of Norway's most famous railway. Fortunately you don't have to choose between them – being a branch line of the Bergensbanen, you'll almost certainly need to catch a train from Oslo or Bergen to ride it. The adventure begins at the junction of Myrdal: from here, northbound trains stop for photos beside the thundering waterfall of Kjosfossen (you'll also spot the hydroelectric plant that helps power the electric locomotives). Continuing downhill, countless more waterfalls tumble from the clifftops into the teal waters of the Flåmselvi River, which accompanies the tracks down to sea level and the sublime shores of the Aurlandsfjord. Look out too for cyclists, who race the trains downhill on the Rallarvegen, the steep road which runs parallel to the tracks.

Start // Myrdal
Finish // Flåm
Distance // 8 miles (13km)
Duration // 1hr

DOVREBANEN

Another intercity adventure, the Dovrebanen connects Oslo to Norway's third city, Trondheim. Hauling out of the capital, the century-old line begins by trailing northward along the shores of Mjøsa, the country's largest lake. Look out for Mjøstårnet – one of the world's tallest wooden buildings, rising over the lakeside town of Brumunddal. At Mjøsa's northernmost tip lies Lillehammer – the city that hosted the 1994 Winter Olympics – which acts as the gateway into the scenic Gudbrandsdalen Valley. Try to spot musk oxen and reindeer herds as you cross the wide-open space of the Dovrefjell plateau – a Norwegian National Park – before making your steady descent towards Trondheim. Most passengers will have their eyes wide-open on this scenic line, but if you want to shut them, one of Norway's surviving sleeper services also runs on the line.

Start // Oslo
Finish // Trondheim
Distance // 340 miles (548km)
Duration // 7hr

RAUMABANEN

A dark horse among Norwegian railway lines and little known compared to its more famous cousins, the Raumabanen still packs a serious punch over its 71-mile (114km) course, with chilly fjords, crashing waterfalls and horseshoe curves allowing trains to adjust to demanding gradients. You reach it by alighting at Dombås, roughly midway along the Dovrebanen. In doing so, you switch from long electric express trains to two-car diesel, but the scenery, if anything, proves an upgrade as the train trundles along the Romsdalen Valley, with the lofty Kylling Bridge particularly impressive. Sheer cliffs close in on both sides as the line begins its final approach to the fjordside terminus of Åndalsnes. Plans originally had the rails running all the way onwards to art nouveau Ålesund; instead waiting buses shuttle passengers to what is perhaps Norway's prettiest town.

Start // Dombås
Finish // Åndalsnes
Distance // 71 miles (114km)
Duration // 1hr 20min

NORD

ALL RAILS LEAD TO ROME: ITALY BY HIGH-SPEED TRAIN

Ride one of Italy's principal high-speed routes from Milan, gliding south through the Tuscan and Umbrian countryside to journey's end among the ancient wonders of Rome.

Crowds of travellers; the chirruping and beckoning of the station announcements; the shushing of opening and closing ticket barriers; the smooth-humming of modern locomotives departing up and down the spine of the country – an Italian railway cathedral in the heat of summer is a vision to sustain the would-be passenger through a long, cold winter.

If that sounds romantic, it's also the reality of a busy Saturday morning at Milano Centrale, my starting point for a sprint to Roma Termini. Milan to Rome is 297 miles (477km) of high-speed fun, connecting the capital of Italy's industrial north with the mother city of the ancient world. It starts at the vast bulk of Centrale. Whatever you do, arrive early to have time to enjoy the station itself. In Milan, only two other buildings come close: the jaw-droppingly ostentatious medieval Duomo and the vast, spaceship-like San Siro football stadium. Centrale has, among other noteworthy features, its own marble-clad colonnade, plus murals and mosaics reflecting the varied influences that came in and out of fashion during its 25-year design and construction period (1906 to 1931). Hidden away out of sight, there's even what was once a waiting room reserved for the king of Italy. Today, Centrale accommodates vast numbers of passengers who, if they're anything like me, feel smaller while crossing beneath its towering ceilings.

In the bright daylight of the five-arched trainshed, my fast train to Rome was ready to board. Milan is a crucial stop on Italy's north–south high-speed line, connecting Turin with Salerno, south of Naples. Given this key role, there were plenty of gleaming red Frecciarossa trains waiting to begin

their journeys south. Dotted among them were Italo-branded competitor services and colourful regional trains heading for Lake Como and Switzerland beyond.

Trenitalia's Frecciarossa trains are a treat in themselves. As well as the 186mph (300km/h) top speed, they rival any of Europe's fast lines for comfort. This being Italy, the buffet car serves a mean espresso, which is best drunk in the national style, standing at the counter while the countryside whizzes past. Not least because doing it any other way risks displeasing the barista who, on the day I travelled, looked like he'd been picked up that morning from a backstreet *tabacchi*, where he could have been dishing out coffees and *cornetti* (croissants) for neighbourhood customers. He also grilled a mean cheese-and-ham panini.

Our departure from Milan was prompt, efficiently on schedule, and soon we passed the vast signal boxes that stood like a gateway to the rest of the country. For the first hour, our route crossed green farmland parallel to Autostrada 1. Both rail and road stick close to the ancient Roman Via Aemilia before arriving in Bologna Centrale. Hopeful of a glimpse of the red rooftops and baroque church cupolas of this beautiful city, I was somewhat disappointed to shunt into a modern underground section of the station. From here, other services head southeast and along Italy's Adriatic coast, veer north to Austria via Bolzano on the dizzying heights of the Brenner Railway, and connect to Florence by three different routes. Also beginning here are the original trans-Apennine line to Florence via Pistoia and its successor, the Ferrovia Direttissima, both representing older engineering feats.

Taking the newest of these routes to Florence, our train pulled out of Bologna and continued on its rapid run to the capital, carving a course across the south of Emilia-Romagna and a whole swath of northern Tuscany; sadly, though, our route sacrificed scenery for speed. At around 40 minutes, this section

MEMORIALE DELLA SHOAH

Binario (platform) 21, beneath the street-level platforms at Milano Centrale, is the home for Milan's Memoriale della Shoah, commemorating Italy's Holocaust victims, many of whom were deported along the station's tracks, never to return. This unique space is a sobering reminder of the tragic events that took place here until as late as February 1945. Reservations are recommended at weekends; check online (memorialeshoah.it) for more information.

Clockwise from top: Milan's Cathedral; a high-speed train in the Italian countryside; the Galleria Vittorio Emanuele II; inside Milan Centrale. Previous page: Rome's Colosseum.

Viacheslav Lopatin/Shutterstock; Matt Munro/Lonely Planet

certainly felt rapid, but most of it was in tunnels – just 2.9 miles (4.7km) saw us in the open air. Like many of the quickest services on this route, my train didn't halt at Florence's Santa Maria Novella, another of Italy's great stations. Pulling in here requires reversing out again, adding complexity and time, so we skirted the city before a blink-and-you'll-miss-it crossing of the Arno. Soon more of the line was above ground – this was the point to put down the timetable and enjoy watching southern Tuscan hilltops give way to Umbria, passing Arezzo, Montepulciano, Orvieto and then entering Lazio, the final province of our journey. We crossed Rome's river, the Tiber, three times in the final miles of the trip, intersecting its meandering course.

Leaving the last high-speed section of the route we crossed Rome's ring road and slowed down on the approach to Termini. Though a definitive full stop on the Italian rail network, the station is, in fact, not named after its status as a terminus. The name comes from the district that Termini was built in and over, and refers to the hot baths (thermae) that ancient Romans would enjoy in these parts. (The Baths of Diocletian were just across the road from today's station.) Terminus or not, Termini is a fantastic place to arrive: a mix of pre-war elements and more modern renovations, including a recent refit to offer huge amounts of retail opportunities. Arriving into the high, airy main hall is one of the best introductions to Rome. It's a calm place despite the crowds – and something of a halfway house between the serenity of the train and Rome's unique and wonderful clamour, just a few steps away. Once outside, the wave of heat, police sirens and noise told me in an instant where I was. Slightly disoriented and thrilled in equal measure by how fast I had got here, the day to explore the Eternal City was still wide open. But first another espresso. **TH**

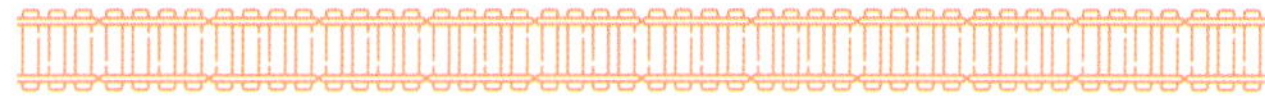

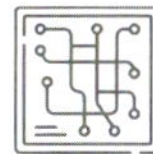

Start/Finish // Milan Centrale/Rome Termini
Distance // 297 miles (477km)
Duration // 2hr 50min
Ticket types // Frecciarossa classes – Standard, Premium, Business, Executive – are roughly equivalent to coach, premium economy, business and first on a plane.
How to book // The useful Trenit app gives a full rundown of options on any given route, plus booking links and reliable journey tracking while on the move. Otherwise, try Trenitalia (trenitalia.com) or Trainline (trainline.com).
When to go // With so many daily trains across Italy, booking a few weeks in advance is usually fine, but add extra time if travelling over Italian public holidays.
Things to know // Trenitalia competitor Italo (italotreno.com) also offers a high-speed Milan–Rome service; from 2026, French company SNCF plans to run Ouigo services in Italy.

Alessia Pierdomenico/Bloomberg via Getty Images; Justin Foulkes/Lonely Planet

Opposite top: Mt Etna in Sicily. Opposite below: The hilltop city of Perugia in Umbria.

MORE LIKE THIS SLOWER ITALIAN RAIL ODYSSEYS

IONIAN RAILWAY

This seven-hour epic, covering 293 glorious miles (473km), runs twice daily between Taranto and Reggio Calabria, the latter best-known as being one end of the boat train to Sicily. The service links quiet seaside towns on Italy's Ionian coast for much of the journey. As you might expect for a railway that doesn't connect major destinations or tourist attractions, this line has low passenger traffic even in high summer, giving it a lazy and slightly secret atmosphere. With imagination, the Ionian Railway can form the basis of a few days of exploration along the line, with stops such as ancient Metaponto and comparatively little-visited coastal cities like Crotone and Catanzaro. For an end-to-end ride, take the afternoon service. You can then put your feet up as this stately service rumbles past endless sea vistas until Sicily looms into view across the Straits of Messina, with sunset as an accompaniment. (It's 23 stops with no dining car – bring a picnic.)
Start // Taranto
Finish // Reggio Calabria
Distance // 293 miles (473 km)
Duration // 7hr

LITTLE RAILWAYS OF SARDINIA

The slowest of Italy's slow trains can be found on Sardinia – and that's precisely the point. Away from mainlines and regional narrow-gauge services are the Trenino Verde (green lines). These seasonal trains – five of which are currently in service around Sardinia – run deep into less explored areas of the island. Travel over venerable tracks, rattling through cork forest and rugged mountain territory, by vintage railcar or in diesel-hauled heritage carriages. Return journeys on these lines, pausing at near-forgotten stations that are only open for the occasion, act as day trips into the otherwise difficult-to-access Sardinian backcountry. Which lines and sections of lines are operating can change. Check online (treninoverde.com) for routes, schedules and bookings.

PERUGIA TO ROME

This backdoor route to Rome can be a little tricky to find on timetables, which will try to send you via the Florence–Rome mainline, a route which involves backtracking to Terontola–Cortona. Instead, board a southbound service from Perugia and sit on the left-hand side of these laid-back regional trains. Rolling through the Umbrian countryside, you'll pass a succession of smaller hill towns – Assisi, Spello and Spoleto included – that from a distance look like they're unchanged since medieval times. With easy bus connections from the stations, a night or two spent exploring these towns makes for a superb car-free Umbrian itinerary. The line then heads into Lazio, past Terni and Orte, before entering the modern world on the approach to Rome. Getting to Perugia Station from the high-altitude hill town is an adventure in itself, with mini self-driving railcars whizzing down the hillside to the mainline tracks.
Start // Perugia
Finish // Rome Termini
Distance // 129 miles (207km)
Duration // 2hr 10min

Locomotive74/Shutterstock; Marco Rubino/Shutterstock

GREEN DAYS ABOARD THE COSTA VERDE EXPRESS

Ride this luxury service along northern Spain's Costa Verde (Green Coast), from the holy city of Santiago to the boisterous port of Bilbao.

Across Galicia I saw many pilgrims: people with callused feet, blistered toes and sunburned necks limping the long miles to Santiago. Some had walked from France to reach this far northwest nook of Spain – a journey of the soul as much as of the feet. I felt a pang of betrayal whenever I saw these exhausted folk on their march to the holy city. But I also felt a smidgen of smugness too.

That's because I was in Galicia not on a pilgrimage, but rather to board the Costa Verde Express – the luxury train that ambles its way along the coastline of northern Spain, cocooning its passengers in the utmost comfort on the way. Its route intersects with parts of the Camino de Santiago pilgrimage network – from the train windows you occasionally see walkers in hiking gear, slogging onward to the city of St James. Those on board, meanwhile, need to make only the slightest exertion to summon a gin and tonic from bar staff. Miles pass effortlessly, watched from under the duvet in your compartment, or else from comfy armchairs in the bar car. Most pilgrims travel westward to Santiago and to the northwestern cusp of Iberia. My trip, however, would be an anti-pilgrimage – an eastward journey enjoying the indulgences of

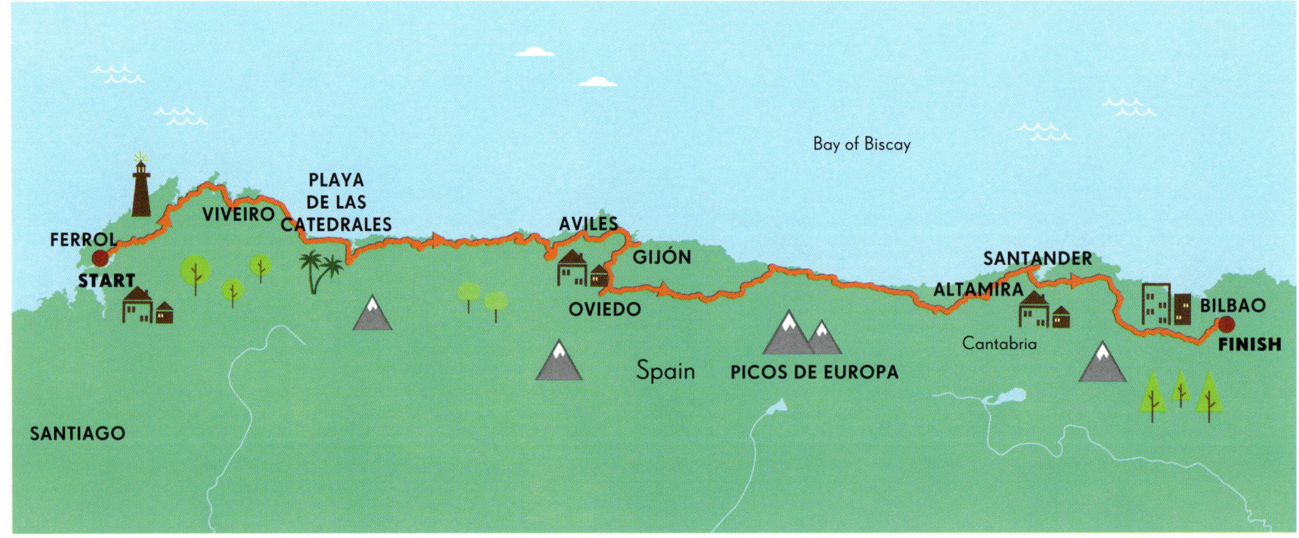

GALINDO
BILBAO

Asturian cider, Cantabrian sunsets and Basque *pintxos*, on the way to Bilbao's urban charms.

The journey began in the industrial port of Ferrol – the starting point for the Camino Inglés, or 'English Way' to Santiago, so-named because it was here that English ships docked and medieval wayfarers would disembark on the last leg to the holy city. In Ferrol Station, staff in crisp uniforms greeted passengers on the platforms. Once aboard, everyone cooed at their suites, decked out with writing tables, double beds and private bathrooms. Plush curtains hung over expansive windows. But, lovely though the interiors were, it was the view that proved more distracting, as we departed Ferrol and struck out towards the tidal shores of the Galician Coast. Most of the passengers on board were Spanish, and for many of them, a journey on the Costa Verde Express reveals a side of their homeland lightyears away from the parched landscapes of Andalucía or Castille. Our train meandered through groves of eucalypts and forests of pine, rumbled through little tunnels of overgrown foliage. Rain showers gusted in from the Atlantic to drum on the roof of our little suites, nourishing a landscape of rich greens. The 'Verde' in Costa Verde Express is no idle brag.

The train follows the same 'cruise ship on wheels' model taken by many luxury trains – rather than a non-stop point to point journey, the (hefty) ticket price includes breaks for off-train cultural excursions and multi-course meals in nearby restaurants. On our first night we alighted in the handsome little town of Viveiro to learn about Galicia's Celtic character, dining on traditional *pulpo a la Gallega* (octopus) as bagpipe music played nearby. The next day we skirted the great *rías* (estuaries) of northwestern Spain, where a succession of green peninsulas reached out to sea, like the fingers of an outstretched hand. The train idled as passengers lounged on the lineside beach of As Catedrais, feeling the sand and the suck of the tide between our toes. Later, we rattled across the border into Asturias, in whose trinity of cities – Oviedo, Avilés and Gijón – I learned the art of pouring cider from a lofty height, allowing the liquid to carbonate slightly. I inhaled some mountain air in the karst heights of the Asturian Picos de Europa range, where we jumped on buses to travel mountain roads no train could negotiate.

"Rain showers gusted in from the Atlantic to drum on the roof of our little suites, nourishing a landscape of rich greens..."

A journey from Santiago to Bilbao can be done by road in a long afternoon – on the Costa Verde Express it unfurls over the best part of the week. This is a long, lazy ride – trains are very often stationary, stopping in sidings for the night to eke out this pocket odyssey. In fairness, the lines travelled by the Costa Verde Express are not exactly built for high-speed travel. These are colloquially known as the 'FEVE' network – a decidedly local grid of narrow-gauge tracks. Costa Verde passengers stretching out their toes in

THE SAME COSTA VERDE FOR LESS

As well as the Costa Verde Express, northern Spain's FEVE lines are also travelled by ordinary passenger services – stopping trains that feel like a country bus, where drivers often know passengers' names. Erratic timetables mean journeys are best done as hops between coastal cities – good staging posts are Ferrol, Avilés, Gijón and Santander. Tickets are refreshingly cheap.

From left: Bilbao's spectacular Concordia Station; the Nervion River snaking through Bilbao; the train passes the beach at As Catedrais. Previous page: Dinner is served on the deluxe Costa Verde service.

the (somewhat compact) double bed will likely also notice this is a slightly smaller train than the mighty machines that shuttle out of Madrid Atocha or Barcelona Sants stations.

Sure it's small, but no less beautiful for that. The penultimate region in our journey was Cantabria, where the focus changed to art. We visited cave systems like Altamira, adorned with 36,000-year-old paintings. We also stopped by the Centro Botín – the ultra-modern Renzo Piano-designed gallery in Santander, whose waterside station lies beside the port for ferries from the UK and Ireland. The coast provided constant company on the journey – the salty air and the call of gulls snuck through open windows. We savoured the bittersweet thrill of seeing beaches of heartbreaking beauty rolling past too quickly.

On the final stretch, we entered the Basque Country and the great port of Bilbao loomed ahead. I got off in the spectacular Concordia Station, whose mint-green arch and classical columns rise over the last meanders of the Nervion River before it washes out into the Bay of Biscay. Here the train would be turned over, the detritus of a journey on the Costa Verde Express revealed to anyone on the platforms – tapas dishes washed, wine bottles discarded, linen tablecloths offloaded to be laundered. Windows would soon be scrubbed, affording passengers pristine coastal views on the return journey to Galicia.

It was truly a train worth making a pilgrimage for. **OS**

Start/Finish // Ferrol (by rail)/Bilbao
Distance // 360 miles (579km)
Duration // 6 days
Ticket types // The one class, 'Gran Class', features double beds and bathroom. Tickets are inclusive of excursions, meals on and off the train and some alcoholic drinks.
How to book // Book at trencostaverdeexpress.com.
When to go // Trains runs May to October. Even in the height of summer, when the rest of Spain swelters in furnace-hot temperatures, the northern coast can be surprisingly cool. There is a flipside – the climate is maritime, so pack a raincoat whichever time of year you visit.
Things to know // Though the FEVE lines don't go particularly near Santiago, Costa Verde itineraries start and end with tours in the holy city, with a bus running to/from Ferrol.

Opposite top: Plush decor on board Al Andalus, which has been operating since 1985. Opposite below: The narrow-gauge El Transcantábrico: the sister to the Costa Verde Express.

MORE LIKE THIS
LUXURY TRAINS IN SPAIN

EL TRANSCANTÁBRICO

The Costa Verde Express' sister service is the El Transcantábrico, a luxury train which predates it, running along the very same FEVE rails since 1983. Look closely however and you spot subtle differences between the two. The itinerary on El T is longer – incorporating an eastward extension to San Sebastián by bus – meaning it unravels over eight days rather than six. The train itself is also more luxurious, featuring original 1920s carriages, while suites are more spacious, boasting small living areas with sofas and armchairs. Tickets cost roughly double, but in all other respects the route is the same and the scenery just as priceless. Look out for the moment when the two luxury trains pass midway on the itinerary – passengers greet each other and staff sometimes hug their comrades on the platforms.

Start // Ferrol (by rail)
Finish // Bilbao (by rail)
Distance // 360 miles (579km)
Duration // 7 days (by rail)

AL ANDALUS

Al Andalus is another of Spanish national operator Renfe's luxury sleeper trains, shuttling between the cultural wonders of – you guessed it – Andalucía. It's another cruise model – itineraries mix journeys with excursions by bus. A classic journey starts in Seville, before detouring south to Jerez, the home of sherry. Trains then reverse to take in the soaring bridge of Ronda and the great Mosque-Church of Córdoba, before passing through a sea of olive trees as the peaks of the Sierra Nevada gather on the horizon. Al Andalus finally shudders to a halt not far from the Alhambra of Granada (after which it's another bus ride to Málaga). Moorish wonders abound, but the train itself is also full of history, formed of historic Wagons Lits carriages. The lounges – named after local landmarks – are particularly evocative, with plenty of lacquered wood and brass fittings.

Start // Seville (by rail)
Finish // Granada (by rail)
Distance // 570 miles (917km)
Duration // 7 days (by rail)

EXPRESO DE LA ROBLA

A tapas dish of a train – compared to the multi-course indulgences of Al Andalus and El Transcantábrico – the Expreso de la Robla offers shorter hops in northern Spain, travelling the hinterland south of the Costa Verde route. Its history is a surprising one. Originally used for teaching students, it's now solely used by tourists and, accordingly, you'll find it's somewhat more functional than other luxury Renfe sleepers, with bunk beds rather than double beds, and more modern decor. The standard three-night itinerary travels the stretch of countryside between Bilbao and León. On the way, visitors stop to admire the beautiful Tobera waterfalls and explore Romanesque churches beside the Camino Francés pilgrimage route. The final destination, León, is one of Spain's most underrated cities, crowned by its Gothic cathedral.

Start // Bilbao
Finish // León
Distance // 211 miles (340km)
Duration // 3 days

OCEANIA

KiwiRail
KiwiRail

TWO OCEANS BY TWO RAILS: THE INDIAN PACIFIC

Journey across the breadth of Australia from coast to coast and discover the stark, wild beauty of the country's hidden interior.

Beyond my window, Earth has lost its features. There are no gentle undulations of terrain. No roads or fences or distant stands of trees bending in a far-off breeze. There is nothing but red soil stubbled with scrub, a horizon that could have been scored along a laser level and a blue sky. The land is so flat it creates an optical illusion, making the vast distances seem oddly truncated. The furthest reaches of my vision appear almost close enough to touch. I feel certain I can see the curvature of the planet.

I'm aboard the Indian Pacific, a railway that crosses the breadth of the Australian continent from, you guessed it, the edge of the Indian Ocean on one side to the Pacific on the other. In a three-night luxury sprint, it covers 2700 miles (4345km) between Sydney in the east and Perth in the west, across some of the country's most inhospitable terrain.

Inhospitable is not how I'd describe the start of my journey though, at Sydney's Central Station. The grand sandstone

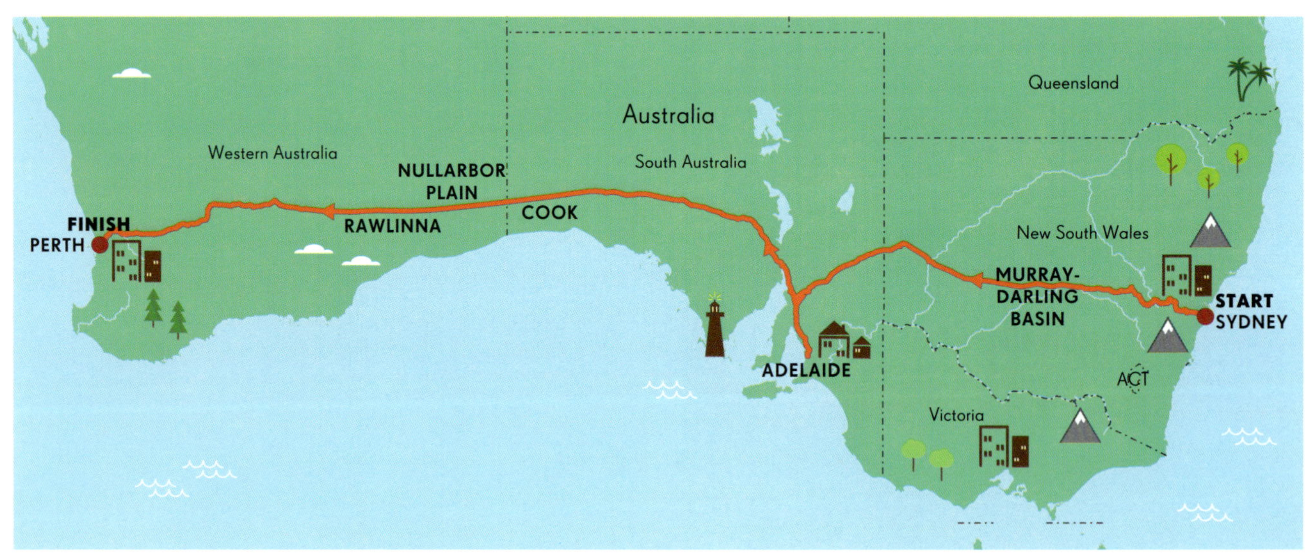

INDIAN PACIFIC
NR27
INDIAN PACIFIC

building looked almost golden in the sunshine, and it buzzed with commuters and chattering day-trippers. There on platform one, humming gently as if in anticipation of the grand journey ahead, was the Indian Pacific – a 2300-foot (711m) streak of steel, with 25 carriages and a sturdy blue locomotive.

I stepped aboard and happily explored my single bunk cabin – opening and closing tiny cupboards and marvelling at how an en-suite bathroom can be squeezed into a space the size of a phone box – when a shrill whistle sounded. The train lurched forward. We were on our way.

Sydney's high-rise buildings flashed past the windows, followed by suburban streets lined with squat bungalows. Somewhere, without me noticing the transition, we entered a different landscape – what Australians call 'the bush', an all-purpose term used to describe areas beyond the urban fringes. Through my window were speed-blurred swathes of eucalypts and colourful bursts of bright yellow wattle and fire-hued banksia.

The route led us up through the Blue Mountains, so named for the vapour that rises when the oil of its countless eucalypts evaporates in the hot sun, forming a bluish mist. Then it was down, into the rolling green farmland of the Murray-Darling Basin, Australia's food bowl – evident from the distant hills lined with orderly rows of fruit trees and the vast fields of wheat and barley waving as we passed.

No doubt some of this produce was served in the Queen Adelaide dining car, a comforting, wood-panelled space of brown leather, brass fittings and white linen. There were canapés of curry puffs scented with native lemon myrtle. Saltwater barramundi, and tender beef from the fields of the Hunter Valley. Plates of seared kangaroo fillet and ravioli stuffed with Hervey Bay scallops. And to drink, a generous list of wines from across the railway's path – from a deeply fruity Barossa Valley shiraz to a citrusy Margaret River sauvignon blanc.

Such luxury on the rails must have been impossible to imagine for those who first dreamed of a cross-continental Australian railway. Work began to unite the east and west coasts in 1912, just a few years after the country's federation. Yet the extraordinary challenges of building a line across mountains, arid deserts and extremely remote topography meant it was nearly six decades later, in 1970, that the first coast-to-coast rail journey took place.

Some of the views may have changed since, but when we left the built-up areas behind after the South Australian capital Adelaide, only the stark, timeless land of the outback stretched ahead of us.

Which brings me to my present view, and that exceptionally barren expanse outside my window. We're crossing the Nullarbor Plain, a prehistoric seabed of solid limestone stretching over 100,000 sq miles (260,000 sq km) and littered with fossils of ancient marine creatures. The name is Latin – literally, 'no trees plain'. But before anyone who spoke Latin stepped a foot on this land, it had another name – Oondoori, meaning 'waterless'.

STARGAZING IN THE OUTBACK

In the deep outback, where outposts of civilisation can be hundreds of miles apart, you'll find almost no light pollution, which means unparalleled celestial displays. The star clusters and nebulae of the Milky Way sweep across the sky, with the bright Southern Cross pointing to true south. Look to the dark spots between the constellations and you might just see the shape of the Great Emu, a creator spirit from the Aboriginal Dreaming.

Clockwise from top: Crossing the outback; lunch in the Queen Adelaide dining car; a dinner stop at Rawlinna. Previous page: The Indian Pacific crossing the Blue Mountains.

Onwards along tracks straight as pins. The Nullarbor is home to the longest stretch of undeviating trainline in the world – 297 miles (477km) of it – a feat made possible only because there are no geographical features to avoid.

An apple-cheeked train manager bustles by in a high-vis vest and notices me staring out in slack-jawed wonder. It's not always the same, she tells me. Sometimes there are wildflowers. Birds and animals crowding around scarce water sources. Dust storms so thick you can barely see. Rains so heavy it floods the tracks. 'I love the Nullarbor', she says, 'because I know every time I come, it's going to be different.'

Signs of civilisation appear at Cook, a near-ghost town in the eastern Nullarbor, and again at Rawlinna, which is little more than a pub by the tracks where jackaroos and jillaroos (cattle handlers) gather from far-flung cattle stations. I become so accustomed to the desert, plain and scrubland that it's a shock when the trees – purple-blossomed jacarandas – return. Then forests as we roll into the Avon River Valley. Houses, which have been so rare for the past two days, appear more frequently, until they merge into a suburban blur on the outskirts of Perth.

After four days and thousands of miles, we come to a gentle stop at East Perth Railway Station. I'm back in the world again, amid the skyscrapers and manicured parks of Perth.

Suddenly my epic cross-continental journey feels like a dream of another world. One of raw nature, red dust, limitless expanses and a distant horizon that I can almost reach out and touch with a fingertip. **CL**

Start/Finish // Sydney/Perth
Distance // 2704 miles (4352km)
Duration // 65hr
Ticket types // Tickets on the Indian Pacific are all-inclusive, covering cabin accommodation, meals, drinks and off-train excursions such as stargazing and vineyard dining. You have a choice between Gold Service, with single or twin bunk cabin and small private bathroom, and the more expensive Platinum Service, with a spacious double cabin, full-size en suite, views from both sides of the train and access to the exclusive Platinum club dining carriage.
How to book // Visit journeybeyondrail.com.
More info // For things to do before and after your train journey, check out sydney.com and visitperth.com.

Opposite top: A Gold Service compartment on the Great Southern. Opposite below: The Overland crossing a dry salt lake in South Australia.

MORE LIKE THIS
AUSTRALIAN LONG-DISTANCE ODYSSEYS

THE GREAT SOUTHERN

The Great Southern is a three-day luxury trip that takes in the best of Australia's southeast, running between the cities of Adelaide in the south and Brisbane in the surf-fringed northeastern state of Queensland. From Adelaide, the Great Southern's bright-orange locomotive heads east, tracing the winelands of the Adelaide Hills towards the mighty Grampians, a mountain range with sandstone escarpments of red and ochre. Next stop is Australia's capital Canberra, and the vine-ribbed hills of the Hunter Valley. Soon after, you arrive at Coffs Harbour, home to some of the most beautiful coastline in New South Wales. Here, you can learn about local wildlife with an expert Gumbaynggirr Indigenous guide before jumping back on the train and heading north to end your journey in booming Brisbane.

Start // Adelaide
Finish // Brisbane
Distance // 1793 miles (2885km)
Duration // 3 days Adelaide to Brisbane/3.5 days Brisbane to Adelaide

SPIRIT OF THE OUTBACK

This rail journey may not be quite as luxurious as the Indian Pacific, but the Spirit of the Outback offers more than its share of quintessential Australian landscapes as it streams through the heart of Queensland. Setting off from Brisbane, you'll head north along the coast via cities like Bundaberg (famous for its sugar cane rum, known locally as 'Bundy') and Rockhampton on the Capricorn Coast, before turning inland. The tracks stretch through green fields towards the Central Highlands, where forested mountains and escarpments give way to arid landscapes and far horizons. The journey ends in Longreach, a classic outback town and original home of Australian airline, Qantas. The train caters for local commuters, so it's possible to jump off at stations along the way – just be sure to plan carefully as the Spirit of the Outback only runs twice a week.

Start // Brisbane
Finish // Longreach
Distance // 825 miles (1300km)
Duration // 26hr

THE OVERLAND

This 10-hour scenic journey takes you from artsy, coffee-loving Melbourne to its refined South Australian neighbour, Adelaide. Make sure to explore the former's laneways, boutiques and restaurants before heading to Southern Cross Station to catch the Overland. The rails progress west from the city, passing through Geelong on the curve of Corio Bay and crossing the wheat fields of the Wimmera region. At the town of Ararat, look out for the Grampians mountain range rising in the distance. Past the aptly named Bordertown (on the border of Victoria and South Australia), you'll approach the rolling vineyards of the Adelaide Hills, before arriving in Adelaide itself. Try to time your visit to coincide with one of the city's many festivals, and catch some of the live music it's famous for.

Start // Melbourne
Finish // Adelaide
Distance // 515 miles (828km)
Duration // 10hr 30min

VOLCANIC MAJESTY ON THE NORTHERN EXPLORER

Take a trip across the North Island of New Zealand, linking two attractive cities via an array of spectacular landscapes including mighty volcanoes.

There's nothing quite like standing on the platform at Auckland's Strand Station, waiting to board the Northern Explorer train for the 11-hour journey down to Wellington. It's an early morning departure, so the air is crisp and the sun just risen, with the glass towers of the city centre looming outside.

The only disappointment is the lack of a grand building to depart from. Sadly, Strand Station is basically a shed. To be fair, its platform did once belong to a marvellous rail terminal, a beautiful beaux-arts building from 1930 which I had walked past earlier. This former main railway station would indeed be the perfect place to begin the long train journey across New Zealand's North Island, but nowadays it's home to apartments. If you have time to spare, you can step inside the lobby and admire the beautiful interior, or grab a bite to eat at the onsite restaurant which is open most evenings.

Station architecture aside, my focus is on the wonderful scenery in prospect for the day as the Northern Explorer forges a path south through the North Island's complex geography.

The train itself is well-suited to an appreciation of the countryside. A diesel locomotive pulls several carriages with big windows, a cafe car and an observation car. Comfortable seats are mostly in pairs facing forwards, with the occasional set of four surrounding a table which would suit travelling groups. Large windows make for maximum visibility, with an additional angled window above them providing a skywards panorama. The roof and walls of each carriage have timber panelling.

The cafe car serves hot meals along with lighter options, and local beverages such as beers from South Island brewer

KiwiRail
4692
KiwiRail

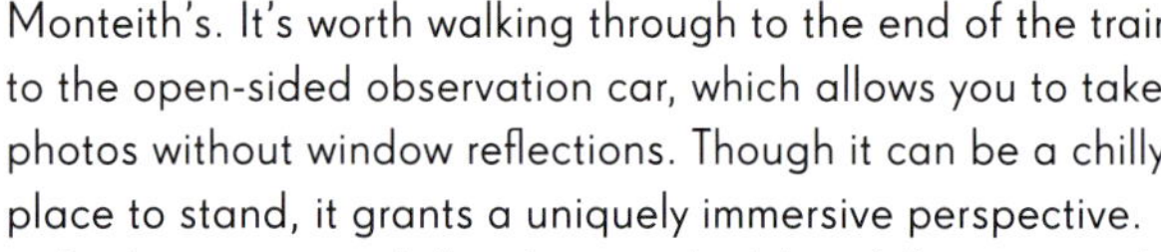

Monteith's. It's worth walking through to the end of the train to the open-sided observation car, which allows you to take photos without window reflections. Though it can be a chilly place to stand, it grants a uniquely immersive perspective.

Back in my seat, I don the supplied headphones to take in the excellent recorded commentary supplied along the journey. As we head out of the city it tells me that Auckland is built on dormant volcanoes and had its own Māori settlements before Europeans arrived. Once we've left the suburbs behind, the landscape grows green and hilly, a series of picturesque undulations wreathed in morning mist.

The land flattens out beyond Hamilton, with the first hint of mountains on the horizon. As we trundle along I get chatting with a group of New Zealanders on an outing to Tongariro National Park for a couple of days, retirees who love the social aspect of trains.

At Te Kuitik I tune back into the commentary which relates the story of a famous local rugby player who used to train with a sheep under each arm. It also talks about the construction of the line in the 19th century, and how a team of railway surveyors was once held captive by a Māori tribe who objected to their incursion. Halfway through the journey to Wellington we reach an engineering triumph, the

"The landscape grows green and hilly, a series of picturesque undulations wreathed in morning mist..."

1898 Raurimu Spiral. This looping section of track allows trains to gradually rise 433ft (132m) up to the Volcanic Plateau at the centre of the North Island. There are regular views of mighty volcanic peaks such as Mt Ruapehu, and the train soon halts at National Park Station where my new Kiwi friends alight.

If you want to break this rail journey into two halves, Tongariro National Park would be the obvious place for a stopover along the way. There are two stations serving the ski slopes and hiking trails of the area, one at National Park and the other at Ohakune, half an hour down the line. Both are adjacent to townships with accommodation and road access to the national park, but Ohakune is the more attractive as a destination in itself. Within walking distance of its station is the glorious Powderhorn Chateau, a character-packed timber hotel, the Ohakune Railway Museum and Ohakune Hot Tubs – a series of wood-fired baths sitting out under the open sky.

I'm tempted by all of these options, but this time I'm continuing onward. After leaving the plateau, slowly curving

HAMILTON HIGHLIGHTS

Although New Zealanders talk down the city of Hamilton, you might like to break your rail journey here. It has appealing gardens and a tea plantation, and is 45 minutes by road from Hobbiton, the set of the Hobbit village which featured in the *Lord of the Rings* movies, now developed into a permanent attraction with beautiful gardens.

Clockwise from top left: The train passing Tongariro National Park; hikers exploring the park; Hamilton Gardens; Wellington station; North Island coastal scenery. Previous page: Passing Mt Ruapehu.

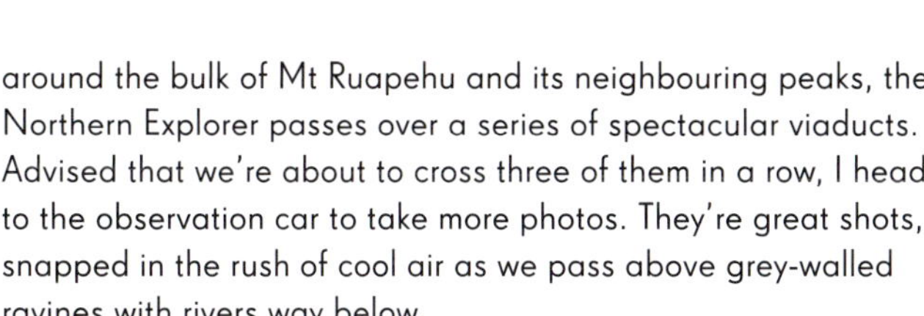

around the bulk of Mt Ruapehu and its neighbouring peaks, the Northern Explorer passes over a series of spectacular viaducts. Advised that we're about to cross three of them in a row, I head to the observation car to take more photos. They're great shots, snapped in the rush of cool air as we pass above grey-walled ravines with rivers way below.

It's around this point that the recorded commentary tells the sobering story of a 1953 disaster in which a Wellington-Auckland night train plummeted from a bridge which had been damaged by flooding. Thankfully, nowadays the line is festooned with modern technology which warns of such pending perils.

The sun starts to set as we reach the Kapiti Coast on the Tasman Sea and the commentary points out the bulky profile of Kapiti Island, nowadays a nature reserve from which predators have been eradicated.

It's dark as we enter Wellington's commuter belt and snake through the city to arrive at Wellington Station, right on time. At last I'm in a magnificent terminal worthy of such a long train journey, a neoclassical beauty opened in 1937 and still the hub of the New Zealand capital's rail network.

Stepping out into the evening to walk to my hotel, I feel I've absorbed both Aotearoa's railway history and natural beauty in my day on the rails. **TR**

Start/Finish // Strand Station, Auckland/Wellington Station

Distance // 423 miles (681km)

Duration // 11hr

Ticket types // There's Scenic Class and, as of late 2024, Scenic Plus Class, which includes hot meals served to your seat. Food served in the cafe car is good quality.

How to book // Reserve at greatjourneysnz.com.

When to go // December to March sees the warmest weather; for the snow sports season visit between July and September.

Things to know // It's not possible to choose specific seats, but you can include seat requests when booking. Seats mostly face forward in pairs, but there are some sets of four facing each other across a table.

More info // newzealand.com

Clockwise from top: The Coastal Pacific south of Oaro; Dunedin's gorgeous station was built with local Oamaru limestone and black basalt.

MORE LIKE THIS
ON THE RAILS IN NZ

COASTAL PACIFIC

If you've arrived in Wellington via the Northern Explorer, you can transfer to another great scenic train journey by catching an Interislander ferry across Cook Strait to Picton on the South Island, taking in the beautiful scenery of the Marlborough Sounds en route. At Picton you can pick up the Coastal Pacific to Christchurch. This train has identical carriages and amenities to those on the Auckland-Wellington service – and equally impressive scenery. It first traverses the Marlborough wine region, with views of grapevines, then passes Cloudy Bay, where one of the earliest settlements of Māori people was founded. Then the train runs alongside the Pacific Ocean, with the Seaward Kaikoura Range of mountains looming on the other side. From Kaikoura the line continues south through a gorge to end at Christchurch, the South Island's biggest city.
Start // Picton
Finish // Christchurch
Distance // 216 miles (348km)
Duration // 6hr

DUNEDIN RAILWAYS

It seems a sad twist of fate that New Zealand's most beautiful train station no longer receives mainline passenger services. Opened in 1906 in a grand Renaissance Revival style with a tall clock tower, Dunedin Station is an impressive structure. Luckily it's still possible to take a trip from here on tourist trains operated by Dunedin Railways. The first, the Inlander, heads to Hindon via the pretty Taieri Gorge, with highlights including the lofty wrought-iron Wingatui Viaduct and a unique one-lane bridge shared by both cars and trains. The Seasider reaches Merton via Seacliff (which has a great local brewery), with views of Otago Harbour and the Pacific on the way. And the Victorian travels along rugged coastline to Oamaru, where you can explore the town's Victorian Precinct and Steampunk Museum.
Starting/Finish // Dunedin
Distance // Varies
Duration // Varies

MARLBOROUGH FLYER

This tourist train offers rail journeys through the hilly countryside of the Marlborough region, famous for its vineyards producing high-quality wines. The distinctively red, restored vintage carriages are pulled by a 1950s DA locomotive, once a common sight on New Zealand's tracks. The standard excursion is the Marlborough Train Tour from Picton to Seddon and back, which passes the Para Wetlands then heads through wine country around Blenheim before crossing the Awatere River on a historic rail bridge. A less frequent option is a return trip from Blenheim to Kaikoura, which travels through the Dashwood Pass into the beautiful Awatere Valley, then passes through Seddon to run between the Pacific Ocean and mountains to Kaikoura. Carriages have open balconies at both ends, which make for great photos.
Start // Picton
Finish // Seddon (Marlborough Train Tour itinerary)
Distance // 66 miles (106km)
Duration // 4hr

COAST TO COAST ON THE TRANZALPINE

The TranzAlpine is a triumphant feat of engineering, a journey past rivers, mountains and lakes, and an unmissable introduction to the South Island's wild West Coast.

I hadn't come to New Zealand's South Island to ride trains. Like most, I came here with dreams of long-distance hikes, vast glaciers, catching sight of a whale's tail, or maybe even hurling myself off a bridge with a bungee rope around my legs. But although the world's 12th-largest island excels at adrenaline-filled fun, it was the TranzAlpine – with five hours of the world's most incredible scenery – that left the longest-lasting impression.

The TranzAlpine is not quite sure if it's part of a passenger network or a tourist train. By necessity, it's a bit of both. This journey passes through deep wilderness and, for many travellers, is the key to unlocking the sparsely populated yet incredibly beautiful landscapes of the West Coast. It provides a vital connection from Christchurch to Greymouth, where hire cars can be collected and onward transport leads to the spectacular sights further south. But this KiwiRail service is also (quite rightly) marketed on the back of the scenery along the line. Train staff point out highlights over loudspeakers, and headsets provide further onboard commentary. Most excitingly, the TranzAlpine has open-air observation cars, where the views can be savoured by those brave enough to endure the cold. Though most passengers are from overseas, the route and the views from it were a significant source of national pride to the Kiwis I met on my travels, and many told me how pleased they were that I was incorporating it into my journey.

But there wasn't much hint of the grandeur to come when checking in at Christchurch. This was no airline-style procedure, just a case of making sure your presence was known and tickets checked. On boarding, I made myself at home in a standard-

CAFÉ
KiwiRail

class (Scenic) carriage. There's a higher (Scenic Plus) class, offering extra legroom, in-seat food and drink and a dedicated observation car. In Scenic, we still had very large windows, a cafe and an observation car – there isn't really a bad way to ride this train.

Rolling out of Christchurch, the city centre gave way to suburbs, then the agricultural scenery of the Canterbury Plains – but after an hour, we reached Springfield, and the journey began defying expectations. Our loco, humming quietly on the platform, seemed ready to charge head-first at the imposing, snowcapped mountains ahead. Instead, we began to ascend the Waimakariri River Gorge, with the first sightings of this open, braided waterway bringing bright-blue water cascading down from the Southern Alps. Along with most other passengers, I duly headed to the observation car. There was a friendly camaraderie as we peered over the railings – designed to discourage getting too close to tunnel edges and the perilously steep drops of the bridges and viaducts we crossed. The most startling was Staircase Viaduct, 236ft (72m) above the gully after which it's named, crossed in an instant in the interval between exiting one tunnel and entering another.

As thrilling as it was seeing all this from the open air, there was no escaping the effect of ascending into the mountains. The temperature was falling fast, and I retreated inside to warm up.

"Our loco, humming quietly on the platform, seemed ready to charge head-first at the imposing, snowcapped mountains ahead..."

We passed from Swiss-style mountain climbing to crossing the high plains around Craigieburn. The openness of the terrain made for excellent peak-spotting, with 6102ft (1860m) Mt Binser standing sentinel in the distance. We paused at Cass, a railway settlement which, remarkably, has a permanent population of one. Fittingly, that one person is an employee of KiwiRail. After donning a few more layers, I returned to the observation car as we made the stately, final crossing of the Waimakariri.

At 2425ft (739m), Arthur's Pass formed a symbolic point to break the journey. A carriage-load of passengers disembarked to ride back to Christchurch; others headed off to explore the hiking trails and mountain ascents of the eponymous national park. I was content with a platform leg-stretch, watching the addition of extra locomotives to the front and rear of our train. This was to guarantee trouble-free passage on the next leg through the Otira Tunnel, which descends 820ft (250m) over 5.3 miles (8.5km), and sees the observation car briefly closed. On exiting, the train emerged on the far side of the Southern Alps and into a lusher, greener, lower-altitude landscape. The Otira River's splintered strands were now accompanied by denser trackside foliage, and the air felt noticeably warmer and more humid.

The scenery had been so consistently lovely that it was tempting, by this point, to dismiss another river crossing or another tiny lineside township as par for the course, and start thinking about the end of the line at Greymouth. As if switching costumes for the finale, the final piece of eye candy was a pair of lakes: smaller Lake Poerua and then Lake Brunner, stretching away to the south and west, the view over the water from the station at Moana dominated by Mt Te Kinga, with higher snowcapped peaks behind. The odd fishing and waterski boat were gliding on the lake as we continued from Moana. Another destination scribbled on my list of places to head back to.

If it felt a little like normal life was returning for the final 23 miles (37km), this was all relative. From Greymouth, the Great Coast Road heads north, offering views as equally sweeping and dramatic as the mountain crossing I'd just undertaken. To the south lay Franz Josef and Fox glaciers, and the highest of NZ peaks, Aoraki/Mt Cook. Beyond that, misty Fiordland. From Greymouth onwards, though, there's only roads – all the more reason to savour this most superlative of trains. **TH**

A WORK OF ART

Hailed as one of the icons of New Zealand painting, Rita Angus' 1936 depiction of Cass station invokes a mood of stoic love of New Zealand's backcountry wilderness. The artwork contrasts the natural beauty of Cass with the humble yet unavoidable signs of human intrusion. It's one of the star works at Christchurch Art Gallery.

Clockwise from top left: Arthur's Pass station; closing in on Cass; crossing the Waimakariri River; Lake Sarah in winter. Previous page; Crossing the Bealey River.

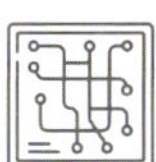

Start/Finish // Christchurch/Greymouth
Distance // 139 miles (224km)
Duration // 4hr 50min
Ticket types // Head to 12Go (12go.com) to book Scenic and Scenic Plus tickets; buy multiday rail tours and other packages from Great Journeys New Zealand (greatjourneysnz.com).
When to go // The TranzAlpine is a lovely trip at any time of year, but book well ahead if travelling in peak season (late December and January).
Things to know // The train can be ridden as a return round trip from Christchurch, either giving four and a half hours at Arthur's Pass or an hour at Greymouth.
More info // newzealand.com is the best place to start planning.

Opposite: the Pyrenean town of Ribes de Freser, a stop on the Barcelona-bound service; the Ribblehead Viaduct counts among Britain's greatest railway architecture.

MORE LIKE THIS
RAILWAYS CROSSING THE RANGES

DENALI STAR, USA

The Denali Star is a vital link for remote communities living away from the road system, as well as transport for hikers heading for Denali National Park. But for many passengers, the main reason for getting on board is a front-seat view of North America's highest peak, 20,194ft (7437m) Denali. The flanks of this iconic Alaskan symbol lie just 46 miles (74km) from the route (keep eyes peeled around the town of Talkeetna), but Denali is just one of many scenic sights on this journey. Look out for panoramas of the Alaska Ranges while crossing Hurricane Gulch Bridge, set 296ft (90m) above a valley, as well as the dramatic section of track along Healy Canyon above the Nenana River. The train, which operates daily, works as a one-day wonder, providing transport for a short excursion in the national park before returning to Anchorage on the same day.

Start // Anchorage
Finish // Fairbanks
Distance // 356 miles (573km)
Duration // 12hr

PARIS TO BARCELONA VIA THE PYRENEES, FRANCE & SPAIN

A journey of two halves begins each evening with an Intercités de Nuit sleeper train heading southwest from Paris. Travelling the mainline from the capital, the service arrives in Toulouse in the early hours before beginning its ascent into the Pyrenees. The high, silent station at Latour de Carol marks the end of the line, and the starting point for Train Jaune services through the mountains to Villefranche-de-Conflent. On a third platform, with a third track gauge, waits the Barcelona-bound Rodalies de Catalunya (Catalan regional) service, which weaves downhill through pretty mountain towns, becoming a suburban commuter train bound for the bright lights of Spain's second-largest city.

Start // Paris Austerlitz
Finish // Barcelona Sants
Distance // 518 miles (834km)
Duration // 15hr 30min

SETTLE TO CARLISLE, ENGLAND

Beautiful, historic and wild, the 'Settle to Carlisle', as it's universally known, is part of the royal family of scenic journeys in the UK. Eight daily services on the line generally start further south in Leeds, with things getting more dramatic on the upland stretch through the Yorkshire Dales National Park. From Settle, the route passes through high open country and past picture-perfect village stations such as Horton-in-Ribblesdale, Dent and Garsdale, perfect for walkers who often combine a ride with a hike between stations. The most dramatic moment is when the train crosses the Ribblehead Viaduct, with the brooding peak of Whernside looming close by. Past Kirkby Stephen, the line rolls on into Cumbria's Eden Valley, before arriving in the border city of Carlisle.

Start // Settle, North Yorkshire
Finish // Carlisle, Cumbria
Distance // 73 miles (117km)
Duration // 1hr 40min

A QUEENSLAND ICON: THE KURANDA SCENIC RAILWAY

Travel along a 19th-century train line through Queensland's rainforest – an environment home to cassowaries and tree kangaroos – to the mountaintop village of Kuranda.

In the 10 years since I moved to Australia, I'd heard countless people rave at length about the Kuranda Scenic Railway. Often visited as part of a day trip to the namesake bohemian hinterland town, the railway line travels through Queensland's UNESCO-world-heritage-listed Wet Tropics rainforest – a lush environment rich in biodiversity, with plant and animal species that can't be found anywhere else in the world.

However, I never really saw the point in riding it. I'd done the drive up to Kuranda, which was scenic enough. Winding upwards into the verdant mountains, the drive felt like travelling back in time to a prehistoric environment where cassowaries – massive flightless birds with brilliantly coloured wattles – look right at home. I wondered: what could a train trip possibly offer that the road trip couldn't? Eventually, however, I suspended my doubts and decided to, quite literally, get on board.

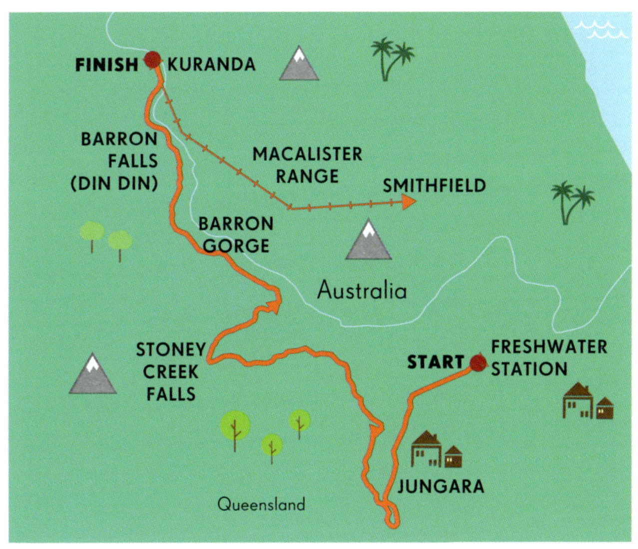

Maurizio De Mattei/Shutterstock; Courtesy of Queensland Rail Travel

It's early in the morning when we arrive at Freshwater Station – about 15 minutes north of the centre of Cairns – but the air is already heavy with heat and humidity. This is Tropical North Queensland after all. Fortunately, we're greeted at the ticket desk with a refreshing drink – a standard inclusion for Gold Class passengers – before boarding the train and finding our lounge-style seats in the refurbished historic carriages. There follows a stream of snacks to accompany the drink, featuring local ingredients such as macadamias and mangos.

When the train slowly pulls away from the station, I feel it in my chest: a vestigial childhood joy for trains, long forgotten, starts to bubble up. I have to refrain from shouting 'Choo choo!' out the window at the well-wishers waving us off. While I'm familiar with the road to Kuranda, which cuts north through the Macalister Range, the train's route starts tracking south of the suburb of Redlynch instead. Then, all signs of the Cairns suburbs are left behind and we begin our slow ascent up through the Barron Gorge. I'm filled with delight again when we start to pass through dark tunnels, but it's not until we reach Stoney Creek Falls – which cascade off the rock face directly beside the train tracks, the mist cooling the carriage's interior – that I realise how foolish I was to assume this experience would be anything like driving.

The falls disappear behind us, and as the train curves around the bend, I can't help but marvel at the tenacity of the people who built this track into the mountainside. It was initially constructed to service communities in the Atherton Tablelands, where deposits of gold were discovered in 1876. Heavy rains during the wet season made roads from the Tablelands down to the coast impassable and with miners unable to obtain supplies, they began to starve. It was soon realised that a rail link would be necessary to support the industry. Surveying for the route began in earnest in 1882, but it wasn't until two years later that a path was identified – the new train line would cut through the Barron Gorge, a steep and landslide-prone environment that rises 1072ft (327m) above sea level. It was a decision that would ultimately create one of Australia's most scenic train routes – but it would also cost time and lives.

The roughly 1500 Irish and Italian men involved in the project were up against slopes averaging 45 degrees covered with up to 23ft (7m) of loose rocks and rotting vegetation. Everything had to be done entirely by hand, from removing those rocks and trees, to hand-carving 15 concrete-lined tunnels and building 39 timber and steel bridges, many hanging high above deep ravines and roaring waterfalls. The Cairns to Kuranda line would take nearly 10 years to construct in its entirety, finally opening to passengers in 1891, and 32 men would die in the process.

But while the environment was hostile to those who built it over 125 years ago, all sense of those hardships slip away as we snake along the track's 93 curves. It's wild, but it's also wildly beautiful. At Barron Falls, we disembark to take photos of

SKYRAIL RAINFOREST CABLEWAY

While the Kuranda Scenic Railway can be travelled both ways, it's best combined with a return journey on the Skyrail – a cable car that travels above the rainforest from Kuranda to Smithfield, a suburb 20 minutes north of Cairns. Stops along the way include Red Peaks, where visitors can take a ranger-guided tour along boardwalks through the rainforest, and Barron Falls, where you'll have a totally different vantage point than the one that you view from the train.

Clockwise from top: Boarding the train; crossing a river; entering Kuranda station; Heritage Class; passing Stoney Creek Falls. Previous page: Kuranda Station.

what will be the trip's highlight for many. Pounding water pours 410ft (125m) from the Barron River down towards the Cairns Coastal Plain. To the Djabuganydji people, who call this site Din Din, it's a sacred place.

Upon arrival at Kuranda's historic railway station, which first opened in 1915, we spend a leisurely afternoon wandering through the town's many markets and along its boardwalks, before heading back towards the railway station. But rather than take the train back down, we hop aboard the Kuranda Skyrail – a gondola that travels through the sky mere feet above the treetops down to the base of the mountain range.

As soon as our gondola starts floating back towards Cairns, I understand why people gush about this experience. On the way up, we were immersed in the rainforest's floor and now we have a cockatoo's-eye view of its canopy, an environment that's home to rare Bennett's and Lumholtz's tree kangaroos. The umbrella trees are in full bloom, their red flowers jutting out like spokes in an umbrella-shaped cluster. And there it is again – Barron Falls below us, an aerial view of a now-familiar sight.

I'd thought that the journey to Kuranda would feel like a well-travelled road. But journeying by train isn't just about immersing yourself in history or feeling the powerful pull of a locomotive – it can also be just the ticket to change what you thought you knew of a destination. **JL**

Start/Finish // Freshwater Station/Kuranda Station
Distance // 23 miles (37km)
Duration // 1hr 30min
Ticket types // Heritage Class is Kuranda Scenic Railway's basic fare. Those looking for a First-Class experience should book 'Gold Class', which includes locally sourced snacks such as cheese platters, and a selection of beers, wines and non-alcoholic beverages.
How to book // Direct at ksr.com.au.
When to go // During the dry season between April and October, temperatures are moderate. However, waterfalls along the Kuranda Scenic Railway are most spectacular from December to March.
More info // For more information on Tropical North Queensland, visit tropicalnorthqueensland.org.au.

Courtesy of Queensland Rail Travel; designium/Shutterstock

Clockwise from top: The Pichi Richi Railway crossing the Flinders Ranges; in the cab on the Mary Valley Rattler; the Puffing Billy crew.

MORE LIKE THIS
AUSTRALIAN TRAIN TREASURES

PUFFING BILLY, VICTORIA

Situated an hour east of Melbourne in the Dandenong Ranges – home to fern gullies, mountain ash trees and mountain peaks up to 1600ft (500m) – Puffing Billy is one of Australia's finest heritage steam journeys. Originally built in 1900 to ferry the local communities around, today this steam train operates daily as a volunteer-run tourist attraction. Running from Belgrave Station (accessed by public transport from Melbourne's city centre) to the historic village of Gembrook, highlights include the timber trestle bridges on the original mountain track. However, the majority of passengers – regardless of age – delight most in dangling their legs out of the open-sided carriages.
Start // Belgrave Station
Finish // Gembrook Station
Distance // 15.5 miles (25km)
Duration // 1hr 50min one way

MARY VALLEY, QUEENSLAND

While Gympie – two hours north of Brisbane – doesn't typically factor in many tourists' itineraries (yet), it played a significant role in Queensland's history. Gold was first discovered here in 1867, and a train line followed in 1881, connecting communities throughout the fertile Mary Valley. This history is celebrated on various excursions including the half-day rail trip, the Classic Rattler Run, which begins at Gympie Station, a timber building constructed in 1913. Passengers then travel in a fully restored C17 steam train across the Mary River and into the surrounding hills. At the tiny village of Amamoor, travellers disembark and are greeted by local musicians and market stalls, while the train engine turns on the turntable before returning to Gympie.
Start // Gympie Station
Finish // Amamoor Station
Distance // 25 miles (40km)
Duration // 3hr round trip

PICHI RICHI RAILWAY, SOUTH AUSTRALIA

Australia's most iconic train journey, the Ghan, runs from Adelaide to Darwin through central Australia's remote outback. However, if you don't have two to three days to spare, there is another option: the Pichi Richi Railway in South Australia. Part of the original Ghan line, this journey aboard restored heritage trains travels between Port Augusta and Quorn, running through the ancient red rocks of the Flinders Ranges. For the full experience, choose the Afghan Express, a full-day journey using the original Ghan steam locomotive and timber-bodied carriages built in the late 1920s. Half-day options include the Pichi Richi Explorer (a steam train ride in 19th-century carriages); the Coffee Pot Experience (an ornate Edwardian-era steam railcar, which is the last operating example of its type in the world); and the Sundowner Explorer (offering a good chance of spotting kangaroos and other endemic wildlife).
Start // Port Augusta
Finish // Quorn
Distance // 48.5 miles (78km)
Duration // 6hr round trip

100
200
300
0
400
psi
WISE

A RED CENTRE EPIC ABOARD THE GHAN

The Ghan is Australia's great north-south train odyssey, connecting the tropical Timor Sea to the wave-lashed beaches of the Southern Ocean.

Look at the logo on the front of a Ghan locomotive and you will see an animal. It's not a kangaroo or a wombat, a dingo or any other stereotypically Australian creature – it is, in fact, a camel. Though they are not native to Australia, there are thought to be as many as 300,000 feral camels wandering the outback – the story of how they came to be there is intertwined with railways.

By the late 19th century, the British Empire had long charted and settled the Australian coast – what lay in the continent's interior, however, remained a source of enduring mystery to London officialdom. Explorers sought answers and many duly strode off heading inland, never to be seen again. To solve the problem, camels were brought over from present day India and Pakistan, along with expert 'Afghan' cameleers to husband them (though they weren't necessarily Afghan). These men rode their great ships of the desert into the 'terra incognita' of the centre, helping map this arid county as they went. By the 1920s a railway followed in the camels' footprints, with fortnightly services named the 'Afghan Express' in honour of those who had blazed the trail.

The original trains were rickety narrow-gauge affairs, prone to endless delays. The Ghan that is their successor, however, is a slick and modern leviathan. The train I encountered on the platforms at Adelaide measured half a mile long – golf buggies were on hand to shuttle passengers to more distant carriages. Soon after I boarded, we hauled out of Adelaide's suburbs and into wide open South Australian scenery, the St Vincent Gulf somewhere to our west and the Flinders Ranges assembling to the north. The green country along the Australian Bight turned to the rusty red of the interior. There remained the best part of almost 2000 miles (3200km)

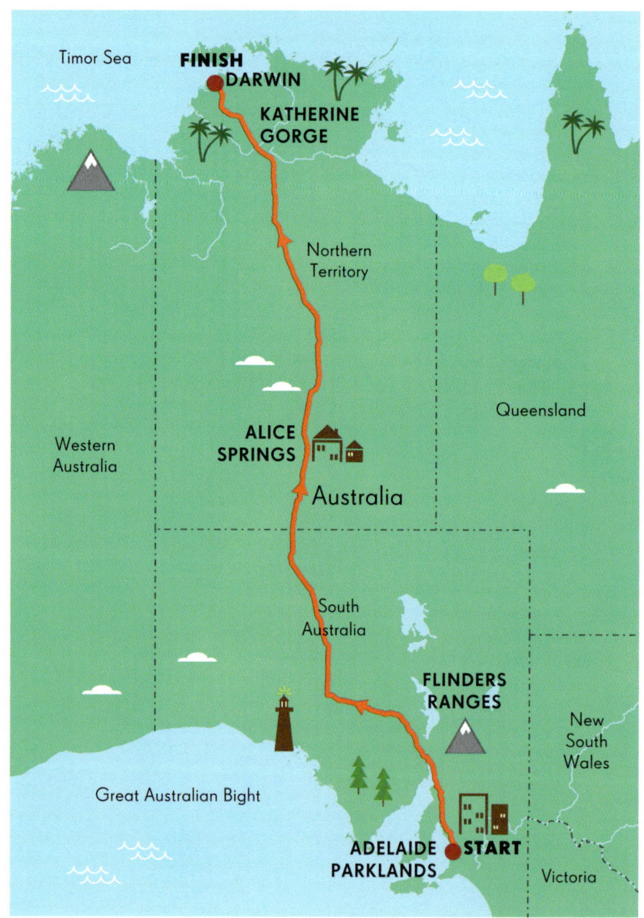

THE GHAN

before we would reach our ultimate destination in Darwin, but supersized landscapes are part of the modern Ghan experience – just like the supersized train that traverses them.

Today's Ghan is a thing of luxury and leisure. Those wishing to travel more quickly between the capitals of South Australia and the Northern Territory can do so in an afternoon by plane – it takes just under four hours to fly from the wine country in the south to crocodile country in the north. The raison d'être of the Ghan, however, is to see the geography of the Australian outback unfurl in real time; to get your own measure of the vastness of this nation.

And, of course, to indulge yourself. Some of my time passes in my compartment, complete with bathroom, large windows and polished wood. It serves as a little living room by day, then is miraculously transformed with comfy beds once the sun has set. More of my time is spent in the communal spaces, such as the Queen Adelaide Restaurant Car, where I dined on fresh seafood, kangaroo steaks and cheese boards paired with South Australian wines. It was here, at the linen-clad tables, that I began to understand the central appeal of the Ghan. You inhabit a narrow enclave of comfort, a slither of luxury living, quietly carving a path through the outback. Meanwhile, on the far side of a pane of glass lies a wilderness of cold nights and merciless midday heat, miles without water or people, horizons hemmed by spinifex and the occasional ghost gum tree. People still go missing in this desert country today, just like those explorers long ago. Peering out of the window brings a perverse kind of kick, like peering over a cliff edge. You count yourself lucky to be on board.

On the second day, we hauled across the border of the Northern Territory, snuck through the narrow cleft of Heavitree Gap and stopped at the unofficial capital of the Red Centre, Alice Springs. Here the train parked for a while so guests could make excursions

THE MAKING OF THE GHAN

The Adelaide to Darwin Ghan railway was more than a century in the making. While building on one of its precursors, the Central Australian Railway, commenced as long ago as 1878, it was only in 2004 that the line's northern section, from Alice Springs to Darwin was fully completed, and Ghan trains could finally complete a truly transcontinental journey. The construction of the route features in Bruce Chatwin's classic book, The Songlines.

Clockwise from top: Lunch is served in the dining car; a southbound service in South Australia; Nitmiluk Gorge; a statue of a cameleer at Alice Springs station. Previous page: Departing Alice Springs.

into the surrounding area. I spent a few hours touring the MacDonnell Ranges on camel with local company Pyndan Camel Tracks. Here the owner Marcus solemnly explained to me that the cameleers of long ago could not bear to see their companions shot dead once their surveying work was done, releasing the creatures to roam forever between the red earth and the blue sky. This is how the feral camels of the outback came to be.

That night our train roamed north from Alice: parting my curtains I saw a cloudless sky become flecked with stars. By the time it brightened again the desert of the centre had begun its miraculous transformation into the verdant north. There were groves of eucalypts and acacias. The riverbeds were no longer so dry. There was time for another excursion at Nitmiluk Gorge, and a chance to appreciate ancient rock art of the Jawoyn people painted onto the canyonside rock. It was a reminder, if it was needed, that tracks were laid across the Australian centre by Indigenous people many millennia before the coming of camels and iron rails. That this country had never seemed empty, desolate or unknown to those familiar with its ways and its watering holes.

The high-rises of Darwin marked the end of the line – the city was named by a crewman aboard Darwin's ship, HMS *Beagle*, which laid anchor here in 1839. By then, I had been fortunate enough to witness the evolution of the Australian landscapes – from coastal green to interior red to green again, culminating with the tropical blues of the Timor Sea. With a window-seat on the Ghan, you see Australia in all its technicolour glory. **OS**

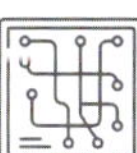

Start/Finish // Adelaide/Darwin
Distance // 1849 miles (2975km)
Duration // 3 days
Ticket types // Classes on the Ghan divide into Gold, Gold Premium and Platinum. All offer comfortable private compartments inclusive of food, drink and some off-train excursions. Platinum compartments are more spacious: guests dine in the plush new Platinum Club dining rooms and are supplied with plenty of champagne. Note the old 'Red' class for budget passengers has been discontinued.
How to book // Book at journeybeyondrail.com.au.
Things to know // As well as travel southward from Darwin, other Ghan packages are available: the Ghan 'Expedition' route is a slow variant that unfurls over four days rather than the usual three, with more time dedicated to off-train excursions. Truncated 'halfway' versions, from Adelaide or Darwin as far as Alice Springs, are also possible.

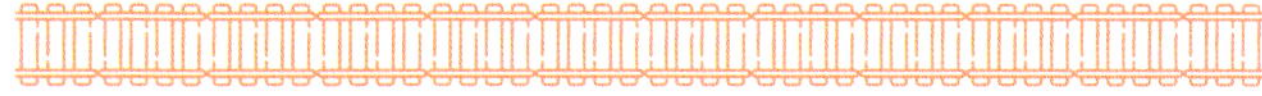

Opposite top: Surfers bound for Bondi Beach, Sydney. Opposite below: Ballooning above beautiful Yarra Valley.

MORE LIKE THIS
THREE SHORTER AUSSIE ADVENTURES

THE SOUTH COAST LINE

Australia has no shortage of long distance journeys like the Ghan and the Indian Pacific, but fortunately a few rail adventures are manageable in a day – and among the best is the South Coast Line. It's an ordinary service that departs Sydney's Central Station to trundle along a scenic slice of the New South Wales coast. After leaving the urban grid, trains skirt the subtropical rainforests of Royal National Park, passing through deep-gouged sandstone cuttings. Passengers are swiftly acquainted with the Pacific and a line-up of surfer beaches roll past the left-side windows. The industrial city of Wollongong and the tidal lagoon of Lake Illawarra soon follow. And while many get off at the end of the electrified line to see the lighthouse at pretty Kiama, real devotees continue in diesel railcars to the buffers at Bomaderry, set on the banks of the Shoalhaven River.
Start // Central Station, Sydney
Finish // Bomaderry
Distance // 190 miles (307km)
Duration // 3hr

YARRA VALLEY RAILWAY

A popular weekend retreat for Melburnians, the Yarra Valley is synonymous with vineyards, cycling trails – and the Yarra Valley Railway, a heritage operation that travels only a few miles from its depot at Healesville, but makes up for it with verdant Victorian scenery and characterful rolling stock too. Passengers board a distinctive Walker railmotor – a 1948-built diesel railcar painted in royal blue and yellow – which rattles its way eastward along the old Healesville line, mothballed in the 1980s but now being restored. The last part sees services hug the Yarra River as forests close in: at the time of writing the railcar stopped at a brick tunnel just short of the TarraWarra Winery, though there are plans to extend it a further 5 miles (8km) to Yarra Glen in the years ahead.
Start/Finish // Healesville
Distance // 5 miles (8km)
Duration // 35min

AUSTRALIND TRAIN

It's fair to say Western Australia doesn't have the same abundance of railway lines as in the country's east. But it can claim the Australind – a train which makes a 103-mile (167km) journey south from state capital Perth to coastal Bunbury, a gateway to the ever-popular Margaret River region. Counterintuitively, it doesn't actually travel along the coast, nor is it a line particularly busy with tourists despite providing an authentic view of bucolic Western Australia, with the Jarrah Forest rising to the east. Trains terminate close to the Indian Ocean waves at Bunbury, which has a fine regional gallery showing Aboriginal art. Note: the line was closed at the time of writing but was due to reopen after maintenance in 2025.
Start // Perth
Finish // Bunbury
Distance // 103 miles (167km)
Duration // 2hr 30min

INDEX

Epic Train Trips of the World
September 2025
Published by Lonely Planet Global Limited
www.lonelyplanet.com
10 9 8 7 6 5 4 3 2

Printed in Canada
ISBN 978 183758614 1

Publishing Director Piers Pickard
Illustrated & Gift Publisher Becca Hunt
Senior Editor Robin Barton
Commissioning Editor Oliver Smith
Editors Cliff Wilkinson, Bridget Blair
Senior Designer Emily Dubin
Layout Designer Jo Dovey
Mapping Wayne Murphy
Image Research Claire Guest
Index Vicky Smith
Print Production Nigel Longuet

Lonely Planet Global Limited
Digital Depot, Roe Lane (off Thomas St),
Digital Hub, Dublin 8,
D08 TCV4
Ireland
STAY IN TOUCH lonelyplanet.com/contact

Authors Akanksha Singh (AS), Anna Kaminski (AK), Austin Bush (AB), Brendan Sainsbury (BS), Chau-Jean Lin (CJL), Christa Larwood (CL), Helen Ranger (HR), Jamie Fullerton (JF), Jamie Lafferty (JLY), Jessica Lockhart (JL), Joe Bindloss (JB), Lauren Keith (LK), Luke Waterson (LW), Monisha Rajesh (MR), Oliver Berry (OB), Oliver Smith (OS), Rebecca Milner (RM), Shafik Meghji (SM), Tim Richards (TR), Tom Hall (TH)

Illustrations by Ross Murray (www.rossmurray.com)